Status and the Challeng

MW00607012

The rise of China and other great powers raises important questions about the persistence and stability of the "liberal international order." This book provides a new perspective on these questions by offering a novel theory of revisionist challenges to international order. It argues that rising powers sometimes seem to face the condition of "status immobility," which activates social psychological and domestic political forces that push them toward lashing out in protest against status quo rules, norms, and institutions. Ward shows that status immobility theory illuminates important but often-overlooked dynamics that contributed to the most significant revisionist challenges in modern history. The book highlights the importance of status in world politics, and further advances a new understanding of this important concept's role in foreign policy. This book will be of interest to researchers in international politics and security, especially those interested in great power politics, status, power transitions, revisionism, and order.

Steven Ward is an Assistant Professor in the Department of Government at Cornell University in Ithaca, New York. He holds an M.A. in Security Studies and a Ph.D. in Government from Georgetown University, Washington, DC, where he won the Harold N. Glassman Award.

Status and the Challenge of Rising Powers

Steven Ward

Cornell University

CAMBRIDGE
UNIVERSITY PRESS

CAMBRIDGE
UNIVERSITY PRESS

University Printing House, Cambridge CB2 8BS, United Kingdom

One Liberty Plaza, 20th Floor, New York, NY 10006, USA

477 Williamstown Road, Port Melbourne, VIC 3207, Australia

314-321, 3rd Floor, Plot 3, Splendor Forum, Jasola District Centre, New Delhi - 110025, India

79 Anson Road, #06-04/06, Singapore 079906

Cambridge University Press is part of the University of Cambridge.

It furthers the University's mission by disseminating knowledge in the pursuit of education, learning and research at the highest international levels of excellence.

www.cambridge.org
Information on this title: www.cambridge.org/9781316633540
DOI: 10.1017/9781316856444

First published 2017
First paperback edition 2020

A catalogue record for this publication is available from the British Library

ISBN 978-1-107-18236-3 Hardback
ISBN 978-1-316-63354-0 Paperback

This book is dedicated to my grandparents.

Contents

Figures and Tables

Figures

Tables

Acknowledgments

Writing a book is an experience that is simultaneously isolating and deeply dependent on a web of intellectual, professional, and personal support. I have many people to thank for contributions without which this book would have been impossible to finish (or even start).

My dissertation committee at Georgetown University deserves enormous credit for shaping my intellectual development and the ideas and analysis that constitute the foundation of this book. David Edelstein is an outstanding mentor, and I am lucky to have benefited from his wisdom, expertise, and support. Andrew Bennett, Keir Lieber, and Daniel Nexon brought an eclectic mix of theoretical and methodological perspectives to the project that deeply influenced the way that I think about theory and how to study international relations more broadly. I also benefited from the larger intellectual environment in Georgetown's Government Department – and especially from the other graduate students in the department, in particular Paul Musgrave, Yu-Ming Liou, and Zacc Ritter.

I have also been lucky to have extremely supportive colleagues at Cornell University. Matthew Evangelista, Peter Katzenstein, and Jonathan Kirshner went beyond the call of duty to read multiple versions of the manuscript; they have each shaped its evolution from dissertation to book. Sarah Kreps, Allen Carlson, and Jessica Weiss also took time to read the manuscript and provided invaluable feedback. Isabel Hull (from Cornell's Department of History) was especially generous and helped to refine my interpretations of the German cases in Chapters 3 and 5.

Cornell's Department of Government generously provided funding for me to hold a manuscript workshop in November 2014. In addition to colleagues from Cornell, five participants from other schools braved early winter in Ithaca to help me begin to think about transforming the partially formed ideas at the core of my dissertation into an effective book. I owe Anne Clunan, Paul MacDonald, Michelle Murray, Randall Schweller, and William Wohlforth a debt that I hope to be able to repay one day.

Chris Layne and Jeff Taliaferro also agreed to read the manuscript, and their reactions and insights helped me improve the substance and presentation of the argument. I am particularly grateful to Jeff. He was my first political science professor and my first mentor. Without his example and support, I would likely not have followed the path that has led me here.

While I was a visiting assistant professor at Georgetown's School of Foreign Service campus in Doha, I employed two talented undergraduates to help with a review of recent work on the consequences of the rise of China for international order. The excellent research of Catherine Lechicki and Khadija Mahsud helped shape Chapter 7.

Finally, this book would not have been possible without the support of my parents and siblings. It takes a great deal of patience to spend nearly seven years writing a dissertation, turning it into a book, and publishing it. It takes even more patience to watch your son or brother spend seven years on a process whose success seems so uncertain for so long. And it takes an enormous amount of faith, tolerance, and love to encourage and support the endeavor. I am very lucky to have the family that I do.

Introduction

One of the most deeply rooted insights from the study of international politics and world history is that the rise of new powers has the potential to cause geopolitical earthquakes.[1] Rising great powers pose deep challenges to international order, which can provoke hegemonic wars and dramatic changes in the balance of power and the normative and institutional character of international politics. This notion drove Thucydides' narrative of the Peloponnesian War; it animated E.H. Carr's analysis of the "twenty years' crisis"; it was at the core of Robert Gilpin's understanding of the engine of change in world politics; and it explains current trepidation about the consequences of the rise of China for the future of the American-backed liberal international order.[2]

Yet this widely held conventional wisdom is puzzling. Over the past two hundred years, every attempt to overthrow the international order has ended with the defeat (and in some cases subjugation) of the challenger. Taking this kind of risk only makes sense for a rising power that is deeply dissatisfied with its stake in the status quo. Uncovering the causes of geopolitical earthquakes thus involves explaining why rising powers occasionally adopt deeply revisionist foreign policy objectives.

Unfortunately, revisionism is a poorly understood concept. It often serves as little more than an ad hoc explanation for otherwise inexplicably aggressive behavior. At the same time, it is a central part of any account of how power transitions work in theory and how the rise of China will play out in practice. The debate over whether China will challenge the

---

[1] The geopolitical "earthquake" metaphor was popularized by Krasner (1982a) as a way of distinguishing between the realisms of Waltz and Gilpin.

[2] Thucydides (1972); Carr (1946); Gilpin (1981). For recent work on the rise of China, see Christensen (2015); Pillsbury (2015); Goldstein (2015); Friedberg (2015), (2011); Steinberg and O'Hanlon (2014); Kupchan (2014a); Luttwak (2012); White (2012); Ikenberry (2011); Mearsheimer (2010); Jacques (2009); and Goldstein (2005). Of course, the even greater trepidation (at least at the moment) about the consequences of the Trump administration's approach to foreign policy for the international order serves as an important reminder that the rise of new powers is not the *only* source of geopolitical earthquakes.

US-backed liberal order – whether the rise of China will provoke a geopolitical earthquake – comes down to a disagreement about the causes of revisionism in rising states. That such a critical question hinges on such a murky concept demands renewed attention to the nature and sources of variation in satisfaction with the status quo among rising powers.

This book offers a novel conceptualization of revisionism and a new theoretical explanation for the sort of dissatisfaction that causes geopolitical earthquakes. I disaggregate the concept and distinguish between two dimensions of revisionism. The first – distributive dissatisfaction – describes a desire to acquire *more* of something: more influence, more territory, more wealth, more status. The second – normative dissatisfaction – describes a desire to protest, delegitimate, or overthrow the rules, norms, and institutions of the status quo order. Distributive dissatisfaction can lead to conflict and war, but it does not in itself cause geopolitical earthquakes because it can often be satisfied within the boundaries of the broader order. But when distributive dissatisfaction is combined with normative dissatisfaction, it produces *radical* revisionism. Radical revisionists not only seek to adjust the distribution of benefits and resources in the system, they also positively value taking steps that signal protest against, delegitimate, or aim to overthrow the status quo order's norms, rules, and institutions. This is the kind of revisionism that helped produce the geopolitical earthquakes that were World Wars I and II: foreign policy in Wilhelmine Germany, Imperial Japan, and Nazi Germany combined commitments to adjusting the distribution of resources in their favor with commitments to overthrowing the normative and institutional foundations of the status quo orders within which each rose to power. Radical revisionism made these three rising powers particularly dangerous because it meant that their drives to expand were relatively unconstrained by a countervailing urge to communicate restraint.

Radical revisionism is as puzzling as it is significant. Rising powers have incentives to signal that they plan to abide by the rules, norms, and institutions that constitute the status quo order even as they seek to increase their power, wealth, territory, and status. Doing so allays the fears of other states and reduces the likelihood that the rising power will face a countervailing coalition. Leaders in China have understood this logic since the time of Deng Xiaoping – and leaders in Wilhelmine Germany, Imperial Japan, and interwar Germany understood it as well. Yet, in the latter three cases, leaders ultimately ignored the logic of institutional restraint and instead took provocative steps that signaled deep dissatisfaction with the foundation of the order. This is the puzzle at the core of this book: why do rising states, which have compelling reasons to signal restraint, sometimes instead pursue policies that communicate a determination to reject and challenge the status quo order – policies that raise the risk of geopolitical earthquakes?

The Argument in Brief

My argument, like Gilpin's, revolves around the idea that *thwarted ambitions* create forces that push the rising state to grow deeply dissatisfied with the status quo. But while Gilpin and other realists emphasize the material benefits of overthrowing the old order, my argument acknowledges that these are rarely worth the costs and risks, especially for a rising power. A satisfying explanation for the pursuit of policies aimed at overturning – as opposed to reforming or expanding within – the status quo order thus has to go beyond rational calculations of material self-interest.

Instead, I argue that obstructed *status* ambitions unleash social psychological and domestic political forces within rising states that push them to reject and challenge the status quo order. Individuals care about the status of their state for the same reason that they care about the status of their hometown baseball team or their alma mater: social identity and its influence on self-esteem. As states become more powerful, their foreign policies often express not only a desire for more power and wealth, but also – in response to demands from nationalist individuals and groups whose social identities are invested in the state's standing – ambitions for higher status. The drive for international status takes the form of policies aimed at acquiring markers of high status – like advanced technology, military victories, and institutional reforms – along with demands that other states behave in ways that recognize the rising state's new position and the rights and privileges it entails.

Sometimes, established powers seem persistently unwilling to do so, which may convince individuals within the rising state that their status ambitions are incompatible with the international order. This constitutes a condition that I call status immobility – the belief that the state faces a status "glass ceiling" – which has two critical consequences for the rising state's foreign policy. First, it contributes to demands from some individuals and groups that the state pursue policies that reject – as opposed to integrate within or reform – the status quo order. The logics that link the perception of an international status "glass ceiling" to a demand for policies that reject the international order are similar to those that motivate disadvantaged social groups *inside* states to protest or secede when they lack an effective legitimate avenue for redressing grievances. Status immobility prompts demands for rejectionist policies both out of a consequentialist drive to remove the perceived obstacle to the state's status ambitions and out of a social psychological need to avoid ratifying an unjust order and prevent the state from participating in its own humiliation. Second, prominent discourses and widespread beliefs about the presence of an unjust, insoluble obstacle to status satisfaction produces political resources that advantage hardliners over moderates in domestic contests over the direction of foreign policy.

In sum, status immobility unleashes forces that undermine the ability of rising states to pursue policies aimed at reassuring established powers that their ambitions are limited. It does so by motivating and incentivizing behavior that lashes out in protest against the status quo order, not necessarily because there is anything material to gain by doing so but rather because defying or attempting to overthrow an unjust order seems more attractive than meekly accepting the rising state's place within it.

Status in International Politics

Apart from proposing a new explanation for an important form of revisionism, the book's most significant contribution is to expand our conception of the role that status plays in international politics. There is nothing new about suggesting that status concerns affect the way states interact. This is a claim that goes back to Thucydides, is an important theme in the work of twentieth-century classical realists and early constructivists, and has generated two modern periods of sustained scholarly interest, one that began in the early 1970s and petered out by the end of the next decade, and the current literature that took off just after the turn of the twenty-first century.[3]

Both of these literatures have focused primarily on how states seek status. This is sensible, and has generated important advances in our knowledge of the way international relations work. For example, scholars have established that states sometimes fight wars in order to achieve higher status, and that they often build weapons not for security reasons but because doing so is a way of performing a claim to membership in a status club.

But status matters in ways that go well beyond its current role as an objective that states pursue strategically. This book suggests two new ways of thinking about status: as the source of a largely non-instrumental demand for revolt against the status quo order, and as a political resource that influences domestic contests over foreign policy.

---

[3] The earlier literature was primarily quantitative and focused on the relationship between status inconsistency and war (Galtung 1964; East 1972; Wallace 1971, 1973; Gochman 1980). The modern literature is more diverse (see Dafoe, Renshon, and Huth 2014; and Larson, Paul, and Wohlforth 2014 for overviews).

Beyond Status-Seeking

The standard model for thinking about the role of status in international politics treats the concept as an objective, and then analyzes the ways in which states pursue it. The focus is usually on establishing that some state took some action not because it wanted more power or more security, but rather because it wanted more status. Scholars have adopted a variety of empirical strategies for defending this claim, and they have done so persuasively across a number of different substantive contexts: wars, arms races, participation in humanitarian missions, and domestic institutional reforms have all been successfully attributed to the ambition for higher status.

This book casts status in a new light. Its role as an objective remains important, but my focus is on how obstructed status ambitions can prompt responses that are not aimed at seeking status but at managing the social psychological and political consequences of being unable to do so. Status immobility produces demands for policies that reject the status quo order not just because this may seem like the only way of satisfying the ambition, but also because defying and delegitimating the order avoids the indignity of being complicit in one's own humiliation. In Chapters 4 and 5, for instance, I analyze the Japanese and German decisions to withdraw from the League of Nations in 1933. Status concerns are implicated in both decisions. Yet it is difficult to see how withdrawal could have helped either state achieve higher status, and this is not how Japanese or German leaders understood it. Instead, withdrawal represented a *protest* against an order that was seen as unjust because it seemed to be incompatible with Japanese and German status ambitions.

This is a critical point because of its relationship to questions about the persistence of international order. Status-seeking often requires that states behave in ways that ratify and reproduce the institutions and norms that constitute the status quo order. This is just as true of peaceful emulation – like Meiji Japan's effort to boost its standing in the world by becoming civilizationally Western – as it is of more conflictual emulation – like Wilhelmine Germany's construction of a fleet of battleships. In either case, the state seeking higher status does things that acknowledge the value of characteristics that the established power has in abundance – this is, after all, partly why these characteristics are status symbols in the first place. What this means is that while status-seeking may cause the international hierarchy to adjust, it also reinforces the deeper normative foundations of international order. Japan's attempt to become institutionally Western reinforced notions about the superiority of Western norms and institutions just as Germany's attempt to equal the British battle fleet reinforced notions about the importance of seapower in world politics. According to the standard model, in other words, status ambitions act as a centripetal force, pulling the international order together even as states compete for position.[4]

In this book, I offer an account of one way in which status ambitions can contribute to the *destruction* of international order. Status ambitions that seem incompatible with the status quo order may not incentivize status-seeking but push toward policies that protest, delegitimate, or aim to overthrow – and thereby weaken rather than strengthen – the foundations of order.

Status and the Second Image Reversed

The theory I develop in this book recasts status in a second novel role: as an international political force that influences domestic contests over the direction of foreign policy. In other words, I build a second-image reversed theory that links status dynamics with the politics of foreign policy in rising states. Unlike other accounts that posit status as an interest that unitary actors pursue strategically, I argue that status concerns often influence policy through pressure on leaders from those outside the regime, and that status immobility serves as a potent weapon for hardliners to deploy against moderates. And because status immobility is partially generated by the behavior of foreign actors, this constitutes one channel through which international political processes influence domestic political processes.[5]

This innovation complicates matters, but it promises significant benefits, one of which is methodological. Theories about how status influences international politics often lack convincing, testable mechanisms, in part because they import insights from fields meant to explain the behavior of individuals – like social psychology – without taking seriously the complications this involves. And the absence of convincing, testable mechanisms means that persuasive qualitative analysis is difficult. This leaves the field to quantitative and experimental analysis, both of which are valuable but inadequate. Quantitative tests of hypotheses about status and international politics are limited because they rely on a particularly problematic measure of status, which is calculated using data on diplomatic exchange. Experimental analysis is useful for testing hypotheses about individual attitudes and decisionmaking, but it can only tell us so much

---

[4] Lebow (2008), p. 67; and Suzuki (2008), p. 60.
[5] On the "second-image reversed," see Gourevitch (1978). For similar arguments, see Evangelista (1993) and Snyder (1989).

about the ways in which status actually matters in international politics. These approaches must be supplemented by rigorous qualitative work, but rigorous qualitative work cannot advance unless theorists more carefully specify the processes through which status influences foreign policy and international politics.[6] This book is, in part, an attempt to address the paucity of convincing mechanisms in analyses of status in world politics by explicitly bringing domestic politics back in.

Outline of the Book

The remainder of the book develops and evaluates the argument using evidence from the most important power transitions in modern history. In Chapter 1, I develop a new conception of revisionism. International orders consist of both a distribution of resources and a set of norms, rules, and institutions that constitute actors, allow them to legitimate action, and regulate state behavior. Rising powers can be satisfied or dissatisfied with the state of either, both, or neither of these dimensions. Chapter 1 explains why policies that simultaneously express dissatisfaction at both the distributive and normative levels – which I call radical revisionism – are dangerous and puzzling. The chapter argues that three existing explanations for shifts toward radical revisionism – based on the costs and benefits of overthrowing the order, the distance between the normative and institutional characteristics of the rising state and the status quo order, and the dynamics of domestic political entrapment – are valuable but inadequate.

Chapter 2 develops the theoretical argument. I begin by defining status and introducing the concept of status immobility. I then lay out the logic linking status immobility to preferences for policies that protest, delegitimate, or overthrow the norms, rules, and institutions of the status quo order; and explain why prominent discourses of and widespread beliefs about status immobility strengthens hardliners at the expense of moderates. The chapter concludes by discussing my strategy for evaluating the theory's ability to explain shifts toward radical revisionism in rising powers.

---

[6] For quantitative work, see fn. 3 and more recently Rhamey and Early (2013); Renshon (2016, 2017); Bezerra et al. (2015); and Miller et al. (2015); for experimental work, see Renshon (2015, 2017). There has been much valuable qualitative work on status published over the past decade (for instance, Wohlforth 2009; Larson and Shevchenko 2010; and Lebow 2008), but it has been less interested in elaborating causal mechanisms than in establishing that states care about status and theorizing about how the status motive might lead to outcomes different than those expected by approaches focused on material motives.

Chapters 3, 4, and 5 constitute the core empirical assessment of status immobility theory. These chapters focus on critical junctures in the histories of three of the twentieth century's most striking revisionist rising powers: Wilhelmine Germany, Imperial Japan, and Weimar/Nazi Germany. For each case, I identify and analyze a shift away from distributive revisionism toward radical revisionism and show that it cannot be understood without taking into account the dynamics that status immobility theory highlights. Chapter 3 examines the origins of Germany's determination to challenge the European balance of power in the years after 1911. I argue that it is impossible to fully understand why many Germans wanted to overthrow the European status quo order without considering the effects of the belief that Germany's ambition to be recognized as a "world power" was incompatible with the institution of the balance of power and especially with Great Britain's role in maintaining it. Moreover, accumulating evidence that the British were unwilling to recognize Germany's claim to *Weltpolitik* – evidence that came in the form of the Morocco Crises and London's response to Germany's naval policy – appears to have substantially weakened the moderate Chancellor Theobald von Bethmann Hollweg's position vis-à-vis German hardliners in the years before the July Crisis.

Chapter 4 investigates the origins of Imperial Japan's turn against the interwar Washington Conference system during the early 1930s. I show that Japan's most visible protest against the interwar order – its 1933 withdrawal from the League of Nations – was the result of outrage against what the Japanese understood to be the West's unwillingness to treat Japan as a full-fledged great power. Japan's withdrawal from the League seems trivial today, but it helped to strengthen Japanese hardliners at the expense of moderates in subsequent fights over other elements of the interwar order.

The shift from Gustav Stresemann's moderate, pragmatic foreign policy to the stridently rejectionist approaches of the late Weimar Republic and Germany under Hitler is the focus of Chapter 5. I show that German radical nationalists demanded, throughout the 1920s, the wholesale rejection of the Versailles settlement and the broader interwar order for reasons linked to status immobility. Stresemann's inability to lift the humiliating sanctions quickly enough through participation in the institutions of the interwar order was interpreted as evidence that Germany faced a status "glass ceiling," which by the end of the decade contributed to political conditions favorable to radical nationalist proponents of rejecting the order. This played a critical role in the rise to power of a leader – Adolf Hitler – who was deeply committed to a radical revisionist foreign policy.

Chapter 6 analyzes the Anglo-American power transition. This is a negative case – one in which a rising great power did not pursue policies aimed at protesting, delegitimating, or overthrowing the order within which it rose. The chapter has two purposes. The first is to explore the sources of British accommodation, and in particular to ask how the British managed the status anxiety associated with being overtaken by the rising United States. The second purpose is to strengthen the case that status immobility matters by using counterfactual methods to establish that it could have exercised a concrete influence on American foreign policy. I accomplish this task by imagining how history might have been different if the British had not accommodated American status claims during the 1895–1896 Venezuela Crisis.

Chapter 7 establishes the importance of status immobility for understanding the consequences of the ongoing rise of China. Will the rise of China bring on the end of the liberal international order? I argue that this depends in part on whether its status claims are accommodated. China has important outstanding status ambitions, which involve – most significantly – the claim to a sphere of influence in East Asia. There are surely also economic and security motives for Beijing's drive to expand its influence in the South China Sea, but status dynamics are implicated because Chinese leaders seem to understand a sphere of influence in their near abroad as one of the rights of a great power. What this means is that accommodating Chinese status claims would likely have to involve a dramatic reduction in the American role as a provider of security and order in East Asia. This would be costly (perhaps prohibitively so), but failing to accommodate would come with its own set of costs – the activation of social psychological and domestic political forces that could advantage Chinese proponents of rejecting the set of liberal norms, rules, and institutions that constitute today's status quo order.

In the conclusion, I summarize the empirical value added by recognizing the role of status immobility in the process of rising power foreign policy change and highlight directions for future research raised by the theory's limitations. The book ends by considering my argument's implications for American grand strategy as it faces a series of rising and reemerging great powers.

1   Revisionism, Order, and Rising Powers

Revisionism is a poorly understood concept. While analysts broadly agree that it refers to dissatisfaction, there is little further consensus. The term captures, in different formulations, anything from a willingness to pay more to change than defend the status quo to a commitment to bringing about a revolution in the international system. There is accordingly little agreement on questions about how to measure or explain dissatisfaction.

Yet revisionism is also one of the most significant concepts in international relations (IR). For classical realists, neoclassical realists, defensive realists, power transition theorists, and hegemonic stability theorists, dissatisfaction is one of the *key* variables in accounts of the causes of major war. This is particularly true for analyses of the international security consequences of the rise of new great powers. There is not *necessarily* any reason to expect rising powers to threaten international order. In fact, states experiencing or expecting relative increases in wealth or military power have incentives to integrate with status quo institutions; this prevents other powerful states from seeking to contain the riser and promises other concrete benefits. Leaders in historical rising states – in Wilhelmine Germany, Imperial Japan, and Weimar Germany – understood these incentives and tried to pursue foreign policies in line with them.

It is when rising powers grow dissatisfied with the status quo that they are dangerous. Dissatisfied states no longer see any value in integrating with status quo institutions and are willing to risk provocation by pursuing increasingly belligerent policies. This, according to many accounts, is what happened to Wilhelmine Germany, Imperial Japan, and Weimar Germany; and it is what some observers worry could happen to China in the coming decades.

For such a potentially consequential concept, we know little about what dissatisfaction is or where it comes from. In this chapter I take two steps that aim to help scholars and policymakers better understand the nature and sources of revisionism. First, I propose a disaggregated way of thinking about dissatisfaction with the status quo. States can be revisionist in two ways: they can be dissatisfied with the distribution of resources in the system, and they can be dissatisfied with the rules, norms, and institutions that constitute and naturalize the distribution of resources and regulate interactions. These two types of dissatisfaction manifest themselves behaviorally as pressure for different kinds of policies, and they combine to form three ideal-typical revisionist policy orientations: *distributive revisionism*, which aims at achieving more of a material, economic, or social resource; *normative revisionism*, which rejects or aims to overthrow the normative and institutional foundation of the status quo; and *radical revisionism*, which combines policies aimed at satisfying distributive ambitions with those aimed at rejecting or overthrowing status quo norms, rules, and institutions.

My second objective in this chapter is to argue that policy combinations that look like radical revisionism are particularly puzzling and dangerous, especially when rising great powers pursue them. These states have incentives to pursue policies aimed at achieving distributive revisionist objectives; they simultaneously have incentives to do things that communicate a willingness to play by the rules and support status quo norms and institutions, since doing so reduces the costs and risks of expanding power, wealth, and influence. A radical revisionist policy mix – which adds normative revisionist policies aimed at *rejecting or overthrowing* status quo rules, norms, and institutions – is puzzling because it is needlessly provocative.

Radical revisionism is also dangerous. Distributive revisionist ambitions and demands for policies that reject or overthrow status quo rules, norms, and institutions interact in ways that push states toward the pursuit of increasingly unrestrained expansion. Leaders in states that positively value rule-breaking and norm violation are likely to calculate that the costs of behaving aggressively are lower than they would otherwise be, and elites who favor less restrained expansion will be less effectively constrained by the objections of more cautious leaders.

In short, my second objective in this chapter is to establish the need for a theoretical account of shifts from distributive toward radical revisionism in rising states: why do rising states committed to achieving limited distributive ambitions while avoiding provocation sometimes abandon the latter commitment and pursue policies that seem to lash out against status quo rules, norms, and institutions? The rest of this book develops and evaluates a theoretical explanation for these dangerous shifts.

What Is Revisionism?

Revisionism refers to an attitude of dissatisfaction with and corresponding desire to change the status quo. It is one pole along a continuum of orientations toward the state of affairs in the international system. The opposite pole – a "status quo" orientation – refers to an attitude of satisfaction with and a desire to preserve the status quo. In the middle of the continuum is an "indifferent" orientation – this refers to an attitude of neither satisfaction nor dissatisfaction, and a corresponding lack of will to either defend or change the status quo.[1]

This simple framework masks many outstanding questions. The most fundamental relates to the nature of the status quo and the corresponding aspirational change that revisionism denotes. There are two distinct ways of defining the status quo in the literature on revisionism.

The simplest and most common is to treat the status quo as a distribution of resources. This often refers to territory or power, but it may also mean the distribution of influence, wealth, markets, ideology, regime type, status, or some other valued good. Revisionism then denotes dissatisfaction with and a desire to change this distribution. This is how Wolfers understood the concept (which he called "self-extension"), and it is also the approach that more recent neoclassical and defensive realist scholarship has taken.[2]

The other way to conceptualize the status quo is as a social order composed of a power and status relationship between states and a set of norms and rules that help constitute and legitimate the order. On this view, revisionism refers to dissatisfaction with the foundation of the order, not with the distribution of resources in the system. In fact a state might seek distributive gains to be better positioned to *defend* the order. This is how Morgenthau (who used the term "imperialism") and Kissinger (who used the term "revolutionary" state) understood revisionism – not as an effort to change the distribution of goods, but as dissatisfaction with a more fundamental set of social relationships and institutions.[3]

Instead of choosing between these two understandings of dissatisfaction, I propose a framework that accommodates both. The status quo, at any particular time and place, consists of *both* a distribution of resources (wealth, military capabilities, status, regime type, access to markets) *and* a set of norms, rules, and institutions that produces order by constituting actors with different statuses and bundles of rights, providing bases for legitimate action in international politics, and regulating behavior and interaction in ways that favor some actors over others.

---

[1] See Carr (1946), p. 53, for an early discussion.

[2] See Wolfers (1962), pp. 91–93. For recent usages consistent with this definition, see Kydd (1997), Schweller (1998), and Davidson (2006).

[3] Morgenthau (1948), p. 57; Kissinger (1957), p. 2; (2014), p. 9. For recent consistent usages of the term, see Legro (2005), Chan (2004), and Buzan (2010).

The distributive element of the status quo is fairly straightforward and needs little elaboration. But the normative element requires greater attention. Norms, rules, and institutions play three roles that are central to understanding how they produce order and stratification in world politics, and why they might prompt dissatisfaction.

First, norms, rules, and institutions produce and sustain social hierarchies by generating intersubjective bases for social comparisons between actors, and by constituting actors with different statuses and bundles of rights.[4] The most obvious and fundamental example is the constitution of the state itself. The institution of sovereignty provides a normative framework that makes possible the social category of the "state" and gives actors in this category certain rights and privileges – for instance, to manage affairs inside borders without interference.[5] But international normative frameworks are also constitutive of different kinds of states with different statuses and bundles of rights. Towns, for instance, has shown that changing norms about the treatment of women are one basis on which states have been categorized as civilized and uncivilized over the last two centuries.[6] Another example is the social category "great power," which refers to an elite club (whose membership criteria have involved a socially constructed mix of material capabilities and civilizational characteristics) in which members have access to certain exclusive rights. Great powers today, for instance, are not just the most powerful states in the system – they are powerful states with rights to legitimately possess nuclear weapons, to privileged positions in global governance institutions, and to intervention abroad for the purpose of maintaining international peace and stability.[7]

Second, norms, rules, and institutions provide the basis for legitimate action in international politics. Leaders draw on normative frameworks (like the idea of the "balance of power," the "responsibility to protect," or the concept of universal human rights) and use formal and informal institutions (like the UN Security Council or the World Trade Organization) to legitimate foreign policies – like military interventions, occupations, economic sanctions, and the formalization of alliance

---

[4] This understanding of the function of norms, institutions, and rules is similar to what Bially Mattern and Zarakol (2016, p. 641) call the "logic of productivity" – norms, institutions, and rules that generate hierarchy do so by producing "both the actors and the space of world politics in which they act." On the constitutive properties of norms and institutions see Barnett and Duvall (2005) and Wendt (1998). For a thorough account of the ways in which norms constitute social hierarchies, see Towns (2010).

[5] See Ruggie (1993).   [6] Towns (2009, 2010, 2012).

[7] On different conceptions of criteria for membership in the great power club, see Neumann (2014). On the rights of "great powers," see Bull (1977), pp. 196–212; Simpson (2004), pp. 70–71; Suzuki (2008); and Heimann (2014).

commitments – for domestic and international audiences.[8] These frameworks and institutions constrain the kinds of actions that can be taken by different kinds of actors – for instance, during the nineteenth century, European great powers invoked the responsibility to maintain stability and defend the balance of power in order to justify intervention in conflicts involving smaller European states. Later, Western actors invoked civilizational standards to justify intervention in and occupation of non-Western states. More recently, Western powers have invoked the illegitimacy of Iranian claims to a nuclear program – which is based on a normative framework that only grants such a right to certain kinds of states – in order to justify sanctions.[9]

Third, norms, rules, and institutions regulate interactions between states. They proscribe certain kinds of behavior and prescribe others.[10] For instance, in the Sino-Centric East Asian order, there were elaborate rules that dictated how other states within that system had to behave during diplomatic interactions in order to receive the benefits of tributary trade with China.[11] Rules may also be less formal – like contemporary customary international law that regulates interstate interaction in the realms of war and commerce.

The normative element of the status quo is not completely independent of the distributive element. There are two important ways in which the two are related. First, norms, rules, and institutions partially constitute and naturalize the status quo distribution of resources.[12] For instance, the normative framework that denies legitimate possession of nuclear weapons to non-NPT nuclear states effectively ratifies the current distribution of nuclear weapons technology. Similarly, the nineteenth-century understanding that the "great powers" had a responsibility to maintain the European balance of power helped to discourage radical changes to the

---

[8] For consistent perspectives, see constructivists like Reus-Smit (1999) and Bukovansky (2002); classical realists like Kissinger (2014); and the English School literature, including among others Bull (1977), Gong (1984), Wight (1977), Watson (1992), and Clark (2011).

[9] Another way to understand this function of norms, institutions, and rules is as a manifestation of what Bially Mattern and Zarakol (2016, p. 641) call the "logic of positionality" – norms, institutions, and rules produce and reflect inequality by "constrain[ing] or influenc[ing] agent choices, behavior, and perceptions."

[10] On this function, see the realist Gilpin (1981) and the neoliberal literature on regimes, including among others Krasner (1982b), (1982a), and Keohane (1984). One might also understand this as a manifestation of what Bially Mattern and Zarakol (2016, p. 636) call the "logic of trade-offs" – norms and institutions "structure action, whether through social or interest-based incentives."

[11] See Kang (2010) and Ringmar (2012).

[12] This was Carr's (1946) point about international "morality" as a means of perpetuating the dominance of the privileged (Chapter 9, especially p. 155). For a related discussion, see Jackson (2011), p. 187.

distribution of capabilities.[13] In short, status quo norms, rules, and institutions help produce an order that strengthens the privileged positions of those at the top.

Second, the character of status quo rules, norms, and institutions is partially determined by the identities, actions, and characteristics of the most powerful actors in the system. For instance, international order is often constructed in ways that reflect the preferences of the victors of major conflicts – as in the wake of the Napoleonic Wars, World War I, World War II, and the collapse of the Soviet Union.[14] Powerful actors also influence the character of order-producing normative frameworks simply by virtue of being powerful. Shared understandings about the criteria for achieving "great power" status around the turn of the twentieth century, for instance, involved the construction of battleships and the acquisition of overseas territories in part because the state at the top of the global pecking order – Great Britain – had these in abundance.

The co-constitutive relationship between the normative and distributive elements of order suggests that often – but not always – the states benefiting the most from the status quo distribution of resources will also have an interest in defending status quo norms, rules, and institutions. And, whether it is true or not, other states often come to the same conclusion about the connection between the status quo distribution of resources and the rules, norms, and institutions that help legitimate it. Late risers throughout history have often inferred that the states most advantaged by the global distribution of power or wealth or status are also those whose interests are most closely identified with the defense and reproduction of status quo norms, rules, and institutions. For instance, many Japanese and German leaders understood the League of Nations and the post–World War I set of institutions as a framework that worked to the benefit of the states that already dominated international politics: the United States, Great Britain, and France. Similarly, some Chinese observers today understand the contemporary set of order-producing norms and institutions as a framework that primarily works to preserve American hegemony.[15]

Still, the reciprocal relationship between the normative and distributive elements of the status quo does *not* mean that dissatisfaction is an all-or-nothing proposition. The distribution of resources and the set of norms,

---

[13] See Mitzen (2013) and Kissinger (2014), Chapter 2, on the functioning of the European Concert system for this purpose.

[14] On this view of international order, see Gilpin (1981) and Ikenberry (2001).

[15] See Chapters 4, 5, and 7. The recent rise of an unmistakable disdain for the "liberal international order" in the United States – which itself built and benefits more than any other state from the contemporary status quo – is an important reminder that rising power is not a *necessary* condition for the emergence of this sort of dissatisfaction. I return to this issue in the concluding chapter.

rules, and institutions that produce order are analytically distinct components of the status quo, and states can be satisfied with one and dissatisfied with the other. A dominant-but-declining state might be committed to defending status quo institutions but calculate that to do so, it must increase its share of the distribution of capabilities. Or a rising state might anticipate benefiting from status quo norms, rules, and institutions once it manages to achieve higher status. Conversely, a state might be dissatisfied with the normative basis of the international status quo but uninterested in changing the distribution of resources.

Distributive and Normative Dissatisfaction in Foreign Policy

Distributive and normative dissatisfaction are analytically distinct, and they manifest themselves behaviorally as commitments to different kinds of policies. Distributive dissatisfaction produces pressure to adjust the distribution of resources in the problematic area. This is straightforward when a state wants more wealth or territory – satisfaction comes through territorial or economic expansion. Ambitions for a more favorable distribution of other kinds of goods – like status or influence – push toward more complicated behavioral responses. These might, for instance, lead to demands for *reform* of international institutions to accommodate claims to a more important voice for the state in global governance – as in the case of Indian, Brazilian, and Japanese ambitions for permanent membership in the UN Security Council. They might also involve other forms of normative or institutional innovation or reform in order to improve a state's position in the system.[16] But this is all ultimately motivated by *distributive* dissatisfaction – a desire for higher status or more influence. It should not be confused with evidence of a fundamental opposition to the norms, rules, and institutions that produce the order itself. In fact, this sort of status or influence-seeking actually signals, at a deeper level, acceptance of the norms and institutions that produce the status quo – states with these sorts of ambitions are happy to play by the rules so long as status quo rules and institutions can be adjusted to accommodate claims to more status or influence.

Efforts at institutional reform depend upon the acceptance of a deeper framework by which states can amend the status quo norms, rules, and institutions – a framework still rooted in the status quo order and the

---

[16] See, for instance, the discussion of Japan's attempt to renegotiate the role of "whiteness" as a marker of great power status in Chapter 4; Towns' (2010, 2012) account of the emergence of gender-based legislative quotas among states hoping to improve their standing; and Larson and Shevchenko's (2003, 2010, 2014) conception of social creativity.

support of its defenders. In the realm of domestic politics, the process by which constitutions provide for their own future amendment is an obvious example, but amendment frameworks exist in international politics as well. Historically, these have included the nineteenth-century European concert system, ad hoc conferences among great powers and other states (like the Congress of Berlin, the Hague Conferences, and the interwar disarmament conferences in Geneva, Washington, and London), and formal institutions – most prominently the UN General Assembly – that provide states with legitimate forums through which to change international normative and legal frameworks. Some institutions – like the UN Security Council and the WTO – even have explicit procedures for effecting institutional changes. The key point is that institutional and normative reforms pursued through these legitimate channels do not represent challenges to the foundation of the status quo order – rather, they strengthen the status quo order by demonstrating that its norms, institutions, and rules are flexible and durable enough to accommodate the changing demands of states.[17]

Normative dissatisfaction runs deeper and pushes not toward pressure for marginal reforms to rules or institutions but rather for policies that deny, challenge the legitimacy of, or aim at overthrowing the norms, rules, and institutions that constitute the status quo order. It manifests itself behaviorally in the form of policies of delegitimation and revolution. States that are deeply dissatisfied with the normative and institutional framework that constitutes the status quo order will not pursue changes within the order (since doing so only strengthens its basis), but rather behave in ways that weaken or destroy the order by protesting, denying its legitimacy, or seeking to overthrow it.[18]

More concretely, deep normative dissatisfaction can manifest itself in a range of provocative behaviors. These include violent attempts to destroy and replace the international order – much like revolutions are violent attempts to overthrow domestic orders. But there are also less extreme manifestations of normative dissatisfaction. Normatively dissatisfied states positively value breaking rules and violating norms because doing so signals protest and weakens the normative foundation of the status quo. Along these lines, states express normative dissatisfaction by refusing to participate in or withdrawing from status quo institutions. Normative dissatisfaction might also push against cooperating with states identified as defenders of the status quo order. Doing so, especially in

---

[17] The distinction here is similar to the one Buzan (1991), pp. 237–246; (2010), pp. 17–18, draws between revolutionary revisionists and reformist revisionists.

[18] This is consistent with Chan's (2004) definition (p. 216), as well as his argument that revisionism can be identified by observing relative levels of membership in IGO's.

Table 1.1 *Ideal-Typical Policy Combinations*

	Accept Status Quo Norms, Rules, and Institutions	Reject Status Quo Norms, Rules, and Institutions
Defend (or Decline to Challenge) Distribution of Resources	Satisfied	Normative Revisionist
Examples	*(Pre–World War I Great Britain)*	*(Tokugawa Japan; early Soviet Union)*
Challenge Distribution of Resources	Distributive Revisionist	Radical Revisionist
Examples	*(Prussia/Germany under Bismarck; post-Meiji Japan; Germany under Stresemann)*	*(Revolutionary France; pre–World War I Germany; post-1933 Japan; Nazi Germany)*

ways that seem intended to participate in the management or governance of the status quo order, at least tacitly signals that the status quo is valuable and the privileged position of its defenders is valid. This message is inconsistent with the demand for delegitimation that is associated with normative dissatisfaction.

Revisionist Foreign Policy Combinations

The two dimensions of dissatisfaction combine to form four ideal-typical orientations toward the status quo (depicted in Table 1.1). These can be understood more concretely as policy combinations. States in the real world will never fit cleanly into any ideal-typical category – ideal types exist only in the form of theories and ideas. But states do pursue policy combinations that resemble (more or less closely) one orientation or another; and it is possible to identify *shifts* from a mix of policies that resembles one orientation toward a mix that more closely resembles another. In other words, this framework is particularly useful for characterizing *changes* in the orientation of a state's foreign policy.

The first orientation is satisfaction with both the distribution of resources in a system and the status quo norms, rules, and institutions. This combination is not revisionist at all; it instead consists of a mix of policies committed to defending the distribution of power and other resources, and upholding the legitimacy of the status quo's normative framework. This approximates Great Britain's orientation toward the status quo during the decades before World War I.

There are three revisionist policy combinations. The first – distributive revisionism – refers to the simultaneous pursuit of a change in the distribution of some resource and a commitment to defending (or at least not challenging) status quo norms, rules, and institutions. This is a common mix. States are frequently dissatisfied with how much of some resource they have, but this does not have to be accompanied by fundamental opposition to the rules, norms, and institutions of the order. In fact, states pursuing distributive revisions have incentives to follow a *logic of institutional restraint* – to avoid provoking others by signaling a broader commitment to keeping competition constrained within the bounds of the order's norms, rules, and institutions.[19] Otto von Bismarck understood this logic and worked to defuse potential opposition from other great powers during the Wars of German Unification by legitimating expansion as a *defense* of the normative and institutional foundation of the nineteenth-century European status quo.[20] Similarly, Japanese Foreign Minister Kijurō Shidehara and Weimar Foreign Minister Gustav Stresemann sought to expand the power, wealth, status, and influence of their respective states, but simultaneously worked to signal acceptance of the normative and institutional frameworks of the post–World War I order as a way of making their distributive revisionist efforts less costly and risky.

The second revisionist orientation – normative revisionism – combines policies that reject status quo norms, rules, and institutions with disinterest in changing the distribution of resources in the system. This is perhaps less common than distributive revisionist orientations, but there are some examples of states pursuing these kinds of policy combinations. Japan under the Tokugawa is one. In the wake of Toyotomi Hideyoshi's failed attempt to invade and conquer Korea and China, it was clear to the Tokugawa that efforts to change the distribution of power, territory, and influence in early modern East Asia were futile and much less important than consolidating domestic authority. Yet the Tokugawa simultaneously refused to participate in the norms and institutions that constituted the Sino-Centric order. Beginning in the early seventeenth century, Japan symbolically withdrew from that order by refusing to engage in tributary trade, participate in the institution of investiture, and use diplomatic language and protocols that signaled subservience to China.[21] Early Soviet foreign policy is another example of this sort of combination. In the immediate aftermath of the Russian Revolution, the Soviet Union eschewed distributive gains while seeking to

---

[19] For similar arguments about the logic of signaling restraint through institutions, see Voeten (2005) and Ikenberry (2001).
[20] Goddard (2009), pp. 126–139. [21] See Toby (1984), pp. 29–94.

overthrow what its leaders saw as a global order produced by the norms, rules, and institutions of global capitalism.[22] Some strains of American isolationist thought have also expressed a preference for policy combinations that reject distributive gains but at the same time withdraw from and delegitimize the status quo order.[23]

The third revisionist orientation – radical revisionism – refers to simultaneous dissatisfaction along both distributive and normative dimensions. It thus results in combinations of policies that aim at making distributive gains and policies that aim at protesting, delegitimizing, or overthrowing the norms, rules, and institutions at the core of the status quo order. This combination – as I detail in the next section – is deeply provocative and thus puzzling, and also deeply destabilizing. Some of the most rabidly belligerent states in modern history have pursued combinations of policies that look like radical revisionism. These include Revolutionary France, which combined a deeply destabilizing challenge to the monarchical status quo with a concerted effort to conquer much of Europe; Wilhelmine Germany, which had similarly aggressive distributive ambitions that coexisted alongside an increasing discomfort with the British-managed "balance of power" European order during the years just before World War I; Imperial Japan, which after 1933 simultaneously pursued policies aimed at expanding in mainland Asia and protesting Western rules and institutions; and late Weimar and Nazi Germany, which by the early 1930s was pursuing increases in military power and territory while simultaneously protesting and delegitimizing the norms and institutions of the interwar European order.[24]

The latter three cases suggest that radical revisionist policy combinations are particularly likely to arise in and particularly dangerous when pursued by rising states. But it is important to keep in mind that rising great powers are not the only actors who occasionally pursue these sorts of policy combinations. Although dominant states often have incentives to defend

---

[22] Jacobson (1994), Chapters 1 and 2.

[23] See Nau (2013), pp. 42–44, for an overview of American isolationism, and Tucker and Hendrickson (1990), pp. 149–150, on Jefferson's simultaneously revolutionary and isolationist strategic thought.

[24] One question that may arise at this point involves challenges for system leadership: should these be classified as distributive (since they involve dissatisfaction over the distribution of power, influence, or status) or should they be classified as radical (since they involve overturning the system's hierarchy)? In a scenario in which a leading and challenging state agreed on what the social and institutional foundations of order in world politics should look like, then we might code the challenger's revisionism as distributive. But since leadership challenges rarely occur in the absence of conflict over the order's normative and institutional foundation (see Gilpin 1981 and the description of Gilpin's account of change below for more on why this is so), in practice the challenger's revisionism will almost always look more radical than distributive.

both the distribution of resources and status quo norms, rules, and institutions, they sometimes behave otherwise. American foreign policy under the George W. Bush administration might be understood as a very mild radical revisionist mix.[25] Many neoconservatives expressed preferences for a combination of policies that aimed simultaneously at expanding American power and influence and delegitimizing the norms and institutions (like the United Nations and the International Criminal Court) that previous American policy had built and defended. And though it is too early to draw firm conclusions about how this will influence American foreign policy, Donald Trump has articulated a worldview that expresses strong dissatisfaction with the normative foundation of the liberal international order and vague ambitions to shift the distribution of resources (including status, wealth, and military power) toward the United States.[26]

Much weaker actors can also pursue radical revisionist policy combinations. The most prominent recent example might be the foreign policy of the "Islamic State" (IS). IS simultaneously seeks to change the distribution of territory and wealth in the Middle East and to overthrow not just the Western normative and institutional order, but also the Westphalian foundation of the state system itself.[27]

Radical Revisionist Shifts in the Foreign Policies of Rising Great Powers

This book does not propose a universal theory of revisionism. States likely pursue different kinds of revisionist policy combinations for many reasons, and trying to capture these in a single theoretical framework would be futile. I do not even attempt to develop a general theory of radical revisionism. Rather, my focus in this book is limited to developing an explanation for *shifts* in the direction of radical revisionist policy combinations among one particular class of actors: rising great powers. Radical revisionism in states whose position in the international system seems to be improving deserves special attention for two reasons, on which I elaborate below. First, because of the incentives that rising states have to behave patiently and cautiously as they grow and expand, that they would adopt such deeply provocative policy combinations is puzzling. Second, shifts in the direction of radical revisionist combinations in the foreign policies of rising great powers are especially dangerous and destabilizing.

[25] See Chan (2004), p. 234, on this point.
[26] For an exhaustive overview of Trump's worldview, see Laderman and Simms (2017).
[27] For an account of the Islamic State's foreign policy ambitions, see Graeme Wood (2015).

The Puzzle of Shifts Toward Radical Revisionist Policy Combinations in Rising States

Rising great powers present challenges and potential threats to states that benefit from the status quo order. As the debate about the rise of China among American academics and policymakers demonstrates, power shifts create uncertainty because of ambiguity about the intentions of the riser and the long-term consequences of its rise. Observers disagree about what China wants, whether it can rise peacefully, and whether it can integrate successfully with status quo norms and institutions. Different answers to these questions have different implications for American policy toward China. Those who think China is likely to pose a deep challenge to the status quo advocate robust military (and even economic) containment, while those who think China can integrate with the status quo order advocate engagement.

Chinese leaders are – as leaders in other rising states have been – aware of the international debate about their intentions and – as leaders in other rising states have as well – understand the corresponding incentives they have to avoid behaving provocatively. In order to weaken the advocates of containment and strengthen the advocates of engagement within potential balancers, rising states have incentives to avoid acting in ways that seem to confirm the fears of those who worry that they may launch revolutionary challenges against the status quo.[28]

This does not mean that rising states should never be expected to pursue any kind of revisionist policy. They may require economic expansion in order to continue growing; they may redefine their security requirements as they grow in ways that push toward territorial expansion; and their leaders and populations may demand increases in status and influence concomitant with their new strength. Leaders might also calculate that increasing capabilities provide new opportunities to pursue a broader range of objectives than they could previously.

But when they do pursue distributive revisions to the status quo, rising states have strong incentives to do so without simultaneously signaling that they are interested in challenging the normative and institutional foundation of the order. Other states are more likely to accept distributive changes when the state pursuing them seems willing to integrate, play by the rules, and cooperate in the governance of the system. States that are satisfied with the norms, rules, and institutions that constitute the status

---

[28] This is one reason why Chinese leaders since Deng Xiaoping have stressed restraint in foreign policy (under labels like "keeping a low profile," "peaceful rise," and "peaceful development"). See Guo (2006), Chapter 1; Deng (2008), p. 41; and Zheng (2011), Chapter 6.

quo order are more likely to be behaviorally constrained by them. They are also unlikely to use any new increases in wealth, power, or influence to try to delegitimize or overthrow the normative and institutional foundation upon which the privileged position of other powerful states is partially based. Conversely, states that are dissatisfied with status quo norms, rules, and institutions positively value violating them and opposing their defenders. They are thus less behaviorally constrained and more likely to be seen as deeply destabilizing threats as they grow more powerful.[29]

In short, leaders in rising states have compelling reasons to behave in ways that reassure more powerful states that they accept the normative and institutional foundation of the status quo order – even as they seek to expand their power and influence.[30] This is precisely why Bismarck invoked the sanctity of a treaty brokered by the British as justification for invading Schleswig-Holstein in 1864.[31] It is also why Bethmann Hollweg tried to mend German relations with Great Britain before World War I, and why Japanese and German moderates objected to violating the rules of the interwar order and to withdrawing from the League of Nations.

History shows, though, that rising states sometimes behave in ways contrary to these incentives. Elites and the public in Wilhelmine Germany developed and expressed a deep antipathy to the British-dominated order that contributed to Germany's reckless foreign policy in the months before the July Crisis; Imperial Japan and Weimar/Nazi Germany took steps that signaled an unwillingness to integrate with the status quo order – steps that leaders in both states understood might lead to unnecessary isolation and disaster. Given the incentives that rising states have to avoid unnecessary provocation, their occasional unwillingness or inability to avoid policies that lash out in protest against the status quo order defies easy explanation.

The Dangers of Radical Revisionist Policy Combinations

Radical revisionist policy combinations are not just interesting because they are puzzling; they are also particularly dangerous in ways that distributive and normative revisionist policies on their own are not.

---

[29] Put another way, states that seem to reject the status quo order may pose what Weisiger (2013), pp. 25–33, calls "dispositional" commitment problems for other states.

[30] The literature on reassurance (Osgood 1962; Etzioni 1962; Stein 1991) suggests that it is easiest to convince others of one's benign intentions if one is willing to use institutions of global governance and respect status quo norms and rules related to international competition. See especially Stein (1991), pp. 432–433.

[31] Goddard (2009), pp. 133–134.

Support for status quo norms, rules, and institutions tends to limit the ambitions of a distributive revisionist. Since the state values the rules and has an interest in strengthening or at least not undermining them, its behavior should be sensitive to the costs of rule-breaking. And since global governance institutions often constitute mechanisms for limiting the extent to which conflicting interests and ambitions threaten other actors and the status quo order itself, a commitment to respecting these kinds of institutions naturally channels dissatisfaction with the distribution of resources in a system toward policies that seek consensual adjustments. This was the intended (and, for a time, actual) function of the Concert of Europe; it was also the intended function of both the League of Nations and the United Nations Security Council. Each of these institutions was meant to help states limit the consequences of inevitable conflicts of interest (which often stem from distributive dissatisfaction). An interest in strengthening these institutions would thus present an important justification for limiting aggressive unilateral action that might simultaneously undermine the institution and threaten other great powers.

Conversely, a *demand* for delegitimation, protest, or overthrow of the status quo order removes this justification for limiting the pursuit of distributive revisions and thus reduces constraints on expansion. Imagine an idealized domestic debate over foreign policy within a rising state. There are two kinds of leaders – moderates, who prefer policies of pragmatic caution; and hardliners, who prefer more aggressive expansionist policies. All participants have to make public arguments to try to win support from other elites and the public. As the case studies in Chapters 3, 4, and 5 show, moderate leaders quite often invoke the costs of international rule-breaking and norm violation as an important argument against hardline policies. But when domestic audiences *positively value* policies that protest the legitimacy of status quo norms, rules, and institutions, that particular moderate objection is not politically sustainable. This empowers the advocates of expansion, whose preferred policies have the benefit of seeming to signal a rejection of the legitimacy of the status quo order. So while normative satisfaction tends to function as an obstacle for proponents of expansion, normative dissatisfaction makes less restrained expansion politically attractive.

This process is implicated in the increasingly aggressive behavior of Wilhelmine Germany, Imperial Japan, and Weimar/Nazi Germany as they grew more powerful. In each case, deep dissatisfaction with the status quo order undermined moderate leaders as they attempted to pursue pragmatic, cautious policies. In Wilhelmine Germany, this hampered Bethmann Hollweg's effort to facilitate a rapprochement with Great Britain and may have contributed to Germany's unwillingness to back down in the last days of July 1914. In Imperial Japan, it forced moderates to accede to hardliner demands for withdrawal from the League of Nations, which in turn empowered advocates of expansion in mainland Asia and unrestrained naval building. In Weimar Germany, increasing anger at the norms, rules, and institutions of the interwar order aided the rise of the NSDAP (the Nazis) and incentivized leaders (even before Hitler) to pursue deeper revisions to the Versailles settlement than pragmatists like Gustav Stresemann would ever have contemplated.

Of course, normative dissatisfaction on its own does not *necessarily* make states particularly dangerous. Depending on its depth and the apparent feasibility of launching a military challenge, it *may* push only toward policies that delegitimize and protest status quo rules, norms, and institutions, and states can sometimes satisfy these drives without acting violently or aggressively. The case of Tokugawa Japan illustrates how this is possible. Beginning in the early seventeenth century, Japan simply stopped participating in the institutions that constituted the Sino-Centric East Asian order. But this did not lead to military conflict – indeed Tokugawa leaders were well aware of how foolish this would be in the wake of Hideyoshi's failed campaign in Korea. Instead, the result was that Japan founded a parallel international order and refused to interact with other Sinic states in particular ways.

But in combination with significant distributive revisionist ambitions, normative dissatisfaction can help produce deeply aggressive postures that are dangerous and destabilizing for the rising state, its neighbors, and the status quo order. This book is devoted to understanding the origins of this explosive mix of revisionist policies.

Existing Explanations for Radical Revisionism

Why do rising states, which have incentives to pursue limited distributive change while expressing support for status quo rules, norms, and institutions, sometimes do things that run counter to this incentive structure? Why do they sometimes pursue policies that protest, delegitimize, or seek to overthrow the status quo order? Why do they sometimes fail to take steps that would make the pursuit of distributive change cheaper and less risky by signaling that they accept the broader legitimacy of the order and are willing to play by its rules? IR theorists have proposed three broad answers to these questions. Realist explanations invoke the costs and benefits of working within versus radically remaking the order; constructivist explanations invoke the normative or ideological distance between the rising state's vision of order and the status quo; and domestic explanations invoke a process in which the way elites with distributive revisionist preferences sell their policies to the public potentially pushes them to act in much more provocative ways. While none of these accounts tells a completely satisfying story, they offer important insights that I draw on as I develop my own theoretical framework in Chapter 2.

Realism and the Costs and Benefits of Revolutionary Change   The most important realist theoretical account of the origins of radical revisionist ambitions in rising great powers is Gilpin's. The conceptual framework at the core of *War and Change in World Politics* is similar in important ways to the one developed above. Gilpin's international systems are defined by distributions of resources and of prestige, and also by sets of rules and institutions that both help produce and are produced by the distribution of resources and prestige. The system's rules and institutions are set up in ways that benefit the actors at the top of the hierarchy of prestige, and these actors work to defend the status quo.

Rising states unsettle the status quo because their increasing power makes it profitable for them to demand and seek change. Gilpin envisions two distinct kinds of changes that rising powers may pursue. The most common is "incremental change." Gilpin describes this as a process of "continuous incremental adjustments within the framework of the existing system."[32] It involves limited shifts in the distribution of territory, wealth, influence, and prestige, and in alliances. This kind of change is best described as evolutionary, and it relieves the "pressure" on the system produced by uneven rates of growth.[33] Incremental change, in other words, is very closely related to the notion of distributive revisionism – rising states quite often seek changes in the system's distribution of resources but in ways that do not threaten the deeper foundation of the order.

The other kind of change is much less common and much more consequential. Gilpin calls this "revolutionary" change. States sometimes "believe that their interests can be served only by more sweeping and more profound changes in the international system."[34] When this is the case what is at "issue is the nature and governance of the system itself and/or, more rarely, the character of the international actors themselves."[35] Crises brought on by this sort of "constitutional" conflict "raise the basic issue of whose security, economic, and ideological interests will be most benefited by the functioning of the international system."[36] Gilpin's "revolutionary" change is closely related to the notion of radical

---

[32] Gilpin (1981), p. 45.   [33] Ibid., pp. 45–46.   [34] Ibid., p. 46.   [35] Ibid., p. 46.
[36] Ibid., p. 46.

revisionism – states with gripes about the distribution of resources also sometimes grow dissatisfied with the deep foundation of the order itself.

The story that Gilpin tells in *War and Change* is ultimately a story about why demands for incremental change sometimes morph into much more destabilizing demands for revolutionary change. His account, in brief, is that insurmountable obstacles to incremental change lead the rising state to grow dissatisfied with the order itself. While incremental changes are cheaper and less risky, the rising state will become willing to challenge the status quo more deeply if its objectives "cannot be realized in the framework of the existing system."[37] For Gilpin, this is typically the case because dominant but declining states are unwilling to make concessions until it is too late to appease the riser. A "disequilibrium" develops, produced by the tendency of the riser to grow faster than the system can adjust to its rise. This situation pushes toward hegemonic war as the increasingly radical demands of the riser convince the declining hegemon that the rising state cannot be appeased in a way consistent with the hegemon's vital interests, and that fighting now is better than fighting later. The outcome of the hegemonic war then leads to the constitution of a new system built to satisfy the interests of the victor, and the cycle begins again.[38]

Gilpin's insight about the relationship between obstructed incremental demands and the emergence of revolutionary demands is critically important and is at the core of the theoretical explanation I develop in Chapter 2. But the claim as it is presented in *War and Change* is problematic because it cannot explain why the rising state would risk disaster to transform the order. For one thing, Gilpin's conception of what rising great powers want is spare. Like many other realist accounts, *War and Change* focuses on demands for economic and security resources. Rising states seek increases in wealth and territory because the economic and security benefits of doing so begin to outweigh the costs.[39] But economic and security calculations are often not enough to explain demands for revolutionary change. As Ikenberry and others have persuasively argued, rising states often profit from free-riding on the institutional and normative frameworks of systems built and maintained by other states.[40] China, for instance, benefits from American-backed international rules and institutions that contribute to a global commitment to open markets, and from the American provision of public goods that keep shipping routes open, ensure the availability of resources like oil, and suppress defense spending in other East Asian states. It is far from clear why a

[37] Ibid., p. 46.   [38] Ibid., Chapter 5.   [39] Ibid., pp. 81–82, 95.
[40] See Ikenberry (2014), pp. 102–104; (2011), pp. 343–344; Schweller and Pu (2014).

Chinese leadership motivated by economic and security concerns would care to challenge American hegemony and the institutions, norms, and rules it maintains. Similarly, many moderate leaders in the rising great powers of the early twentieth century understood that their economic and security interests were better served by working within the existing order than by challenging it. This implies that we may need to go beyond wealth and security-seeking to explain demands for revolutionary change by rising great powers.

Moreover, Gilpin's conception of states as basically rational actors does not sit well with the claim that they respond to obstructions by escalating their demands.[41] According to Gilpin, the expanding objectives of states as they rise are the result of an evolving cost/benefit calculation. States begin demanding change when the benefits exceed the costs, and they continue to do so until the costs exceed the benefits. These same "hyper-rational" cost/benefit calculators are supposed to respond to obstructed incremental demands by making more radical demands. But it is not obvious why a rational actor would do this. Demands for revolutionary change, in Gilpin's framework, raise the probability of hegemonic war. And hegemonic wars are costly, messy, and unpredictable affairs, which is why Gilpin appeals to non-rational mechanisms – emotions like anxiety, and the tendency for events to "escape from human control" – to explain their initiation.[42]

This creates significant ambiguity within Gilpin's account: why would a rational actor respond to obstructed incremental demands by making revolutionary demands that convince other states that it cannot be appeased and thereby raise the probability of apocalyptic conflict?[43] Moderate leaders in early twentieth-century Germany and Japan raised similar objections to what they thought were unnecessarily provocative moves that seemed to promise only isolation and eventual disaster. What this implies is that we need to go beyond mechanisms that appeal to rational cost/benefit calculations to understand why obstructed incremental demands sometimes lead states to make demands for revolutionary change.

Normative Distance and International Order Constructivist explanations for radical revisionist policy combinations appeal to the ideological or normative "distance" between the rising power and the status quo order. The clearest exposition of this approach is Kupchan's

---

[41] See Kirshner (2014), pp. 142–151, on this critique.

[42] Gilpin (1981), p. 202; see also Kirshner (2014), pp. 156–157.

[43] Perhaps this behavior is a form of brinkmanship, though this interpretation does not appear in Gilpin's account.

recent work on the social foundations of hegemony.[44] Kupchan's argument is straightforward. States have varying ways of ordering political, social, and economic relations within their own borders. Some value democratic institutions and market economies; others practice authoritarian rule and have command economies; states also vary in the way their domestic social institutions express cultural values, like religion. As states become more powerful, they seek to export these normative "packages" as ways of ordering international politics within their spheres of influence. They do this both because leaders in the "metropole" believe their normative packages are the most appropriate, and because these packages are the visions of order with which elites are most familiar and comfortable.[45]

This means that hegemonic transitions "entail competition over norms and rules as well as position and status."[46] The more different the dominant normative "package" is from the riser's preferred package, the more likely the rising state will seek deep changes in status quo rules, norms, and institutions. When a rising state and a dominant state have similar visions of domestic order, their visions of international order will also coincide and the transition should not destabilize the normative foundation of the status quo. Kupchan suggests, along these lines, that the peacefulness and normative continuity of the Anglo-American power transition may be attributable to the Anglo-American consensus about the "Anglo-Saxon" vision of order.[47] Conversely, incompatible visions of order lead the rising state to reject status quo norms, rules, and institutions and turn the transition into an ideological conflict – by way of example Kupchan cites the competition between fascism, communism, and liberal democracy between the beginning of World War II and the end of the Cold War.[48]

The study of hegemonic transitions has been dominated by scholars interested in material sources of conflict, and Kupchan's argument is an invaluable corrective. But the focus on the normative distance between the rising state and the status quo order as a driver of conflict obscures two critical parts of the story. The first is that competing visions of order are contested domestically, not just internationally. Fascism may have contributed to the radically revisionist orientations of Imperial Japan and Nazi Germany prior to and during World War II. But during the 1920s and early 1930s, proponents of the fascist vision of order existed in Germany and Japan alongside proponents of alternative visions that were more compatible with the norms, rules, and institutions of the interwar status quo.

---

[44] See Kupchan (2012; 2014a; 2014b). See also Haas (2005) and Owen (2010).
[45] Kupchan (2014b), pp. 25–26; (2014a), pp. 225–226.   [46] Kupchan (2014b, p. 26).
[47] Ibid., p. 21.   [48] Ibid., p. 26.

There was nothing inevitable about the eventual dominance of the normatively distant fascist vision. Visions of domestic order – along with their implications for the way a state approaches the question of international order – are subject to domestic political contestation. This means that invoking ideological distance to explain why a rising state might challenge status quo norms, rules, and institutions entails not just identifying the sources of normative difference, but also accounting for the domestic victory of one vision of order over the alternatives.

The second complication follows directly from the first. Domestic visions of order have implications for foreign policy and international politics. But international politics also influence domestic contests over competing visions of order. Proponents of competing normative "packages" frequently base their foreign policy prescriptions on predictions about the behavior of other states and the feasibility and profitability of integrating with the status quo order. This means that foreign behavior can provide resources that actors in other states might be able to deploy to gain political advantages. The end of the Cold War provides a particularly striking example of this process. Gorbachev and his allies were committed to implementing a more open domestic political and economic order that would be ideologically closer to (and thus more compatible with) the Western international order. They were opposed, though, by Soviet hardliners who rejected both domestic reforms and rapprochement with the West. In order to prevail over the hardliners, Gorbachev needed to be able to demonstrate the feasibility and profitability of rapprochement, which meant that the Reagan administration's increasingly friendly treatment of the Soviet regime during its second term was critical both to the reform of the Soviet Union's domestic order and to the end of the Cold War.[49] Conversely, I show in Chapter 5 that proponents of the normatively distant fascist vision of order in Weimar Germany drew upon what they interpreted as unfair treatment by Western great powers to discredit moderate proponents of a more liberal vision.

This "second-image reversed" element implies that the relationship between normative distance and deep challenges to the status quo order is complicated by a reciprocal relationship between international politics and domestic visions of order. Normative distance may matter, but if it is partially (at least in some cases) caused by other factors, then there is more to the story. The theoretical account that I develop in Chapter 2 is sensitive to this complexity and proposes one particularly important process through which the behavior of foreign actors influences domestic contests over how to approach the status quo international order.

[49] See Evangelista (1993, p. 176); Brands (2014), pp. 126–139.

Entrapment and the Domestic Politics of Radical Revisionism The most relevant domestic theoretical frameworks are not pitched as explanations for policies that express deep dissatisfaction with the status quo order, but rather as explanations for "over-expansion," understood as unnecessary, self-defeating aggressive behavior.[50] Still, they are worth considering because radical revisionist policy combinations are a form of sub-optimally aggressive behavior.

Domestic accounts of over expansion vary tremendously in their conceptions of the sources of individual and small-group interests in aggressive foreign policies.[51] What they share is a commitment to a common mechanism that explains how aggressive elite interests produce self-defeating grand strategy: political and rhetorical entrapment. Snyder and Kupchan, for instance, both argue that elites with expansionist interests propagate "myths" or "images" about the relationship between security and expansion that help them convince the public to support aggressive foreign policies. But later, when it becomes clear to them that their policies are self-defeating and need to be adjusted, they find themselves trapped by the dominance of the very same myths and images they helped produce.[52] Christensen similarly invokes entrapment to explain why a leader who must oversell an expensive policy to a hesitant public by exaggerating moral or ideological threats might then be forced to pursue a sub-optimally aggressive grand strategy "in order to maintain the appearance of consistency between rhetoric and practice."[53]

It is not difficult to see how the mechanism of entrapment could help explain why rising powers might pursue radical revisionist policy combinations. In order to sell expansionist policies to the public, elites might try to propagate ideas about the undesirability of supporting status quo norms, rules, and institutions. If they succeed, they may be forced to actually take steps consistent with this rhetoric, like withdrawing from an international institution. They could also be prevented from taking steps – like cooperating with states committed to defending the status quo – that might make sense for strategic reasons but be inconsistent with the notion that the international order is illegitimate.

The domestic entrapment story is compelling and powerful, and a closely related set of mechanisms plays an important role in the theoretical

---

[50] See especially Snyder (1991), Kindle location 1282; Christensen (1996), p. 14; and Kupchan (1996), Chapter 2.

[51] Snyder locates them in parochial interests; Kupchan locates them in cognitive biases associated with perceptions of vulnerability; and Christensen locates them in realist calculations about the national interest.

[52] Snyder (1991), Kindle location 931–946; Kupchan (1996), pp. 87–92.

[53] Christensen (1996), pp. 16–17.

account I develop in the next chapter. But the conditions under which the entrapment mechanism – as it is deployed in these prominent accounts of over expansion – operates to push states toward sub-optimally aggressive policies require greater theoretical attention.

The root of the problem is that Snyder, Christensen, and Kupchan all model foreign policy legitimation as a fundamentally top-down process. Elites, who are either already in charge of foreign policy or who gain control through processes that are independent of legitimation games, develop a policy program and then work to gain support for it by bamboozling the public. They eventually succeed, and are then constrained in the future by their own success.

This model stands in contrast to another depiction of legitimation: as a contest between groups of elites who have opposing policy programs and draw on competing sets of rhetorical and political resources to gain the upper hand. Victory in these contests does not automatically go to the side advocating the more aggressive policy, but is rather influenced by variables like the elites' institutional positions, the character of preexisting discursive frameworks, and the kinds of arguments each side is able to draw upon.[54] Another way to put this is that aggressive myths, images, and mobilizing rhetoric do not always resonate with publics, and do not always trump the rhetorical and political efforts of elites pitching more moderate visions of the state's interests and grand strategy. Hitler's anti-status quo rhetoric did not launch him to prominence in Germany until the very end of the 1920s, even though he had been making similar arguments since the NSDAP was founded. Japanese militarists' loud campaign against status quo institutions did not overcome moderate objections to withdrawing from naval arms conventions and leaving the League of Nations until 1933.

What this suggests is that domestic explanations for over expansion based on the rhetorical and political appeal of expansionist myths or images need to be supplemented by an account of the conditions under which deeply aggressive policies are likely to be more easily sold than moderate policies. In the next chapter, I propose that widespread pessimism about the possibility of achieving status ambitions functions as one important rhetorical and political resource that produces advantages for advocates of provocatively aggressive policies over advocates of moderate policies.

---

[54] On this view of legitimation, see Krebs and Lobasz (2007), Krebs and Jackson (2007), Jackson (2006).

2   Status, Foreign Policy, and Revisionism

Rising powers have incentives to pursue policies that express demands for limited changes in the status quo distribution of resources while signaling support for status quo rules, norms, and institutions. But sometimes they pursue policies that express demands for much more radical change. They take steps that aim at protesting, delegitimating, or overthrowing status quo norms, rules, and institutions, and they fail to behave in ways that could make distributive gains easier and cheaper. As I showed in Chapter 1, these radical revisionist policy combinations are puzzling and particularly dangerous and destabilizing.

In this chapter, I develop a theoretical explanation for shifts from distributive to radical revisionist policy combinations in rising great powers. My account builds directly on Gilpin's insight that obstructed demands for "incremental" change can push rising states to demand deeper changes. But I part ways with Gilpin in two important ways. First, I argue that it is not obstructed economic and security ambitions but rather the appearance of permanently obstructed status demands that push states toward radical revisionist policy combinations. Second, I appeal to social psychological and domestic political mechanisms to explain how permanently obstructed status ambitions contribute first to individual demands for policies that reject status quo norms, rules, and institutions and then to state behavior that expresses these preferences.

My argument, in short, is that status immobility unleashes social psychological and political forces that push rising states toward radical revisionism. The belief that the rising state's status claims cannot be accommodated can produce preferences among individuals for policies that reject the status quo order. The more prominent the idea of status immobility is in the elite beliefs and foreign policy discourse of a rising state, the harder it is for moderate leaders to justify policies that participate in status quo institutions, follow status quo norms and rules, and cooperate with states identified as defenders of the order. This dynamic creates political advantages for hardliners, who can influence foreign

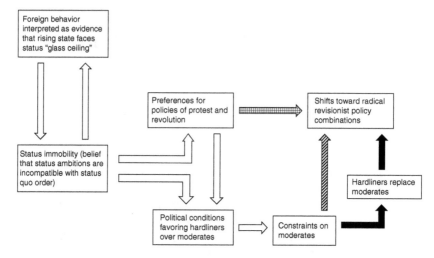

Figure 2.1 Status Immobility and Foreign Policy Change

policy even when they are not in power by pressuring moderate incumbents or by contributing to their political defeat. The result is a set of processes that push toward deeply (and sub-optimally) aggressive and provocative policy combinations. Figure 2.1 – to which I refer throughout the discussion below – summarizes these causal sequences.

The argument also complements the constructivist and domestic accounts reviewed in the previous chapter. Normative distance may well contribute to rising state dissatisfaction with status quo norms, rules, and institutions, but I argue that the appearance of permanently obstructed status claims can contribute to the dominance of distant visions of order in rising states. This is clearly not the only possible source of ideological differences between rising states and hegemons, but I show in Chapter 5 that it helps explain the rise to prominence and ultimate victory of Hitler's vision in the early 1930s. Similarly, my argument is consistent with domestic stories that involve rhetorical and political entrapment. But it clarifies an important ambiguity related to these approaches by proposing beliefs and discourses about status immobility as one condition that favors hardliners over moderates in rhetorical and political contests over policy.

The chapter proceeds as follows. I first define status and explain why states – especially rising states – want it and how they acquire it. I then introduce the concept of status immobility – the belief that a state's status ambitions have been permanently and unjustly obstructed. I develop the argument that status immobility produces shifts toward radical revisionism in two steps. First, I draw on insights from social psychology to argue that status immobility can cause individual demands for policies that reject status quo rules, norms, and institutions. Second, I argue that widespread beliefs and prominent discourses that the state faces a condition of status immobility change political conditions in ways that strengthen hardliners and weaken moderates. The chapter concludes by laying out my strategy for assessing the theory in light of evidence from the behavior of historical rising powers.

Rising Powers and Status Ambitions

Status refers to an actor's position within a social hierarchy. It may mean either membership in a highly regarded group or category of actors (like the "Big Ten") or rank within a group. Unlike other resources like wealth or power, status has to be recognized by other actors in order to be experienced as real. When an actor seeks a particular status, this entails an effort to achieve the markers of that status – the consensually valued characteristics that serve as prerequisites for membership – in order to convince others to behave in ways that signal that the status claim is legitimate.[1]

For example, an individual seeking the status of "professor" would go about accruing the markers of that status by achieving the characteristics of a professor and behaving like a professor. This might involve standing up and lecturing in a classroom twice a week. But if other actors do not respond appropriately – if students, for instance, refuse to pay attention or show up at all – then the aspiring professor will not experience the status as real.

This point is worth restating in more general terms. Whereas other kinds of ambitions can be satisfied unilaterally (as long as an actor is capable and committed enough) status ambitions are different. Their satisfaction depends upon the willingness of other actors to accommodate or recognize them by behaving in ways that ratify the claim.[2]

---

[1] For recent definitions, see Dafoe, Renshon, and Huth (2014), pp. 374–375; Larson, Paul, and Wohlforth (2014), p. 7; Neumann and de Carvalho (2015), pp. 4–7.

[2] The literature on recognition in international politics is concerned with the same fundamental issues as is the literature on status, but it differs in two primary ways: its self-conscious focus on the *performance* of identity claims, as opposed to the acquisition of status markers or consensually valued resources, and its attentiveness to the consequences of misrecognition (as opposed to status inconsistency, dissatisfaction, or anxiety) for foreign policy. See Ringmar (1996), Murray (2010), Lindemann (2010), Ringmar (2012), Daase, Fehl, Geis, and Kolliarakis (2015), and Lindemann and Ringmar (2016).

There is substantial evidence from social psychology and other fields that human beings identify with groups and care not just about their own individual status but also about the status of the groups that make up their social identities.[3] Understanding why this is so – and in particular why individuals care about the status of the state with which they identify – is critically important to the argument that I develop later in this chapter. There are three potential explanations.

First, it is likely that – in some contexts – groups with higher status provide the individuals that identify with them with better life chances. Attending a university with higher status provides certain material advantages; so does identifying (and being identified) as a member of a high status ethnic group.

Some scholars have analyzed the role of status in world politics primarily from this materialist perspective. Gilpin, for instance, suggested that the status of hegemon confers on its holder the right to order the international system in ways that benefit itself above other states. Others argue that high status increases power, influence, credibility, or coercive leverage, and thus that it has a positive effect on a state's welfare and security.[4]

But there is no reason to presume that status matters to states primarily because of its material significance, or to take this notion as a default theoretical starting point. For one thing, the claim that status boosts influence, credibility, or coercive leverage has never been demonstrated empirically in the context of international politics. It is, at this stage of the research program, no more than an assumption.[5] Moreover, a common finding of research on status in IR is that its pursuit often comes at the *expense* of welfare or security.[6] And individuals seem to care about the

---

[3] See Frank (1985); Goethals and Darley (1987); Berger and Zelditch (1998); Berger et al. (1998); Loch et al. (2001).

[4] Gilpin (1981); Dafoe, Renshon, and Huth (2014); Renshon (2016, 2017); Sambanis, Skaperdas, and Wohlforth (2015).

[5] Renshon (2017) asserts that status has instrumental value in the context of international politics and that this means that we should build theories about status-seeking on rationalist or strategic foundations, rather than by appealing to what he calls "weak" mechanisms related to frustration or other emotions. But it is striking that he provides no evidence that the former claim is true. Indeed, the way that he discusses his experimental results (Chapter 3) leads to the interpretation that status concerns reduce the quality of decision-making; there is no attempt to establish a link between status and outcomes like success in coercive bargaining in the quantitative section of the book (Chapters 4 and 5); and in each of the four historical cases that he analyzes (pre–World War I Germany, Russia during the July Crisis, Great Britain during the Suez Crisis, and Egypt's intervention in Yemen beginning in 1962), status-seeking did not lead to any concrete instrumental advantage, but rather to disaster (Chapters 6 and 7). Moreover, Mercer (2017) has recently provided compelling theoretical and empirical reasons to think that, far from having instrumental value, status is an illusion that states pursue at their peril.

[6] See Murray (2010); Ward (2013); Wolf (2014).

status of groups with which they identify even when this has no plausible effect on their material welfare. Whether the Yankees win the World Series in any given year has material significance only for the club's employees and for people whose businesses might benefit from a long playoff run. Fans nonetheless remain deeply emotionally invested in the performance of their team. If the status of an athletic team matters to human beings for reasons that have almost nothing to do with material welfare or instrumental value, then it makes little sense to assume that a state's status is primarily significant because of its utility for the pursuit of other objectives.

A second explanation is that the status of a group is significant for the self-esteem of the individuals that identify with it. This is the position of much social psychological research – especially the body of it known as social identity theory (SIT). Developers and users of the SIT framework have demonstrated experimentally that individuals exhibit ingroup bias, even when group membership is minimally constituted and even when favoring members of the ingroup over members of the outgroup has no plausible link to any materially significant outcome.[7] The implication of these findings is that group status matters because it influences how individuals feel about themselves. Being a member of a respected group generates positive emotions like pride; being a member of a disrespected group generates negative emotions like shame and, under some conditions, anger and frustration.

From this perspective, individuals care about the status of the state because the status of the state influences their self-esteem. This, of course, is not true of all individuals all the time – some people will simply not spend much time thinking about what it means to be American or French or Canadian, and others may actively object to such categorizations. But some people do identify strongly as members of states – this is a defining feature of nationalists. And for these individuals – according to the insights of social psychologists – the status of the state is important not (or not mostly) because of its material significance, but because of its significance for identity and self-esteem.[8]

The third reason that the status of a state might matter to an individual is related to the second, but it applies specifically to leaders: status might be important because of its significance for domestic political legitimacy.

[7] On SIT, see Tajfel (1978a, 1978b, 1982); Tajfel and Turner (1979); and Hogg and Abrams (1988).

[8] For a review of social psychological perspectives on nationalism, see Druckman (1994). This perspective is common within parts of the IR status literature, most notably in the work of Larson and Shevchenko (2010, 2014), but also in recent work on stigma and social hierarchy (Zarakol [2011], and Adler-Nissen [2014]).

The link between status and the legitimacy of a leader runs through the preferences of nationalists and the nature of predominant identity narratives or claims: if, as suggested above, nationalists care about the status of the state and prefer higher to lower status, or are attached to a particular understanding of what status the state deserves, then demonstrating a commitment to raising or maintaining the state's status is critical for any leader at least partially dependent on their support. Presiding over a decline in status or a failure to satisfy ambitions for higher status leaves the leader vulnerable to charges of having failed to secure the state's rightful place in the international system – which may undermine his or her legitimacy and position.

Status may matter to states for all three of these reasons. Yet the second and third are critical to the argument I develop below. If status were *only* important because of its value in terms of wealth and security, then it could be bought and sold without much difficulty. A state whose status ambitions seemed incompatible with the status quo order could be compensated in other ways. It is the emotional and domestic political significance of status that makes this difficult and that makes status distinct from other kinds of resources. Appearing to bargain away a claim to equal or superior status might be seen as unacceptable for reasons that have nothing to do with welfare or security, which may make it a dangerous proposition for a leader. In short, status may indeed make a state wealthier and more secure; but privileging this understanding of status' role in IR is unwarranted and leaves one with an anemic view of its potential consequences for foreign policy.

Establishing that status-seeking often motivates foreign policy has been one of the most important achievements of the growing literature on status in international politics.[9] This scholarship has identified status-seeking as the driver of policies and outcomes that include among others the initiation of major war, great power rivalry, construction of certain kinds of weapons, attempts to join or reform international organizations, and involvement in peacekeeping and humanitarian missions around the world. Status is obviously not the *only* resource that motivates states, but it is a prominent and underappreciated one. And it holds the potential to help us understand otherwise unintelligible behaviors, like Germany's

---

[9] Thucydides (1972), I: 76, acknowledged the status motive, as did Hobbes (1985), p. 185, Machiavelli (1996), p. 219, and Rousseau (1991), p. 48. See also Slomp (1990), p. 566; and see Markey (1999, 2000) on status in the thought of classical authors. But with some notable exceptions (for instance, a short-lived research program that began in the 1970s, Gilpin's [1981] invocation of "prestige" in *War and Change*, and a short discussion in Nicholas Onuf's [1989], Kindle location 5310–5538, foundational exposition of constructivism), the concept has not attracted sustained attention from IR scholars until recently.

obsession with building battleships before World War I or Norway's insistence on "punching above its weight" in world politics.[10]

Clearly not all states' foreign policies are equally concerned with status-seeking. Some seem deeply concerned – like contemporary China – while others – like, say, Canada or Switzerland – seem not to care as much. This is not a simple matter of power: small states sometimes have foreign policies that are deeply concerned with issues of standing.[11] The literature on status in IR has not developed a comprehensive account of variation in the salience of status concerns, and I do not do so in this book either.[12]

What previous scholarship *has* established, though, is that status is often an especially salient concern for states whose material capabilities are rising. Increasing wealth and military power make a rising state more like established high status powers in significant ways, which prompts people who identify with the riser to expect – and demand – convergence in terms of standing, influence, and rights as well. This dynamic is at the core of claims by contemporary Chinese elites for a renegotiated pattern of relations between Beijing and Washington: China's growing economy and improved military mean that it deserves to be treated like an equal, rather than like a subordinate regional player.[13]

But status attribution or recognition often lags behind increases in economic and military power.[14] This observation – which is at the core of Gilpin's framework in *War and Change* – explains why rising states sometimes seem so preoccupied with their place in the world. Rising

---

[10] For a review, see Dafoe, Renshon, and Huth (2014). On status and conflict, see Lebow (2008), (2010b); Wohlforth (2009); Larson and Shevchenko (2010); and Onea (2014). Others have argued that status partially explains why states build nuclear weapons (Hummel 2016), battleships (Murray 2010), and aircraft carriers (Ross 2009; Pu and Schweller 2014). On status and international organizations, see Larson and Shevchenko (2010, 2014a); Paul and Shankar (2014); Heimann (2014); and Pouliot (2014). On status and involvement in peacekeeping operations and humanitarian efforts, see Suzuki (2008), and in the context of Norwegian foreign policy, Graeger (2015) and de Carvalho and Lie (2015).

[11] On small-state status-seeking, see de Carvalho and Neumann (2015).

[12] Renshon (2017) has recently made a start by arguing that the salience of status concerns is fundamentally a matter of unmet expectations, though there remain a large number of outstanding questions.

[13] The most prominent articulation of this argument is in Gilpin's *War and Change* (1981). More recently, see Renshon (2016, 2017) and Volgy et al. (2014). Though Renshon attributes the link between increasing capabilities and status ambitions to a combination of perceived opportunity and grievance (due to being denied the status appropriate to the state's "asset level"), Mercer's (2017) recent critique implies that it may have more to do with emotional psychology: increasing capabilities may generate pride that then translates into heightened expectations about the state's status. On Chinese status expectations, see Deng (2008).

[14] On the "stickiness" of attributed status, see Renshon (2017), Chapter 5.

status expectations result from rising (or apparently rising) material capabilities, but status does not follow automatically. It has to be granted through acts of accommodation – actions by high status states that confer on the rising power particular rights and privileges that are associated with the status it seeks. Status expectations can outpace acts of accommodation for many reasons. Established powers might not understand the nature of the rising power's demands; institutional inertia could delay accommodation; or – most simply – the established power might be uncomfortable acknowledging that the rising power deserves the status, rights, and privileges that it claims.[15]

This should not be taken as an argument that rising power is the *only* source of concerns about status. Explaining the origins of status ambitions involves, at root, explaining the origins of the way that people imagine their state's place in the world. This process is clearly driven by much more than changes in material capabilities: other factors – like representations of national history, collective understandings of identity, and the idiosyncratic personalities and choices of leaders – also matter. My claim is simply that – whatever else might be at work – rising power often drives rising status expectations. This means that the theoretical dynamics that I develop below are particularly relevant for understanding the foreign policies of rising powers.

Whatever their source, status expectations that outpace accommodation result in the condition of *status inconsistency* or *status dissatisfaction*.[16] Status inconsistency is politically and psychologically uncomfortable – individuals feel that the state with which they identify deserves more respect than it gets, and may also feel that their leaders are failing to secure it. Leaders, for their part, may feel pressure to address concerns about the state's status through policies aimed at securing recognition from other states. The conventional wisdom in the IR status literature is that policies intended to correct a condition of status inconsistency or dissatisfaction typically entail conflict, violence, and war.[17] But this is not

---

[15] See Wohlforth (2014) on uncertainty about status ambitions and Onea (2014) on the dominant state's disinclination to recognize the riser's claims. Mercer (2017) suggests that reluctance to recognize claims to higher status may also be driven by psychological mechanisms that bias actors toward discounting the achievements of rivals. On accommodation more broadly, see Paul (2016).

[16] Lenski (1954). Status inconsistency has often been linked to demands for social change and violence. See Galtung (1964); Stryker and Macke (1978); and Gould (2003). On status dissatisfaction, see Renshon (2017). I use status inconsistency and status dissatisfaction interchangeably.

[17] The link between status inconsistency and war originated with Galtung (1964), and spawned a large quantitative literature during the 1970s, 1980s, and 1990s (East 1972; Wallace 1971, 1973; Ray 1974; Gochman 1980; Volgy and Mayhall 1995). More recently, see Wohlforth (2009); Volgy et al. (2014); and Renshon (2016, 2017).

always true. The way in which a demand for status influences policy depends upon the particular markers associated with the aspirational status category, and these are social constructions that vary across time and space.[18] A state aspiring to great power status may need to fight and win wars, but only if demonstrating the ability to do so is understood as a prerequisite for membership in the great power club. In different contexts, the markers of great power status have included the possession of particular kinds of weapons systems (battleships around the turn of the twentieth century; nuclear weapons after 1945; and aircraft carriers today), the possession and administration of colonial territory (until the post-1945 era), and certain civilizational and institutional characteristics (which have varied over time). States seeking this particular status will do so by pursuing a mix of policies intended to increase the similarity between themselves and existing great powers along all relevant dimensions. Status-seeking only entails violence to the extent that violence is necessary to achieve status markers.[19]

The record of Japanese status-seeking after the Meiji restoration is a useful example. As I detail in Chapter 4, Japan aspired to membership in the club of Western great powers that included Great Britain, France, and the United States (and at various times Germany, Russia, Italy, and Austria-Hungary). Achieving this status entailed a mix of policies. Some of these involved violent conflict, such as the wars against China and Russia that earned Japan its first overseas possessions. But status-seeking also involved efforts to reform Japanese social and political institutions to bring them in line with Western norms, as well as a concerted effort to participate in the management of the post-World War I order by joining the League of Nations as a permanent member of the League Council. All of this was in large part motivated by a desire to achieve for Japan the same rights and privileges afforded other great powers.[20]

The Japanese efforts highlight another important point. Status-seeking itself does not push states to adopt radical revisionist policy combinations. Indeed, to the extent that seeking status motivates states to participate more deeply in status quo institutions and ratify (by their behavior) status

---

[18] For example, see Towns (2010) for a thorough account of the changing function of gender norms as markers of status in world politics, and the varying ways in which this influenced policy toward women in states positioned differently in the international hierarchy.

[19] See, for instance, Barnhart (2016) on the role of collective understandings about the value of colonial territory in explanations in constituting imperial competition as a response to status anxiety among late nineteenth-century European powers.

[20] See also Ward (2013).

quo norms, it actually strengthens the normative element of the status quo order.[21] It is, in the conceptual vocabulary introduced in Chapter 1, a form of distributive revisionism.

Status Immobility

Recent scholarship on status in IR has made important contributions to our understanding of the ways in which states seek status and some of the links between status dynamics and conflict. It has also left important questions unanswered. One of the most significant relates to the consequences of persistently denied status claims. Since the satisfaction of status claims depends upon recognition by other states, this raises the possibility that persistent denials could convince elites and others in a rising state that their status ambitions are fundamentally inconsistent with the status quo order. I call this pessimism about the prospects of securing recognition *status immobility*.

Status immobility refers to the belief that a state's status ambitions face an obstacle that is fundamental to the status quo order and cannot be overcome from inside of it. Two parts of this conceptual definition require clarification. First, the concept does not refer to an objective condition. Certainly objective conditions are significant – the behavior of other states, for instance, is an important source of information about the possibility of achieving membership in an aspirational status club. But what really matters is how individuals and groups within the rising state interpret international conditions and foreign behavior. This means that beliefs about the severity of the obstacle the rising state faces can vary across actors *within* the rising state.

Second, status immobility refers to the appearance of obstacles that originate within the political, normative, or institutional structure of the status quo order; it does not refer to obstacles related to the incompetence or unwillingness to invest of the status-seeker. The key difference is that status immobility involves the notion that exclusion from the aspirational status club is *unjust*.[22] In this sense, status immobility can be understood as a status "glass ceiling." The problem is not that the rising state has not yet accumulated the requisite markers of status and thus does not deserve membership; it is instead that the state *does* deserve membership, but other states seem fundamentally unwilling to treat it as a full member of the club.

---

[21] See also Wohlforth (2015), pp. 149–152.
[22] For an important treatment of justice in international relations, see Welch (1993).

The processes through which perceptions and discourses of status immobility arise are complex and multiple. They are rooted, in part, in actions by other states – especially by established members of elite status clubs – that seem to signal a firm commitment to refusing the rising power's claims to higher standing. Put more concretely, foreign behavior may contribute to the emergence of beliefs and the production of discourses about status immobility when it seems to deny the status-seeker rights and privileges claimed as inherent to the aspirational status, and when it seems to reflect a basic disposition against recognizing the rising power as an equal, rather than a simple conflict of interest in some specific context. These two elements are worth unpacking at more length.

First, for an act to be interpreted as evidence of status immobility, it needs to appear to be an act of status denial. To understand what this means, it is helpful to think of status as a role identity associated with a bundle of rights and privileges: "great power" status, for instance, is an identity that has made it possible for states to whom that identity adheres to legitimately take certain actions – like intervening in their near abroad or possessing particular kinds of weapons – that would be illegitimate for other kinds of states. There are, in other words, certain rights and privileges – which are historically contingent and have evolved over time – to which only states in the "great power" club have legitimate access.[23]

In concrete terms, then, an act of status denial is an act by one state that seems to deny that another state has access to a right that it claims as part of a claim to a particular status. The US Navy's freedom of navigation (FON) operational assertion program nicely illustrates the sort of act that might be interpreted as evidence of status denial. Under the FON program, the navy sails warships through maritime zones in which other states have claimed rights to restrict navigation that exceed the limits set out in the UN Convention on the Law of the Sea. In other words, FON operational assertions assert the right to freedom of navigation while signaling a denial of the target state's right to restrict navigation. When the target state's claim is implicated in a broader claim to standing – as it arguably is in the case of Chinese claims to a sphere of influence in East Asia and the South China Sea – an operational assertion may seem to be an act that denies not only the right but also the associated claim to status.[24]

Second, in order to be interpreted as evidence of status immobility, an act of status denial has to seem to reflect a fundamental inability or

[23] For consistent treatments, see Bull (1977), pp. 207 and 212; Simpson (2004), pp. 68–71; Suzuki (2008), p. 47; Heimann (2014); Larson, Paul, and Wohlforth (2014), p. 10; Neumann (2014); and Paul (2016), p. 5.

[24] On the FON program, see Etzioni (2015).

unwillingness to accommodate the rising power. Not all acts of status denial are equally easy for observers who identify with the rising state to assimilate into a narrative about the basic injustice of the status quo order. Some may seem to be one-off consequences of circumstance, or they can be explained away as nothing more than the result of the bargaining and haggling that characterizes the typical nature of international politics.

Two characteristics make acts of status denial easier to see and characterize as evidence that a state faces a condition of status immobility. First, an act that seems to be part of a *pattern* is easier to interpret as evidence that the status quo is unjust than is an act that seems to come out of the blue. This is an obvious but important point, and it implies that perceptions of status immobility take time to emerge and are path-dependent – if leaders or elites have characterized foreign behavior as an act of status denial in the past, it will be easier for them or others to interpret a new act of status denial as reflective of a disposition against treating the state justly.

Second, acts of status denial are easier to interpret as evidence of status immobility when they can reasonably be presented as the consequence of a salient structural condition that prevents the state from being treated fairly.[25] This, too, is a straightforward point: an act of status denial is more likely to seem like a reflection of systemic injustice when it appears to be driven by a deep, difficult-to-change feature of the international environment than when it seems explicable as a result of the disposition of a particular leader or the nature of a temporary set of circumstances. When acts of status denial can be attributed by observers to factors like inflexible alliance commitments, discrimination based on identity cleavages, or institutional arrangements, they are likely to contribute to pessimism about the possibility of achieving the state's status ambitions without a drastic change in the character of the status quo order.

But acts of status denial merely provide the raw material out of which beliefs about and discourses of status immobility emerge. The ways in which leaders and other political elites publicly interpret the meaning of what happens abroad is also important. This may have more to do with short-term political incentives than it does with genuine beliefs about the injustice of the international status quo, and it is heavily influenced by the rhetorical and political resources elites have available to them as a result of the way that they (and their predecessors) have interpreted the state's history. A leader in a status-seeking state might, for instance, have an

---

[25] See Zarakol (2011), Kindle locations 2428–2610, for a discussion of the ways in which social conditions can seem to impose insurmountable obstacles to advancement.

incentive to publicly make sense of some crisis or diplomatic defeat as evidence of a discriminatory disposition on the part of other states in order to deflect attention from the incompetence or overreaching of the government. And doing so might be easier if the allegedly obstructionist state seems to have a record of behaving in ways that seem unjust, unfair, or discriminatory to the status-seeker. This means that the process by which status immobility becomes prominent in any state is path-dependent. This complication has methodological implications to which I return at the end of the chapter.

This discussion raises a puzzle: why do established powers not attempt to accommodate the status claims of rising powers and thereby short-circuit or minimize the negative consequences that – I argue below – emerge from the production of status immobility? This is an important question, in part because it has implications for the ability to distinguish – in practice – status immobility theory from standard realist accounts of conflict driven by power transitions. These might contend that established powers deny the status claims of rising powers because accommodation is incompatible with a commitment to opposing or containing the expansion of the rising power's material capabilities or influence, and, as a result, that accommodation threatens the established power's welfare or security.[26] Thus conflict over status is inevitable, but epiphenomenal: it is merely a product of conflict over security or wealth, and thus does not merit attention in its own right.

It is worth taking very seriously the possibility that accommodation failure is nothing more than the consequence of a commitment to the material containment of a rising power, and that conflict over status is reducible to conflict over wealth or security. This view implies that accommodation and containment represent opposite poles along a continuum of policy options available to established powers confronting rising powers – thus, to choose containment is to reject accommodation (and thus commit to status denial), and vice versa.

But accommodation and containment are better understood as positions along *two distinct* dimensions of policy. Accommodation refers to behavior that signals to the riser that it has legitimate access to some claimed right or set of rights associated with a particular status category. Status denial refers to actions that signal the opposite. Containment, on the other hand, refers to actions aimed at halting or restricting the expansion of a rising power's material capabilities. Its opposite is retrenchment: the reduction of security commitments and the resultant

---

[26] See Paul and Shankar (2014) and Lobell (2016) for arguments about security concerns as an obstacle to accommodation.

(at least tacit) acquiescence to the rising power's growing material power and influence.[27]

These are separate analytical dimensions, and established powers can, and sometimes do, adopt policy orientations that approximate all four possible combinations. This implies that status denial is not always caused by a commitment to containment. For instance, I show in Chapter 4 that Western policy toward interwar Japan combined status denial – in the form of behavior that seemed to reject Tokyo's claims to a variety of status-related rights in world politics – with a refusal to materially oppose the expansion of Japanese power and influence in East Asia. Similarly, I argue in Chapter 5 that the Allied powers pursued a combination of status denial and retrenchment toward interwar Germany – they acted in ways that seemed to reject Berlin's claims to the rights of a great power, but they also refused to contain its growing material capabilities. In neither of these cases were acts of status denial caused by the pursuit of policies aimed at containment.

In fact, acts of status denial can be driven by a variety of dynamics. Established powers may suffer from their own status anxieties – perhaps exacerbated by the nature of the rising power's demands – which might make acts of accommodation difficult; domestic political obstacles unrelated to status concerns might prevent accommodation in some cases; and established power leaders may even simply fail to correctly perceive the nature of the rising power's demands. The upshot is that even if acts of status denial are sometimes caused by the commitment to containment, the origins of status immobility are separate from – and thus not reducible to – conflict over power and security. The sources of status immobility are diverse.

Ultimately it is the consequences of status immobility – not its causes – that are central to my argument in this book. Analysts of status in world politics have thus far not developed a consistent and satisfying account of what happens when a state's status ambitions are obstructed. The most common argument is that obstructed status claims lead states to abandon peaceful status-seeking strategies in favor of geopolitically competitive or violent ones.[28] There are several problems with this proposition. First, geopolitically competitive forms of status-seeking often precede perceptions of status immobility, for the simple reason that military power, territory, and economic resources are common markers of status.[29]

---

[27] On containment, see Art (2003), pp. 111–120; on retrenchment, see MacDonald and Parent (2011).

[28] Larson and Shevchenko (2010, 2014a, 2014b); Murray (2010); Wolf (2014); Lee (2016).

[29] See, for instance, Barnhart (2016), Volgy et al. (2014), Renshon (2016).

Thus geopolitical competition is often the result of an attempt to achieve higher status, rather than a response to the perception that doing so is impossible.

Second, in most cases status-seeking – even vigorous and violent status-seeking – *strengthens* the normative and institutional elements of the status quo, and thus the foundation of the privileged position of its defenders. It has this effect because – as the Japanese example briefly discussed above shows – it accepts and ratifies the legitimacy of existing markers of high status.[30] Even Germany's deeply conflictual effort to catch up with Great Britain in terms of battleships and colonies cannot but have signaled that Germany accepted the legitimacy of battleships and colonies as valued attributes – the same valued attributes that constituted Great Britain as the state at the top of the global hierarchy.

A state facing a situation in which its status ambitions appeared *incompatible* with the status quo order – or an individual who believed the state faced a status "glass ceiling" – would thus confront a dilemma: policies aimed at status-seeking by acquiring consensually valued characteristics might simultaneously be futile and reproductive of the unjust order. They may, as a result, be doubly unattractive. In the next section, I propose instead that status immobility pushes toward policy responses that protest, delegitimize, or overthrow the normative foundation of the status quo order.

A third problem with existing treatments of state responses to concerns about status is that they almost invariably treat states as if they were people, which leaves the mechanisms at the heart of these accounts ambiguous. One prominent approach, for instance, has been to take the insights of social identity theory – a social psychological framework that is intended to explain how individuals manage status anxiety originating in group membership – and use them to explain how *states* manage status anxiety.[31] But individuals within states may hold very different ideas about what the state's status ambitions should be, how important they are relative to other goals, and how likely they are to be achieved within the bounds of the status quo order. In order to link beliefs about status "glass ceilings" to foreign policy, we need to incorporate status dynamics into a model that takes seriously the politics of making policy. The theoretical framework that I develop in the next section does this by proposing that status immobility has the potential to influence policy not only by motivating leaders but also by changing the balance of power between moderates and hardliners inside states.

---

[30] Lebow (2008), p. 67; Suzuki (2008), p. 60; Zarakol (2011), Kindle location 2234.
[31] See Larson and Shevchenko (2003, 2010, 2014a).

Status Immobility, Demands to Reject the Status Quo Order, and Foreign Policy

This book's central argument is that status immobility produces social psychological and political forces that push rising states toward adopting policies that reject – rather than seek to adjust or rise within – the status quo order. There are two important elements of this argument. The first is an account – rooted in insights from social psychology – of the origins of individual preferences for policies that reject the status quo order. Put simply, the perception of persistent, unjust status denial can produce demands for actions aimed at overthrowing, withdrawing from, or protesting status quo rules and institutions. These dynamics are most likely to affect those who identify most strongly with the group – which, in the context of international politics, means strong nationalists. Thus, the first element of the theory establishes its micro-foundations: a social psychological link between perceptions of persistent status denial and an interest (especially among nationalists) in policies aimed at rejecting international order.

Of course, foreign policy will not always reflect the preferences of frustrated nationalists. Leaders have competing interests to balance, and may be more sensitive to the (domestic and international) costs and risks that rejectionist policies entail. Thus, the second element of the theory draws on insights from research on the politics of legitimation to build an account that links preferences for rejectionist policies to concrete policy change. The argument is that widespread beliefs about or discourses of status immobility constitute a domestic political resource that benefits actors with hardline foreign policy preferences. It can be invoked to weaken incumbents – especially if they prefer to pursue moderate policies – and to strengthen the proponents of aggressive policies, regardless of where aggressive preferences originate. And anticipation of these effects on their political survival can push moderate incumbents to pursue rejectionist policies against their own better judgment. Thus the social psychological consequences of status immobility can be harnessed by political entrepreneurs to effect foreign policy change and advance their own interests, even if they themselves evidence no great concern with the state's status. This dynamic makes the state's foreign policy more aggressive and more reflective of the preferences of those frustrated nationalists demanding rejection of the status quo.

Status Immobility and the Social Psychology of Rejection

Previous scholarship has drawn upon social identity theory to derive three logics of identity management, or strategic responses to low state status.

The standard model distinguishes between *mobility* (emulating the values and institutions of the members of the elite club to join its ranks), *creativity* (altering the markers associated with membership in the elite club), and *competition* (attempting to equal or outdo a higher status state in the areas on which its dominance is based). This is a valuable taxonomy, but it is incomplete. Each of these responses to status anxiety depends, in the end, on the recognition of existing members of the elite club; each also at least implicitly accepts and therefore ratifies and reproduces the prevailing institutions and rules that constitute the elite club as elite. This is most obviously true for mobility, but it is also true for creativity – which aims at the reform of the status quo from within – and competition – which takes for granted that the advantaged position of the dominant actor has a legitimate basis and merely seeks to beat the dominant actor at its own game.[32]

What the taxonomy is missing is an account of how actors respond when gaining status through these three avenues seems to face an unjust, externally imposed, and insuperable obstacle. What is needed, in other words, is an account of how actors respond to status *immobility*. I introduce a new logic of identity management – the logic of rejection – that addresses this neglected dilemma.

First, though, a note on what I mean by "logic of identity management" is in order. I depart slightly from the standard model (which treats mobility, creativity, and competition as strategies from which unitary *states* choose) and define a "logic of identity management" in international politics as a way of dealing with low state status that an *individual* who identifies with that state may pursue or promote in response to the way in which the individual understands the international social conditions that the state faces. Two individuals may at the same time promote two different responses – one may advocate that the state compete for status; the other may promote creativity because competition seems infeasible or unwisely provocative.

In terms more familiar to students of international politics, a logic of identity management is analogous to a grand strategy – while a grand strategy is a theory about how a state can secure its material existence and welfare, a logic of identity management is a theory about how a state can best secure its identity and status. And just as individuals often promote different grand strategies based on their varying ideas about factors like the nature of the national interest or the utility of force, individuals also

---

[32] Part of the problem with this taxonomy is that it is based on a mistranslation of social identity theory. See Ward (forthcoming).

promote different logics of identity management based on their varying ideas about the international social conditions the state faces.

The familiar identity management strategies of *mobility, competition,* and *creativity* are all based on the logic of recognition. They can only resolve a condition of status dissatisfaction by convincing relevant others to recognize the rising state's claims, and their pursuit has centripetal force: each of these responses, in an important sense, accepts (thereby ratifying and perpetuating) the rules, institutions, and social hierarchy that constitute the status quo. Mobility does this by emulating consensually valued cultural and institutional forms; competition by tacitly accepting the legitimacy of the status hierarchy's foundation; and creativity through its dependence on existing "top dogs" to acknowledge the legitimacy of some reinterpretation of the comparative situation. Thus, there is good reason for someone who believes that the state faces a condition of status immobility to oppose these three responses. If the rules seem to be fundamentally unfair, then playing the game according to the rules will not only be futile, it will also reconstitute the rules, the game, and the unjust social hierarchy these produce.

Instead, the condition of status immobility leads to pressure for a response that *rejects* the status quo order. A response aimed at rejection is distinct from one aimed at recognition in two ways. First, its immediate aim is not to convince relevant others to grant the state higher status – whether in the form of membership in a high status category or club or of status-linked rights and privileges. This, after all, is thought to be impossible absent some dramatic change in conditions. Second, it explicitly rejects playing by the rules of the status quo order. Undermining the rules and institutions that constitute the order would run contrary to the requirements of mobility, competition, or creativity; but a belief in status immobility is equivalent to a belief that the rules are hopelessly unfair – thus, rejection *values* undermining the foundation of the status quo order.[33] Table 2.1 summarizes the three logics of recognition and contrasts them with the logic of rejection.

Research in the field of social psychology shows that individuals tend to support actions that reject status quo rules, norms, and institutions when faced with unjust, persistent denial of status. There is evidence to support this notion from both laboratory experiments and observational studies in a variety of substantive contexts. Beginning in the middle of the 1980s, a series of related studies (called the Five-Stage Model or FSM

---

[33] See Zarakol (2011), Kindle locations 2460–2610 on the fundamental difference between trying to advance within a social hierarchy and rejecting the order as distinct logics of identity management.

Table 2.1 *Logics of Identity Management*

Logic	Description	Nature of Solution
Mobility	Aims to gain entry into elite club by emulating its members' norms and institutions	Recognition by relevant others of new hierarchy
Competition	Aims to achieve higher status through geopolitically competitive practices	Recognition by relevant others of new hierarchy
Creativity	Aims to achieve higher status by changing collective understandings about what constitutes a status marker	Recognition by relevant others of legitimacy of new status criteria and new hierarchy
Rejection	Aims to protest, delegitimize, or overthrow status quo norms, rules, and institutions	Removes obstacle to achievement of status ambitions; expresses frustration, anger, resentment; avoids indignity of participation in own humiliation

studies) investigated individual emotional and behavioral responses to varying perceptions of the justice and flexibility of status hierarchies. Researchers manipulated individual beliefs about whether their placement in a low status group was just, as well as whether the higher status group was open to new members. Participants could choose to respond to their condition with "normative" action – for instance, accepting their placement or requesting a re-assessment of their individual merit for membership in the higher group; or they could choose a "non-normative" action – for instance, protesting their placement in the lower status group. Subjects were told that "non-normative" responses were seen as "unacceptable" to the members of the high status group. Results of these studies suggest that individuals facing a condition in which a high status group seems to be "closed" – especially those who believe they deserve membership in that group – are particularly likely to prefer "non-normative" behavioral responses. This may be due to consequentialist reasoning: if accepted practices leave no path to status advancement, then these practices must be circumvented or undermined. But it may also be due to affect: results of the FSM studies suggest an association between the perceived closure of the high status group and feelings of frustration and resentment – especially for subjects who felt they were better qualified for membership in the high status group.[34]

---

[34] Taylor and McKirnan (1984); Taylor et al. (1987); Wright et al. (1990); Kawakami and Dion (1995); and Boen and Vanbeselaere (1998, 2000).

Observational studies – mostly conducted within the relative deprivation (RD) research program – provide additional evidence of a link
between perceptions of persistent, unjust status denial and support for
actions that reject status quo rules, norms, and institutions. Relative
deprivation refers to a condition of perceived injustice: an individual
believes that he or she suffers from some sort of deficit, not relative to
what is needed for survival, but rather relative to a reference group or
expectation-level. The experience of relative deprivation has been linked
to a wide range of "non-normative" behavioral responses. For instance,
in one of the most famous applications of relative deprivation theory
(RDT) to a question of interest to political science, Ted Gurr invoked
relative deprivation as part of an explanation for rebellion. Others
have more recently noted a particular link between "collective relative
deprivation" – that is, the belief that a group with which one identifies
suffers collectively from RD – and protest "orientations" among members
of disadvantaged groups within states, as well as support for "secessio-
nist" or separatist movements.[35] The political scientist Justin Gest has
extended a similar argument to the context of American and British
politics and found compelling evidence that support for "anti-system"
political parties in the United States and the United Kingdom is driven by
perceptions among members of the white "working class" of "relative
social deprivation" rooted in lost status in domestic class and racial
hierarchies, along with pessimism about the prospects for future gains.[36]
Again, there are multiple potential explanations for these findings, but
researchers working within the RDT research program tend to focus on
affect: the emotions of frustration and resentment that arise from the
experience of collective relative deprivation are the proximal causes of
"separatist attitudes and engagement in collective protest actions."[37]

What do these findings mean for international relations? Status
immobility is, in part, a form of collective relative deprivation: it is a belief
that the state with which one identifies does not enjoy the position that it
deserves. Moreover, status immobility denotes a belief that the state's
status ambitions are incompatible with the status quo order – that there
are no "normative" pathways that are likely to successfully alleviate the
situation. For some individuals, this condition may not seem particularly

---

[35] For prominent early articulations of the RDT framework, see Runciman (1966) and
Walker and Pettigrew (1984). See Gurr (1970) for the application of RDT to the study of
revolutionary movements.
[36] Gest (2016).
[37] Abrams and Grant (2012), p. 4; see also Dube and Guimond (1986); Walker and Mann
(1987); Grant and Brown (1995); de la Rey and Raju (1996); Grant (2008); and
Stekelenburg (2011).

significant: there are surely more important things for many Chinese people to worry about than whether China is receiving its due in international politics. But for committed nationalists – "high identifiers" in the parlance of social psychology – the state's status has deep significance for self-esteem, and the condition of status immobility demands a response.[38]

The social psychological research discussed above suggests that that response is likely to take the form of some sort of rejection of the international order's rules, norms, and institutions.[39] There are two ways in which rejection might seem to be an effective or satisfying reaction to the experience of persistent, unjust status denial. The first is based on the notion that overthrowing or revolutionizing the status quo order might destroy whatever element of the system is obstructing the satisfaction of the state's status ambitions. This is akin to the argument that protest or secession movements are motivated by the desire to fundamentally transform an institutional order in a way that removes the source of injustice or deprivation. In the context of domestic politics, the ultimate manifestation of this drive is armed revolution: if the system is so corrupt that reform is impossible, then blowing it up is a necessary step toward a better future.

In the context of international politics, the desire to destroy a status quo order in order to rebuild it may – but does not have to – motivate a preference for hegemonic war. The objective of such a war is not to achieve membership in a high status club. Launching a major conflict against the most powerful defenders of the status quo is a counterproductive way of securing admission to their ranks via recognition. Rather, the point of a hegemonic war fought to "revolutionize" an international order is to remove some element of the order that seems like an impediment to the satisfaction of the state's status ambitions. This might involve destroying the power of an actor or constellation of actors whose influence seems to prevent others from granting recognition; or it might involve demonstrating the bankruptcy of an institution or principle that seems to be the source of the state's status immobility.

The drive to overthrow or revolutionize an international order represents a gamble that destroying the order will also destroy an obstacle to the satisfaction of the state's status ambitions and thereby facilitate a

---

[38] The degree to which individuals identify with a group is a key intervening variable in research on social identity. See, for instance, Branscombe and Wann (1994); Doosje, Ellemers, and Spears (1995); Ellemers, Spears, and Doosje (1997); Spears, Doosje, and Ellemers (1997).

[39] Though Zarakol's (2011) argument is not pitched in social psychological terms, she concurs with the notion that perceived obstacles to status advancement lead to responses that reject international order. See especially Kindle locations 2594–2610.

better future. This function does not *have to* be performed violently – states may be able to weaken or undermine status quo institutions through diplomacy, by intentionally sabotaging them through habitual norm violation or withdrawal, or by the construction of parallel institutions. And it is also worth noting that the link between overthrowing the old order and establishing a better one does not need to seem reasonable from the perspective of an objective analysis of costs and benefits in order for a frustrated nationalist to genuinely *believe* that it is a reasonable (and perhaps the *only* reasonable) response to the condition of status immobility. This is especially the case when the frustrated nationalist's valuation of the status quo itself is particularly low – that is, when the status quo seems intolerable. Thus rejection may seem attractive to some frustrated nationalists because it simultaneously represents action to undermine an unacceptable status quo and the possibility of securing a more satisfying future.

Rejection may also seem attractive for a second reason. Just as individuals can be motivated to protest or support separatist movements as means of expressing frustration and resentment with status quo institutions, a foreign policy aimed at rejection might seem attractive to a frustrated nationalist for reasons related to affect and emotion, rather than consequence and calculation. Rejection – whether it takes the form of violent conflict, a withdrawal from an institution, or a policy that explicitly ignores and invalidates international rules and norms – is a way of lashing out against the status quo order. It constitutes a salient signal that the state does not accept the legitimacy of some set of arrangements.

This is likely to be emotionally satisfying for a frustrated nationalist whose state seems to face the condition of status immobility for two related reasons. First, doing nothing may seem to amount to a tacit acceptance of the situation. Remaining fully engaged in the very institutions that appear to be perpetuating the state's status deficit might seem humiliating or threatening to an actor's dignity. Thus, protesting through some form of rejection – via withdrawal, rule-breaking, or in some other way – at least prevents the state from participating in its own humiliation. Second, rejecting status quo rules, norms, and institutions may be attractive as a means of actively expressing the negative emotions – anger, frustration, resentment – that are generated by the experience of status immobility. In short, rejection functions here less as a way of changing the prevailing order than as a way of managing its social and political consequences for the dissatisfied state.[40]

---

[40] This is in the spirit of Zarakol (2011) and Adler-Nissen's (2014) conception of ways of dealing with imposed "stigma" through strategies that may not remove the stigma but rather manage its negative social consequences.

Two caveats are in order. First, the consequentialist and emotional elements of rejection are likely to overlap in practice – that is, when an individual expresses a preference for a foreign policy of rejection, he or she may very well do so for both of the reasons discussed in the preceding paragraphs. They are analytically distinct, but in practice they reinforce each other. And, as social psychologists know, disentangling emotional and practical motivations for protest is inherently difficult.

Second, I do not assume that policies or leaders are ever actually motivated by the social psychological dynamics described above. The argument so far is simply about the genesis of a certain type of policy preference – in favor of rejecting central elements of the status quo order – among a certain type of actor – strong nationalists – in response to perceptions of status immobility. No doubt some leaders are strong nationalists and are subject to the same kinds of dynamics. But this is not always the case. And even when it is, leaders also face incentives to pursue objectives that have nothing to do with the state's status, which often point in different policy directions. To draw a straight line from the social psychological processes that link status immobility to preferences for rejection among nationalists directly to policy leaves out critical parts of the story. Instead, I conceptualize the social psychological conse-quences of status immobility not (or, at least, not mostly) as a factor that directly motivates policy change, but rather as a factor that influences the domestic political environment that leaders and elites – both in and out of power – face as they compete over policy and position.

Status Immobility and Domestic Contests Over Foreign Policy

Leaders typically have to legitimate what they do – to provide public reasons in support of decisions and actions. But leaders cannot say what-ever they want – public talk is constrained in various ways. It is constrained by the state's rhetorical environment – that is, by collective understandings about what kinds of things are appropriate and inappropriate to say; by the degree to which events seem consistent or inconsistent with a particular narrative or legitimation strategy; and by the speaker's institutional position. And since the limits of what can be legitimated impose limits on what can be done, these kinds of factors influence domestic political contests among elites and, ultimately, the direction of a state's foreign policy.[41]

---

[41] On legitimation and rhetoric in foreign policy, see Krebs and Jackson (2007); Krebs and Lobasz (2007); Goddard and Krebs (2015); Krebs (2015b), (2015a); and Copenhagen School work on "securitization" (e.g. Williams [2003]).

This logic underlies an important mechanism through which status immobility influences foreign policy: it makes it harder to legitimate moderate foreign policies and easier to legitimate aggressive ones, especially policies that seem to reject status quo norms, rules, and institutions.[42] Put concretely, widespread concerns about status immobility reflect and contribute to the production and prominence of discourses about the injustice of the status quo order. These make it harder to publicly justify participation in and respect for status quo institutions, rules, and norms, and easier to publicly justify policies that seem to lash out at the status quo. Status immobility has this effect for two related reasons.

First, dominant narratives or discourses – along with the policies that they make possible – can be undermined by the appearance of inconsistency with conditions or events.[43] In a rising state with unsatisfied status ambitions, leaders interested in pursuing moderate policies will have to explain how that course is consistent with the objective of achieving higher standing. This means making a plausible case that a patient, cautious approach that respects the rules of the status quo order and seeks to rise within the existing social hierarchy will pay off in the form of concessions from other states. The development of a prominent discourse of status immobility amounts to the development of the rhetorical material necessary to construct an effective counterargument against this claim. It can be invoked by *anyone* who opposes a moderate foreign policy – not just by proponents of rejection as a response to status immobility. Elites can make use of these resources to undermine the credibility of an incumbent leader for reasons of political ambition, or to promote foreign policy objectives that have nothing to do with status but that require that the cautious approach be undermined. Whatever the case, the more prominent and resonant is a narrative of status immobility – and the more easily its users can invoke foreign behavior as evidence of its validity – the more effective are the potential rhetorical and political weapons that can be wielded against an incumbent leader pursuing a moderate policy abroad.

Second, status immobility produces a natural constituency for actions that seem to lash out against the status quo order, and thus makes it easier to legitimate and politically beneficial to support aggressive policies – regardless of whether proponents of such policies care about status. A

---

[42] For similar arguments about the international production of domestic political resources, see Snyder (1987, 1989); and Evangelista (1993).

[43] The idea that rhetorical possibilities are constrained by the degree to which events seem to line up with what an actor wishes to argue is obvious, but worth emphasizing. See also Legro (2005), Williams (2003), Goddard and Krebs (2015), Krebs (2015b).

militarist might, for instance, be interested in building a larger arsenal of some sort for reasons having nothing to do with status. Others might oppose such a policy because it would run afoul of some element of the rules, norms, and principles of the status quo order – perhaps in the form of an arms control regime – and thus provoke suspicion in foreign capitals. In a state characterized by a prominent discourse about the fundamental injustice of the status quo order, the militarist could fruitfully sell a violation of or withdrawal from the arms control regime as an act of rebellion against a rigged global hierarchy. This would engage the support of frustrated nationalists with preferences for acts of rejection. And – because of the dynamic described in the paragraph above – a moderate opponent would have a more difficult time defending the merits of playing by the rules than would be the case if there were not a widespread sense that the state's status ambitions were incompatible with the status quo order.

It is also, of course, possible that the political resources produced by discourses of status immobility might be harnessed by elites whose aggressive policy preferences *do* flow from the social psychological dynamics described above. But the theoretical account I develop is agnostic about the sources of the preferences of leaders and other elites. Status immobility makes it easier for *anyone* with aggressive policy preferences – regardless of their origins or motivational foundation – to undermine moderate leaders and policies and advance their own agendas, so long as they are willing and able to package them as or together with acts that seem to lash out against an unjust status quo.

Why would arguments in favor of an aggressive, rejectionist foreign policy couched in the language of status immobility not be effectively parried by moderate counterarguments based on pragmatic concerns about cost and risk? Sometimes, they may be. But recall from the discussion above that nationalists care about the state's status for reasons beyond its effect on security or wealth. This means that to legitimate any foreign policy to an audience made up of nationalists, a leader has to make a compelling argument that the policy is consistent with the pursuit or performance of the state's rightful place in the international hierarchy – that it is compatible with the nationalist vision of the state's place in the world. When status immobility is a prominent interpretation of the international context the state faces, it is difficult to package a moderate foreign policy – one that does not appear to reject or lash out against the status quo order – in a way that meets this requirement.

Moderates are left with two options. One is to deny that the state's status ambitions are incompatible with a moderate approach to revising the status quo – or attempt to demonstrate that they are not. This will be less compelling the more prominent and widespread is the notion that some element of the status quo is fundamentally stacked against the state in question. Moreover, it may contribute to an even greater political advantage for hardliners, if attempts to prove the viability of a moderate approach to advancing the state's status raise expectations only to fail in the end.

The second option is to stress the other advantages of a moderate foreign policy: it may not help advance the state's status ambitions, but it could still promote trade and wealth, prevent isolation, and reduce the risk of unnecessary conflict. This effectively pits what analysts of rhetoric call an "epideictic" argument – one that involves questions about the state's identity – against a "deliberative" argument – one that involves questions about the best means of pursuing some objective. Put differently, status immobility-based arguments against moderate policy amount to arguments that doing something is incompatible with the state's identity; deliberative arguments to the contrary are arguments that doing the same thing is expedient. Analysts of rhetorical contests – including those working in IR – suggest that arguments based on identity claims often have an advantage over arguments based on expediency claims.[44] This is especially likely to be the case when nationalists – who should, all else equal, care more about status than others – represent a significant part of a leader's governing coalition.

Pathways to Policy Change and Exogenous Vulnerability

The two elements of the theory developed above – the social psychological and domestic political dynamics produced by beliefs and discourses about status immobility – can combine to influence policy through three distinct causal pathways, which are laid out graphically in Figure 2.1. In the first pathway (denoted by the checkered arrow), leaders themselves develop and act on preferences for rejectionist policies that emerge as a result of the social psychological consequences of status immobility. In an ideal-typical manifestation of this pathway, the domestic politics side of the story plays a limited role. This scenario is unusual for reasons laid out above. Leaders – even if they share the sensibilities of strong nationalists – have real responsibility for governing and thus have more than status to worry about. They also may be more sensitive than those outside the government to the concrete costs of pursuing rejectionist policies and to the benefits of restraint. Still, some leaders – for instance, as I show in Chapter 3, Kaiser Wilhelm II – do display evidence of being at least

[44] See Krebs and Lobasz (2007), p. 434; and Lawson-Tancred (1991), pp. 104–110.

partially motivated by the social psychological dynamics brought on by the perception of being unjustly denied status.

The other two pathways describe situations in which the elites in control of policy remain committed to a moderate, integrationist course and status immobility works by empowering their opponents. In the second pathway (denoted by the diagonally striped arrow), moderate leaders change course and adopt rejectionist policies against their own preferences because moderate policies become politically unsustainable. The specific form of political unsustainability varies according to institutional context – it may involve elite pressure in less open regimes and public pressure in more open regimes. In either case, the preferences of those outside power win out because moderate, integrationist policies become prohibitively difficult to defend.

The third pathway (denoted by the solid black arrow) is similar to the second but the mechanism of change is different. Here, moderate leaders do not respond adequately to demands for policies that appear to reject the status quo order, and are consequently replaced by leaders committed to pursuing a more radically revisionist approach. Depending on the state's institutional context, this could happen electorally, through elite negotiation, or through a coup.

Though these three causal pathways are analytically distinct, in practice they often overlap. Governments are often composed of groups of individuals who disagree amongst themselves about the state's strategic direction. When this is the case, different pathways can operate simultaneously – for instance, in the case of Wilhelmine Germany prior to World War I, there were hardliners within the government whose own aggressive preferences at least in part stemmed from status concerns, but there were also moderates who felt pressured by nationalists to pursue a more provocative foreign policy. And the second and third pathways may operate in sequence: moderates might initially be constrained by external pressure and then be replaced by still-dissatisfied hardliners. Nonetheless, for the purposes of theory building, it is useful to distinguish analytically between these three separate processes.

The extent to which these three pathways are likely to operate in different contexts depends in part upon another variable: the government's exogenous political vulnerability. Political vulnerability denotes the susceptibility of incumbent leaders to pressure from other domestic actors – for instance, from political opponents, interest groups, the media, or parts of the public.[45] But *exogenous* political vulnerability refers only to vulnerability that is not a consequence of dynamics associated

---

[45] On elite vulnerability, see Schweller (2006), Chapter 2.

with status immobility. Exogenous vulnerability may stem from a variety of sources – from institutional arrangements to economic crises to electoral defeats – that reduce the security, popularity, and legitimacy of an incumbent leader.

Exogenous vulnerability is not the focus of my argument, but it is worth flagging for attention because it influences the degree to and manner in which status immobility matters for foreign policy. When exogenous vulnerability is low – that is, when incumbent leaders are secure and mostly insulated from external political pressure – the second and third causal pathways described above are unlikely to be particularly significant. If status immobility matters at all, it will matter, by and large, via the first causal pathway: its direct influence on the attitudes, preferences, and actions of the leaders themselves.

As exogenous vulnerability increases, the relevance of the second and third causal pathways increases along with it. When leaders are more vulnerable to pressure from opponents and less secure from replacement by rivals, they will become more constrained by the need to placate various domestic constituencies – which may include frustrated nationalists clamoring for a forceful response to a status quo that they think is rigged against their state. Legitimation will matter more and be more open to contestation, and leaders will be more vulnerable to being overthrown by outsiders with different policy commitments. Thus exogenous vulnerability may enhance the potential influence of status immobility on foreign policy.

The historical episodes that I analyze in Chapters 3, 4, and 5 display different levels of exogenous vulnerability and – as a result – demonstrate the operation of different combinations of causal pathways. In each case, the social psychological and domestic political dynamics of status immobility contributed to a significant policy shift, but at a juncture during which leaders were vulnerable to external pressure in part for reasons unrelated to status immobility. Chancellors in Wilhelmine Germany were in some ways less institutionally vulnerable than were leaders in the Weimar Republic or Imperial Japan, but Bethmann Hollweg grew increasingly dependent upon nationalist conservative groups and the kaiser for legitimacy after the 1912 election made the Social Democrats the largest party in the Reichstag. This made him more vulnerable than he might otherwise have been to demands for provocative policies from groups like the Pan-German League. Still, the story of Wilhelmine Germany's shift toward radical revisionism is one that is as much (if not more) about the first causal pathway as it is about the second: many German leaders themselves (especially the kaiser) cared deeply about German status and resented what seemed to be British obstructionism.

This had serious consequences for German foreign policy apart from any domestic political pressure.

Exogenous vulnerability was higher in the other two cases. Combined with the fact that incumbent leaders in both Japan and Germany during the 1920s had moderate preferences, this means that status immobility's influence in these cases comes mostly through the second and third causal pathways. Moderate leaders in Imperial Japan became increasingly vulnerable to pressure from militant challengers due to the growing prevalence of threatened and actual assassinations, and in the wake of crises like the Great Depression and the Mukden Incident. This eventually helped make them responsive to nationalist demands that Japan leave the League of Nations. Incumbent leaders in the late Weimar Republic were very vulnerable to pressure from hardline outsiders. Much of this was endogenous to status dynamics, but some was not. Germany's dysfunctional government and the acute economic problems that struck after 1929 combined with anger and frustration related to the status implications of the Versailles settlement to destabilize the Weimar coalition and create the opening that Hitler jumped through to become chancellor in 1933.

Cases and Evidence

Empirically assessing theoretical accounts of international political phenomena often involves – at least in part – demonstrating the existence of a constant conjunction between causal and outcome phenomena: variation in the theory's independent and dependent variables must be correlated in the direction the theory implies they should be. This sort of analysis is popular in both quantitative and qualitative work: in the former, it appears as large-n regression analysis, while in the latter, it aims, in some form, to specify and observe within a small number of cases the presence of patterns of evidence – typically including a correlation between causal and outcome variables – predicted by various theoretical explanations.[46]

The theoretical argument that I have developed above has characteristics that complicate and reduce the value of the search for a correlation between status immobility and radical revisionism. The most obvious problem is that the theory's central causal variable – status immobility – is difficult to quantify in a way that is valid across time and space. Status itself is notoriously hard to quantify. Scholars have attempted to do so

---

[46] See, for instance, King, Keohane, and Verba (1994); and George and Bennett's (2004) discussion of "congruence" tests.

through the use of data on "diplomatic exchange," based on the theory that higher status states tend to be more attractive hosts for diplomats from abroad.[47] Diplomatic exchange, though, is a problematic way to measure the global status hierarchy. It is driven by a range of non-status factors (for instance, geographical proximity); it is strongly related to the material capabilities of the state sending representatives abroad, which means that diplomats from the highest status states in the system (which should, in theory, be the most meaningful) are the most common and thus convey relatively little information about the status of the states that host them; and data coverage is inconsistent.[48] Moreover, even assuming that diplomatic exchange does a reasonably good job of proxying status (which is an open question), a measure of status immobility would remain out of reach: this requires interrogating beliefs and discourse regarding the plausibility of achieving some ambition within the constraints of the status quo order.

Another complication is that the theory does not imply that there should necessarily be a straightforward association between status immobility and change in foreign policy. This is because of the central roles that path dependence, exogenous vulnerability, and agency play in the theory. First, the process through which beliefs and discourses of status immobility emerge and influence political contests is path dependent – it is easier to interpret foreign behavior as evidence of status immobility the more this has been done in the recent past, and vice versa (which is why, in Figure 2.1, the relationship between interpretations of foreign behavior and beliefs about status immobility is reciprocal). This means that we should not expect a straightforward conjunction between acts of status denial and the pursuit of revisionist policies, or between acts of accommodation and the pursuit of moderate policies.[49] Second, regimes vary in the degree to which they are vulnerable to political opposition: strong regimes may be relatively unaffected by critiques of foreign policy rooted in status immobility, but this can change rapidly if events conspire to increase the regime's vulnerability. Third, the choices of individuals – leaders and political elites – are critical. Status immobility can be a potent political and rhetorical resource, but in order to exert influence on outcomes, individual human beings have to fashion it into an effective assault

---

[47] For descriptions, see Singer and Small (1966) and Small and Singer (1973); for recent applications, see Renshon (2016, 2017), Miller et al. (2015), Bezerra et al. (2015).

[48] The second problem means that Renshon's (2016, 2017) recent effort to improve the diplomatic exchange indicator by weighting hosted diplomats more heavily the higher the status of the state that sent them has the effect of increasing the empirical leverage of the least informative observations.

[49] On the methodological implications of path dependence, see Bennett and Elman (2006).

against moderate policies and their proponents. Taken together, these characteristics of the theory depict a model in which policy change happens not continuously but in fits and starts, and in which the timing of change is difficult to predict. Evidence related to correlation or congruence between independent and dependent variables is unlikely to be particularly illuminating.

Instead, I evaluate the theory by looking for evidence that the processes developed above operate in ways that contribute to concrete shifts toward radical revisionism in the foreign policy orientations of rising great powers.[50] This strategy raises two questions: first, what counts as evidence in favor of the operation of status immobility theory's processes and mechanisms? Second, in what cases should we look for such evidence?

The first question calls for an articulation of status immobility theory's observable implications. When we investigate shifts away from moderate, distributive revisionist foreign policies toward radical revisionist foreign policies, what kind of evidence would indicate that status immobility played a significant role? Three kinds of evidence are important. First, there should be evidence that at least some prominent political actors – leaders, elites, or opinionmakers – believe or talk publicly about the existence of an unjust, insurmountable obstacle to the state's status ambitions. Establishing the presence of status immobility requires first establishing that the state's foreign policy expresses status ambitions, which is straightforward because these are often publicly articulated by leaders and elites in the course of legitimating or arguing over foreign policy. Whether this is purely instrumental or reflects real beliefs is inherently difficult to determine, but also not crucial, since the appearance of talk about status indicates at the very least the presence of a discursive environment that requires or rewards it.

How do we know the difference between a concern for status and a concern for some other good, like security or wealth? One clue is to look for evidence that actors are concerned about rights and justice in the state's foreign relations. A claim to status is fundamentally – and concretely – a claim to a particular role identity along with a claim to the rights that the role implies. To seek status is to seek the role identity and set of rights that the state deserves on the basis of its characteristics and accomplishments. When actors speak in terms of the rights that the state is owed on the basis of its position, they are articulating a claim to status.

Of course, actors may speak the language of status in support of policies that they really care about for other reasons. This is still evidence that actors find it politically beneficial to invoke unmet status ambitions – in

---

[50] On process-tracing, see George and Bennett (2004).

doing so they simultaneously reflect and reinforce expectations about the state's proper place in the world and the role of a particular policy in securing it. But to strengthen the claim that a state's foreign policy is at least partially motivated by status ambitions, I adopt a strategy familiar to analysts of status in IR: I show that at least some elements of the state's foreign policy that evidence suggests are attributable to status concerns cannot be explained by ambitions for security or wealth. This involves considering both the actual consequences of particular actions – whether they benefited the state's economic or strategic condition – as well as the reasoning of actors who argued for and against them.

But evidence of status immobility is distinct from evidence that a state is pursuing status ambitions. To ascertain the existence of status immobility, I look for evidence of people – whether leaders, political elites, members of the media, or parts of the public – interpreting foreign behavior as confirmation that the system is rigged against their state. This involves articulations of pessimism about the possibility of being treated fairly, as well as evidence of beliefs and discourse about the source of the obstacle – for instance, the presence of a prominent argument about national discrimination or the unfairness of a particular institutional arrangement. Again, this sort of talk may be entirely instrumental; this does not reduce its evidentiary significance, given the import of legitimation in the theoretical framework.

The second kind of evidence that supports the theory relates to the link between status immobility and preferences for policies aimed at rejecting status quo norms, rules, and institutions. The theory implies that nationalists should develop preferences for rejectionist policies as responses to status immobility. To evaluate this element of the theory, I investigate the objectives and motivations of individuals and groups who demanded radically revisionist policies – policies aimed at protesting, withdrawing from, or overthrowing status quo norms, rules, and institutions. The key question is whether these policy demands seem to have been motivated by or framed in ways reflective of the social psychological link between status immobility and rejectionist impulses developed above. This may take one or both of two forms: an argument in favor of overthrowing the order as a gamble aimed at removing the obstacle to the state's status ambitions; and an argument against participation in key elements of the order to avoid the indignity of being complicit in the state's own humiliation. The presence of one, both, or some combination of these arguments in the record of what revisionists thought or said as they developed and articulated demands for rejectionist policies constitutes evidence in support of the theory.

The theory's third set of observable implications relates to the domestic political consequences of status immobility. The theory suggests that status immobility can influence policy by contributing to the abandonment of moderate positions or the fall of moderate leaders. This implies that we should find evidence that 1) moderate leaders understand the value of participating in status quo institutions, following status quo rules, and cooperating with states identified as status quo defenders; 2) proponents of more provocative policies – regardless of where these preferences originate – frame arguments against moderation in terms of the impossibility of achieving just treatment within the status quo, and benefit politically when foreign behavior seems to confirm these fears; 3) when moderates pursue or accede to policies favored by hardliners (and especially policies valued and promoted by hardliners for reasons related to the logics of rejection), they do so for reasons at least partly related to pressure from domestic hardliners or to the fear of a domestic backlash; and 4) hardliners are strengthened politically – and moderates weakened – by conditions that make more resonant and sustainable the argument that the state faces an unjust, insurmountable obstacle to recognition of its proper place in the world.

As well as investigating the observable implications of status immobility theory itself, it is also important to consider its role alongside other potential drivers of shifts toward radical revisionism. It is entirely possible that there might be plentiful evidence that the processes at the heart of the theory operated, but that they made little difference to the outcome. In other words, evidence that status immobility produces preferences for rejectionist policies and helps hardliners is not evidence that status immobility matters much relative to the causal factors highlighted by alternative approaches. My response to this problem is not to argue that these other factors – like power, domestic political dynamics, and ideology – do not matter at all. Indeed, the theoretical framework developed above acknowledges that they do. Nor do I attempt to assess the relative "causal weight" of these explanatory phenomena. Instead, I identify critical, concrete episodes during which foreign policy shifted visibly and significantly in the direction of radical revisionism, and ask whether these specific episodes can be adequately explained by prominent existing approaches. By demonstrating that they cannot – and then by showing that status immobility can make sense of these episodes – I establish that status immobility was an indispensable part of the process by which the states I examine abandoned moderation and moved toward broadly challenging the status quo order.

The second question that my empirical strategy raises is related to case selection. The theory's scope, as developed above, is limited to rising powers – states in which growing material capabilities produce rising status ambitions and expectations but, simultaneously, incentives for caution in foreign policy. Given my focus on process evidence, investigating the full universe of cases is impossible and unnecessary. Generalizability – not selection bias – is the most important case-selection problem for a study whose logic of inference is based on causal process observation rather than on controlled comparison. This concern places a premium on selecting cases whose features maximize the ability to argue that the study's findings have significance beyond their boundaries.

In the chapters that follow, I analyze three cases in which rising powers launched broad challenges against the status quo order: Wilhelmine Germany, Imperial Japan, and Weimar/Nazi Germany. These cases are valuable for two reasons. First, they are the paradigmatic examples of rising power revisionism in modern world history. The development of each state's foreign policy orientation began with a moderate approach championed by leaders who understood the value of participating in status quo institutions, playing by the rules, and aiming not to provoke other great powers. In each case, the moderate course was challenged by hardliners and ultimately abandoned in favor of a course that was significantly less concerned with demonstrating restraint. In other words, these three cases embody the puzzle at the core of this book: why do rising states, which have incentives to behave cautiously, sometimes adopt foreign policy orientations that challenge the foundation of international order?

Only two other cases of revisionism in foreign policy come close to the depth and significance of these: Revolutionary France and the early Soviet Union. Revolutionary France is an interesting case, but its turn against the status quo order *preceded* its rise to power. This was not a case in which a rising state that had incentives to behave moderately ignored them, but rather a case in which a domestic revolution – prompted in part by overextension and economic crisis – produced international conflict for ideological reasons. Similarly, the Soviet case does not provide an appropriate context for assessing a theory about why a rising great power would turn against the normative foundation of the status quo order because the period during which it most clearly did so came in the immediate wake of the Russian Revolution, not during a sustained period of increasing wealth and power. Both of these cases importantly remind us that there are potential causes of radical revisionism other than the status concerns of rising powers. In this book, I do not claim to have discovered a necessary condition for broad challenges against the status quo order. But both of these cases fall outside the scope of the theory developed in this chapter.

The second reason for analyzing these three cases is that other prominent theories already claim to explain most of their important features.

Wilhelmine Germany's turn against the status quo is frequently invoked by structural realists as a paradigmatic case of either opportunistic hegemony-seeking or preventive war.[51] Imperial Japan's turn against the status quo is, similarly, often invoked as a case of overexpansion driven by domestic political dysfunction.[52] Nazi Germany's revisionism seems easily explained by ideological distance.[53] What this means is that these are three hard cases for status immobility theory. Demonstrating that the processes described above play critical roles in foreign policy shifts that seem well explained by other factors should increase our confidence that status immobility may matter in other cases as well.[54]

My focus in these three cases is on analyzing the origins of perceptible, concrete shifts away from moderate, distributive revisionist policies toward radical revisionist policies. Wilhelmine Germany's policy orientation changed around 1912 from one focused on seeking "world power" status to one that expressed a deeper dissatisfaction with the status quo order. In this case the change is subtle, but visible in German leaders' increasing willingness to contemplate overthrowing the European balance of power (which was, during this period, not just a geopolitical characteristic but also an important status quo institution) and decreasing willingness to openly cooperate with the British (who were identified as a defender of the status quo order), submit issues affecting their vital interests to ad hoc conference arbitration (another important institution of the pre–World War I status quo order), and back down during crises. This shift is the focus of Chapter 3.

The Japanese and Weimar/Nazi shifts are more easily identified because the interwar order was characterized by a set of formal institutions. Japan's foreign policy shifted between 1931 and 1933 from a distributive revisionist approach aimed at increasing Japanese economic and military power and status by working within the Western status quo order to a radical revisionist mix much less concerned with respecting status quo norms, rules, and institutions. The most obvious concrete rejectionist policy came with Japan's withdrawal from the League of Nations in 1933, and this is the focus of Chapter 4. Weimar/Nazi Germany's foreign policy began to shift away from Stresemann's moderate attempt to achieve piecemeal revisions to the Versailles settlement even before Hitler became chancellor in 1933. But once Hitler took over, German foreign policy – like Japanese foreign policy – became significantly less concerned with respecting the norms, rules, and institutions of

---

[51] See Mearsheimer (2001), p. 188; and Copeland (2000), Chapters 2 and 3.
[52] See Snyder (1991), pp. 120–150.   [53] See Haas (2005), pp. 107–109.
[54] For a discussion of this sort of "critical" case selection logic, see Eckstein (1975).

Table 2.2 *Summary of Cases and Evidence*

Rising Power	Timing of Shift	Aspirational Status	Outstanding Rights Claims	Source of Beliefs about Immobility	Elements of Order Challenged	Foreign Policy Consequences
Wilhelmine Germany	Post-1911	World Power	Equality in naval arms; compensation for territorial adjustments	British objection to German fleet; Anglo-French collusion (Morocco Crises)	Institution of the balance of power; ad hoc conference system	Inability to cooperate openly with British; willingness to contemplate war to reorder system; unwillingness to use conferences
Imperial Japan	1931–1933	Great Power	Equal treatment of population; sphere of influence; equality in naval arms	Racial discrimination; Lytton Report	Interwar security institutions	Withdrawal from League of Nations; withdrawal from Washington conference system; increasing influence of militants
Weimar Germany	1929–1933	Great Power	Sovereignty; self-defense; administration of territory abroad	Sluggish Western adjustments to Versailles settlement	Interwar security institutions	Rise of Hitler; unilateral rejection of Versailles restrictions; withdrawal from the League of Nations
United States	No shift	World Power	Sphere of influence in Western Hemisphere	None (ambitions accommodated after 1895)	No sustained challenge to British-dominated order	Accommodation failure could have contributed to stronger American opposition to British policy during the Second Boer War and World War I

the interwar European order. Germany withdrew from the League of Nations in September 1933 and subsequently took a number of other provocative steps. My focus in Chapter 5 is primarily on explaining how Hitler – who obviously had deeply aggressive foreign policy ambitions and is indispensable to any account of Nazi Germany's foreign policy – emerged as a viable alternative to the mainstream German right.

I also investigate, in Chapter 6, the case of the Anglo-American power transition. This is a negative case – the rising United States had clear, outstanding status ambitions but did not experience a shift toward radical revisionism. It is the best modern example of a peaceful power transition. While the case is different in important ways from those that are the focus of Chapters 3, 4, and 5, I argue in Chapter 6 that the processes at the heart of status immobility theory could have had a significant influence on American foreign policy, had American status claims not been effectively accommodated by the British beginning in the decade before the turn of the twentieth century. Table 2.2 summarizes the critical elements of the four cases that I examine in the chapters that follow.

3 "World Power" and Revisionism in Wilhelmine Germany

World War I signaled the end of a relatively peaceful and stable European order that had lasted since Napoleon's defeat just under a hundred years earlier. To be sure, nineteenth-century Europe saw territorial adjustments, competition over power and status, and even war between major powers. But between 1815 and 1914, no great power threatened the central normative foundation of the European status quo – the collective commitment to preventing any single state from dominating the continent.

Historians and political scientists broadly agree that one of the reasons that order broke down in July 1914 was that challenging the European status quo had by then begun to look like an attractive option to many German leaders.[1] One does not have to accept the most extreme version of this argument – that Germany planned for and conspired to bring about World War I – in order to acknowledge that German revisionism played an important role in generating conditions that made continental war likely.

There is less agreement about what kind of revisionism pre–World War I German foreign policy expressed, and where to locate the origins of German dissatisfaction. Did Germany merely want *more* – more power, more territory, more colonies, more battleships, more status – or was it also dissatisfied with the normative and institutional foundation of the order itself? And *why* did German foreign policy seek the kinds of changes that it did? Was it, as many realists maintain, security concerns that made Germany aggressive? Or did something else drive German revisionism?

This chapter aims to illuminate the nature and sources of Wilhelmine Germany's revisionism by applying the framework developed in Chapters 1 and 2. I argue that German foreign policy started off as an attempt to achieve changes in the global distribution of power and status. Particularly important was the policy of *Weltpolitik*, which aimed at achieving recognition that Germany had the same status and rights in world politics that Great Britain had. Almost immediately after this effort began, though, suspicions arose that Germany might not be able to achieve "world power" status

---

[1] See, for instance, Copeland (2000), Chapters 3 and 4; Mearsheimer (2001), pp. 188–189, 215; Strachan (2001), p. 46; and especially Röhl (2014).

70

within the bounds of the European status quo order. German leaders, elites, and parts of the public increasingly came to see Great Britain's commitment to maintaining the European balance of power as a policy of unjust discrimination against Germany's status claims. This belief contributed – for some influential elites and leaders – to demands for a foreign policy aimed at overthrowing the European balance of power, and a preference against using the institutions of the status quo order (in particular the consultative conference system) to manage conflicts. Many nationalist elites, in other words, advocated that Germany respond to apparent status immobility through policies that expressed a logic of rejection.

Evidence of status immobility also imposed constraints on German leaders who had more moderate preferences, especially after 1911. This pulled German foreign policy toward a radical revisionist combination that was manifest in an increasing willingness to consider hegemonic war as a viable policy tool, an inability to make concessions to the British in the face of a strategic environment that seemed to call for just that, and a disinclination to make use of consultative conferences to manage conflicts.

The chapter proceeds as follows. The next section describes the pre–World War I European order and the evolution of German foreign policy from one that mostly expressed demands for incremental changes in the system's distribution of resources to one that demanded revolutionary change. The rest of the chapter documents the rise of status immobility in Germany in the years before the July Crisis, establishes its close relation to the foreign policy preferences of deeply revisionist elite groups and individuals, and explores its contribution to Germany's increasingly radical orientation toward the status quo after 1911.

German Foreign Policy and the Pre–World War I Order

European order in the century before World War I involved a normative and institutional framework that facilitated the management by the "great powers" of the continent's balance of power. When the Concert of Europe emerged in the wake of Napoleon's defeat, it comprised an explicit commitment to preventing instability and major war by managing conflicting interests through the institution of consultative conferences among great powers. While the Concert system had begun to fray during the second half of the nineteenth century, great powers continued to attempt to manage international politics through conferences, and leaders continued to talk about a Concert of Europe and a common European interest in stability through 1914.[2]

---

[2] On this point, see Ikenberry (2001), p. 81, fn. 1; Holsti (1992), p. 50.

The normative foundation of this order consisted more specifically of two related institutions. The first was the balance of power. While the *distribution* of power is clearly an element of the distributive status quo, the *balance of power* – that is, the preservation of the system through the prevention of preponderance – was one of the central *normative* components of the European order after 1815. Maintaining the balance of power was understood in nineteenth-century Europe as a normative objective that Europe's great powers held in common – similar to the way today's great powers understand non-proliferation or the protection of human rights – and it thus constituted both an important justification for restraint and a means of legitimating action abroad. This did not mean that incremental changes in territory or influence were prohibited. It only meant that Europe's great powers shared a normative commitment not to try to overthrow the system and establish continental hegemony – as Napoleon had – and to prevent such challenges from emerging from elsewhere.[3]

The second element of the order constituted the means by which great powers went about managing the system: consultative conferences. This institution set in stone the rights and responsibilities of different classes of states (with the greatest of these going to the great powers), and created a mechanism through which the system could be adjusted to account for changes in power or conflicts of interest. Great power conferences were employed to manage a variety of changes, including those stemming from the revolutions of the 1830s and 1840s, colonial expansion later in the nineteenth century, and the Balkan Wars before World War I.[4]

There was also a distributive component of the European status quo, and it was the consequences of distributive shifts and demands for distributive changes that the Concert system was designed to help keep under control. European states competed over power, territory, wealth, ideology, and status, but did so in ways that were at least partially bounded by the commitment to preserving the system through the balance of power and the mechanism of great power conferences.

The state at the top of the nineteenth- and early twentieth-century global hierarchy – and thus the state most readily identified as the defender of the normative and institutional order – was Great Britain. The European order between 1815 and 1914 is commonly referred to as the Pax Britannica because a British victory created the conditions for

---

[3] On the balance of power as an institution, see Bull (1977), pp. 68–71 and 101–102; and Little (2007). Chapter 5, especially p. 135. On the collective commitment to preventing preponderance as a normative element of the nineteenth-century European order, see Holsti (1992), p. 60; Ikenberry (2001), Chapter 4; and Kissinger (2014), p. 60.

[4] On consultative conferences in the "Concert" system, see Mitzen (2013).

its constitutional moment and British power, status, and leadership underpinned its functioning.[5] This made it easy for leaders in other states – especially those in Berlin and especially in the last decade and a half of its existence – to identify the maintenance of the order as an especially British interest.

Germany's Approaches to European Order

Germany's orientation toward the European status quo changed dramatically in the years between the Wars of Unification and World War I, which is a central part of the story of the geopolitical earthquake that marked the end of the Pax Britannica. From the time of Bismarck through the first decade of the twentieth century, German leaders sought incremental changes in the distribution of resources but did not threaten the normative foundation of the order itself. Bismarck, even as he unified Germany, signaled restraint by communicating that he accepted the sanctity of treaties negotiated by other great powers. After German unification, Bismarck's primary objective was to manage a system of alliances that would be in Germany's favor, but he did not threaten to overthrow and reorder the system. In the 1890s, German foreign policy became obsessed with achieving other kinds of distributive changes – in particular, acquiring colonies and building battleships in order to achieve higher status. Still, the point of this policy – known as *Weltpolitik* – was to achieve for Germany a better position within the European status quo order, not to destroy it.

In the years between 1905 and 1914, though – and especially after 1911 – German foreign policy shifted in the direction of a combination of policies that expressed both dissatisfaction with the distribution of power, territory, and status, *and* a deeper dissatisfaction with the basic terms upon which the European order itself was founded. Prewar German policy at least partially reflected an increasingly widely held calculation that the institutional foundations of the order – the normative commitment to maintaining a continental balance of power and the collective mechanisms through which Europe's great powers managed European politics – were no longer consistent with German interests or dignity. There were two concrete manifestations of this shift. First, German leaders became increasingly skeptical of the value of using consultative conferences to manage conflicts of interest; second, German leaders and other elites became increasingly willing to seriously consider major war to overthrow the system.[6]

---

[5] See Ikenberry (2001), Chapter 4.
[6] Berghahn (1973), pp. 131–155, describes this as a shift from *Weltpolitik* (aimed at achieving world power status) toward *Kontinentalpolitik* (aimed at preparing for major war – and challenging the balance of power – on the continent).

Evidence of these deeply revisionist preferences can be found in the writings of widely read authors like Friedrich von Bernhardi, radical nationalists like Heinrich Class and other Pan Germans, and in the diaries, memoranda, and speeches of German leaders like Kaiser Wilhelm II, Chief of the General Staff Helmuth von Moltke, and Naval Secretary Alfred von Tirpitz. Bernhardi's bestselling *Germany and the Next War* disparaged the balance of power as a tool of British domination and advocated a war for German hegemony; the kaiser interpreted moves that the British justified by invoking the importance of upholding the European balance of power as evidence of anti-German bias, expressed similar sentiments about the British-led multilateral effort to manage the consequences of the Balkan Wars, and by December 1912 had begun to seriously contemplate a major war to overturn the balance of power.[7] There were still moderate voices – like those of Chancellor Bethmann Hollweg and Foreign Secretary Gottlieb von Jagow – advocating rapprochement with Great Britain due to fear of the consequences of major war. But moderates came under heavy challenge by frustrated nationalists who expressed deeper dissatisfaction with the European status quo and preferred more provocative policies.

These concrete manifestations of German dissatisfaction with the foundation of the European status quo – the growing enthusiasm for war to overthrow the balance of power, and the declining confidence in the institutions of the "concert" system – had important consequences for the stability of the order. It is controversial to claim that German leaders worked intentionally to bring about World War I. Available evidence does not permit a confident verdict on the question of whether Germany sought the war or simply failed to avoid it.[8] Either way, the influence of leaders and other elites who believed that the balance of power had to be overthrown at the very least made the July Crisis significantly more dangerous than it would otherwise have been. Similarly, the belief that multilateral solutions were hopelessly biased against Germany rendered unattractive options that could have prevented or short-circuited the crisis. While status immobility did not on its own cause the geopolitical earthquake that was World War I, major conflict would likely have been avoided in August 1914 if German leaders had been less willing (or enthusiastic) to risk major war over the satisfaction of Austrian demands for the punishment of Serbia, or if they had been more open to British calls for multilateral great power crisis management.

---

[7] Bernhardi (1914b); on Wilhelm's attitude, see Röhl 2001, 2014.

[8] Recent accounts of the origins of World War I (2010; Clark 2012; McMeekin 2013; Otte 2014a; Martel 2014) reject the intentionalist interpretation of the Fischer school (Fischer 1961, 1965, 1969; Geiss 1967, 1976) but acknowledge that German foreign policy was reckless. For a notable exception, see Röhl (2014), p. 1020; and (2015).

The Puzzle of German Revisionism

The shift in Germany's orientation toward the status quo – from distributive revisionism toward radical revisionism – is as puzzling as it was significant. As a rising economic powerhouse in a strategically difficult position, Germany had much to gain from a foreign policy that avoided provoking Europe's other great powers. Yet provoke them it did.

The most prominent explanation for increasing German revisionism in the years before World War I is that German security was incompatible with the European balance of power. Different versions of this realist argument emphasize Germany's vulnerable geographic position, its worries about the rise of Russia or the decline of Austria-Hungary, and the opportunity stemming from its rapidly growing capabilities as the factors that fostered dissatisfaction with the European order and motivated German leaders to overthrow the European balance of power.[9] Copeland, for instance, in the most stridently articulated of such arguments, suggests that security concerns related to the rise of Russia were what drove German leaders to become deeply dissatisfied with the European status quo – Germany could not satisfy its need to contain the Russian threat without in the process challenging the normative commitment to maintaining a balance of power.[10]

There is no doubt that these kinds of concerns played some role in the calculations that German leaders made about the value of overthrowing versus incrementally changing the European order. But to claim that Germany sought to overthrow the European balance of power primarily or even mostly because of concerns about its physical security goes too far. There are two problems with this position.

First, it is not clear that Germany's security requirements were *actually* incompatible with the European status quo order, or even that most German leaders thought they were. To be sure, soldiers like Moltke and Falkenhayn obsessed about the rise of Russia and preferred preventive war, the sooner the better, but other leaders and elites were either more optimistic about Germany's economic prospects, or did not think that the rise of Russia necessarily required preventive war. As I detail below, German Chancellor Bethmann Hollweg was deeply pessimistic about the consequences of Russia's rise for Germany's prospects. His preferred

---

[9] Not all realist accounts of World War I emphasize German revisionism – interpretations based on multipolarity, the security dilemma, and the offense-defense balance (Waltz 1979; Jervis 1978; Christensen and Snyder 1990) posit that Berlin did not seek but was forced into the conflict. Still, because of the focus of this book, my most important realist interlocutors are those – like Mearsheimer and Copeland – whose accounts of World War I center on German dissatisfaction.

[10] Copeland (2000), p. 57.

approach to dealing with the problem was not to prepare for war but to pursue warmer relations with Great Britain. Indeed, Bethmann Hollweg thought the consequences of a major European war were incalculable, and he vigorously opposed the naval arms race with the British because the resultant Anglo-German antagonism made managing Germany's more dangerous continental rivals unnecessarily difficult.

Even among those who did develop preferences for a policy aimed at overthrowing the European balance of power, it is unclear that physical security was the only or even the most important concern. Authors like Bernhardi, radical nationalists like Heinrich Class, and leaders like Tirpitz and Kaiser Wilhelm all thought there was something wrong with the status quo order. But they expressed the problem in terms that implied that the source of dissatisfaction was that the order was incompatible with Germany's dignity or with its historical, civilizational mission, rather than with its physical security requirements.

The second problem is that while the broad pattern of the development of German revisionism seems to line up with realist expectations, micro-level evidence about process and timing is difficult to square with the contention that it was fear of the rise of Russia or a growing consciousness of opportunity that led German leaders to become more aggressive and finally to orchestrate the outbreak of World War I.

For instance, the so-called War Council of December 8, 1912 is a critical piece of evidence for realists who argue that German leaders wanted major war for reasons related to either fears about the future or consciousness of opportunity. It suggests to them a picture of the German leadership coolly plotting a war for European hegemony within eighteen months because a window of opportunity was threatening to close.[11] The problem is that the logic of stories about German aggression as security-seeking implies that the meeting should have been called either as a response to news that Russian military capabilities were growing unexpectedly quickly, or to new evidence that a German bid for European hegemony might be cheaper and easier than expected. In fact, the kaiser called the meeting in response to news of a conversation between the German ambassador in London and British War Secretary Haldane in which Haldane reiterated London's determination to support France in the event of a Franco-German war. This should – if anything – have acted as a deterrent, but instead it provoked the kaiser to take a step toward major war. I argue below that the War Council's place in the story of prewar German foreign policy cannot be understood without taking into account a factor that many realists ignore: the kaiser's anger and indignation at British obstructionism.

[11] See especially Copeland's (2000) discussion beginning on p. 65.

There are similar problems with the way many realist accounts of German aggression interpret the July Crisis as the orchestration of German leaders who had already decided on war against (at least) Russia.[12] The evidence does not allow one to draw this conclusion. At the time that the "blank check" was proffered to Count Hoyos and Ambassador Szogyeny, German leaders did not expect – nor desire – Russian intervention. What they wanted was a quick Austrian strike against Serbia, which would forestall any interference from other great powers and keep the conflict localized.[13] What needs to be explained, then, is not why German leaders wanted major war in 1914, but rather why they were willing to risk it, and why they were unwilling to take steps that might have kept the crisis from escalating.

It is also worth noting that arguments about the role of domestic interest groups in this case are incomplete. Snyder's account – which is the most prominent and compelling – is that influential interest groups (the Junkers, the industrialists, and the army) engaged in "logrolling." This produced an overly expansionist – and provocative – foreign policy by marrying high grain tariffs, a large fleet, and the Schlieffen Plan. To legitimate this constellation of policies, leaders engaged in "mythmaking" aimed at the masses – the effectiveness of these myths then prevented German leaders from changing course once it became clear that the foreign policy created through logrolled interests was producing adverse consequences.[14]

Snyder's account works reasonably well as an explanation for *Weltpolitik* (although it ignores the significance of *Weltpolitik* as a claim to a particular status) and for its persistence even after it became clear that it was having counterproductive consequences. But it is unable to unravel the puzzle at the core of this chapter: why German policy shifted after about 1911 toward radical revisionism. Rhetorical entrapment probably did play a role in, for instance, Bethmann's inability to cooperate with the British in the years after the Second Morocco Crisis. But it is difficult to explain as a function of parochial interest or internalized myth the genesis of the sort of rejectionist preferences that nationalists outside the government (and even some inside of it) expressed. Snyder's "myths of empire," once internalized, may be able to explain why "the elite coalition of iron

---

[12] Mearsheimer (2001), p. 188, for instance, writes in the main text of *Tragedy of Great Power Politics* that Germany's objective in July 1914 was "to redraw the map of Europe to ensure German hegemony for the foreseeable future"; yet, in a footnote (fn. 45, p. 469) he acknowledges that "at the start of the crisis in July 1914, Germany wanted a local war in the Balkans involving Austria-Hungary and Serbia."

[13] For recent work supporting this depiction of German intentions in early July, see Clark (2012), pp. 416–417; Martel (2014), p. 108, pp. 158–159; and Otte (2014a), p. 171.

[14] Snyder (1991), Chapter 3.

and rye found it impossible to retreat from an imperialist" foreign policy.[15] But they cannot explain the significant *change* that German foreign policy underwent in the years before the July Crisis.

Status, Order, and German Revisionism

In March 1915, Kaiser Wilhelm II told a visiting Danish diplomat that the eight-month-old European war was the fault of an English king who had been dead for half a decade. Edward VII – the kaiser's uncle – had worked to "keep [Germany] down, & in this way to hamper her peaceful world development." He "had treated Germany with great arrogance and contempt." Any negotiated peace would have to be "concluded on a dignified basis for the German people and in harmony with the sacrifices made by them. This comprised Great Britain admitting German equality and not to regard her as an inferior partner ... who had to enquire first in Great Britain if, and when, Germany might build ships."[16]

The kaiser's words should be taken with a boulder of salt. World War I was not Edward VII's fault, and Germany was not a blameless victim of British bullying. Yet the sentiment that Wilhelm expressed should also not be dismissed as post-hoc justification. The kaiser's feeling of indignation at being denied equal rights in the British-dominated European order far predated the war and was expressed by many other influential German leaders and elites in the years leading up to the July Crisis.

I argue that this widespread belief that Germany faced a status "glass ceiling" due to Great Britain's unwillingness to treat her fairly had real and dangerous consequences for German foreign policy. Status immobility produced pressure within Germany for policies that would protest, delegitimate, or remove the obstacle to German status ambitions – the European balance of power and the system of great power management that helped maintain it. The belief that German status ambitions were incompatible with the European status quo contributed to the development of preferences among German elites – including the kaiser – in favor of an effort to overthrow the status quo order, and opposed to the use of consultative conferences to manage crises. Apparent evidence of British obstructionism throughout the prewar years weakened moderates who did not share these preferences and pushed German foreign policy toward radical revisionism.

In the rest of the chapter, I develop this argument in three steps. First, I establish that German foreign policy was concerned with achieving recognition of world power status, and delineate the particular rights

---

[15] Ibid., Kindle location 2456.   [16] Quoted in Röhl (2014), p. 1138.

that German leaders claimed as part of this status. I also document the rise of the belief that this ambition was out of reach because of British obstructionism. Second, I explore the origins of the preferences of leaders and elites who demanded rejectionist policies, and show that these preferences were at least partly driven by the belief that German status ambitions could not be satisfied within the bounds of the European status quo order. Third, I show that developments that seemed to confirm this belief (especially after 1911) weakened moderate leaders and helps explain the German government's increasing comfort with the idea of major war, its inability to improve relations with Great Britain, and its hesitance to submit disputes to multilateral arbitration.

Status, "World Power," and the Fate of Weltpolitik

Germany's obsession with international social status beginning in the 1890s is well-documented by historians and political scientists.[17] Declarations by the kaiser and his new Foreign Secretary Bernhard von Bülow between 1896 and 1897 that Germany would henceforth pursue a policy of *Weltpolitik*, aimed at achieving its "place in the sun," represented a significant shift from Bismarck's objectives. Germany would now seek to become a world power by securing colonial possessions and building a blue-water navy composed of state-of-the-art battleships (an effort known as *Flottenpolitik*).

Twelve decades later, there remain significant questions about what Germany was after as it pursued *Weltpolitik*. Realists argue that it was wealth, power, and security, but this is unconvincing.[18] Germany's

---

[17] Fischer (1961, 1969) was the first to emphasize the drive for "world power" status in German foreign policy. See also Strachan (2001), Chapter 1; MacMillan (2013), Chapter 4; Röhl (2001, 2014); and Hull (2015). Among political scientists, see Larson and Shevchenko (2014a, p. 39); Murray (2010, 2016); Wolf (2014), Fikenscher, Jaschob, and Wolf (2015); and Renshon (2017), Chapter 6.

[18] Copeland (2000), p. 76; and Mearsheimer (2001), p. 188. Renshon (2017), Chapter 6, has recently asserted that *Weltpolitik* is actually best understood as an effort to increase Germany's position in the world (including its material position) via the achievement of improved status. Status, on this view, induces deference, which means that it is instrumentally useful and thus may be expected to yield long-term material benefits. This, in essence, is a more complicated, better-specified version of the arguments of Copeland and Mearsheimer. More specifically, Renshon interprets the two Morocco crises as successful efforts at improving German status (pp. 199–206), and defends the obsession with battleship building as a nearly successful effort to coerce London into granting Germany coequal status (pp. 206–216). This interpretation is at odds with the consensus of historians and other political scientists, and Renshon does not offer evidence that the status gains that Germany allegedly made during the *Weltpolitik* period provided *any* concrete benefits, let alone that they provided (or even seemed likely to provide) benefits that could plausibly have outweighed the enormous economic, strategic, and opportunity costs that their pursuit required.

colonial empire was never particularly relevant for its economy. On the eve of World War I, it "covered a million square miles, attracted one in a thousand of Germany's emigrants, absorbed a paltry 3.8 percent of Germany's overseas investments, and accounted for 0.5 per cent of its overseas trade."[19]

The case for *Weltpolitik* as security-motivated expansion is even weaker. Colonial expansion served little purpose for a state facing primarily continental threats, and the naval race Germany initiated with the British was one of the most important causes of the Anglo-German antagonism and the formation of the Triple Entente.[20] By 1908, the British response to *Flottenpolitik* – including increased spending levels and the introduction of the *Dreadnought* class – had made it clear that Germany would be unable to compete with Great Britain for naval supremacy (and thus prevail in or deter a naval confrontation), yet the arms race continued.[21] In a late 1908 exchange with Tirpitz, Bülow – who knew Germany had lost the race – suggested that resources be redirected away from battleships and heavy cruisers toward improved coastal defense and commerce raiding capacity.[22] Tirpitz refused, not primarily because he thought German security would be harmed by ending the naval race, but because doing so "would be taken and felt at home and abroad as a humiliation for Germany."[23]

Historians today agree that *Weltpolitik* seems to have been a scatterbrained policy without a coherent strategic objective, and contemporary skeptics shared that sense. Eugen Richter, leader of the German Progress Party in the Reichstag, described German foreign policy during the early twentieth century by saying that "whenever something was happening, anywhere in the world, Germany had to be there too."[24] Former chief of the General Staff Alfred von Waldersee wrote in 1901: "We are supposed to be pursuing *Weltpolitik*. If only I knew what that was supposed to be."[25]

Weltpolitik *and the Rights of a "World Power"*   While many factors may have made *Weltpolitik* attractive to different actors, one common

---

[19] Strachan (2001), p. 10.

[20] Kennedy (1980), Chapter 20; MacMillan (2013), Chapter 5.

[21] Kagan (1995), p. 154; Mommsen (1995), p. 92. See also Steinberg (1965), Glaser (2004), Kennedy (1970), Murray (2010), and Fikenscher, Jaschob, and Wolf (2015) on the strategic illogic of Germany's fleet program.

[22] Bülow to Tirpitz, December 25, 1908, in *German Diplomatic Documents* (Dugdale 1930), vol. III, pp. 331–333.

[23] Tirpitz to Bülow, January 4, 1909, in *German Diplomatic Documents* (Dugdale 1930), vol. III, pp. 335–340.

[24] Quoted in Mommsen (1995), p. 82.   [25] Quoted in Clark (2012), p. 151.

concern was to convince other states – especially Great Britain – to acknowledge that Germany had the rights and privileges of a world power. Germany had come late to the colonialism party, but now wanted what it felt was its due as one of the most powerful states in Europe. In short, *Weltpolitik* was a policy aimed at achieving recognition of a claim to a particular status and the package of rights that went along with it.

The term "world power" was never defined precisely, but it was a common feature of prewar German foreign policy discourse and appears to have referred to a state with global interests, a colonial empire through which to spread its influence and civilization, and a strong navy. Early twentieth-century American author Wolf von Schierbrand attributed the initial use of the term in Germany to the kaiser himself, in the context of an announcement that Germany "must extend her political and commercial influence all over the world, and must have ships on every sea as well as merchants in every port."[26] In 1899 German historian Hans Delbrück wrote that "we want to be a World Power and pursue colonial policy in a grand manner."[27] Twelve years later, Friedrich von Bernhardi's influential *Germany and the Next War* juxtaposed continental great power status against world power status and identified Great Britain and France as members of the latter club. He linked this particular status category to its members' possession of colonies and of naval power, and argued that Germany had to acquire the same in order to be a world power.[28] Bernhardi's analysis was influenced by the thought of Heinrich von Treitschke, who decades earlier had argued that Germany had to work to catch up with other European powers, which were dividing the world among themselves.[29]

Acting out world power status did not just involve seizing colonies and building a strong navy. It also required securing recognition from the other world powers that Germany had the same rights that they did. Two in particular were paramount for German leaders and elites. First was a right to have German interests taken into account in the same way that the other world powers accommodated each other when they made territorial gains abroad. The desire to establish this right partially explains Germany's seemingly senseless tendency to impose itself in colonial disputes that had very little strategic importance.

References to a "right" to overseas expansion were common from the inauguration of *Weltpolitik*. An 1896 memo written by the future chief of the Naval Cabinet laid out the case for building colonies and argued that Germany "stands far ahead in the need and indeed the right to

---

[26] Schierbrand (1902), pp. 1–2.   [27] Quoted in Welch (1993), p. 96.
[28] Bernhardi (1914b), pp. 81, 239. Bernhardi seems to treat "great power" and "world power" as equivalent.
[29] See Hausrath (1914), pp. 195–216; and Mommsen (1984), p. 10, fn. 40.

expand."[30] Bülow's declaration of *Weltpolitik* in the Reichstag in December 1897 followed the infamous claim to a "place in the sun" by elaborating that that meant that "In East Asia as in the West Indies we shall endeavor ... to protect our rights and our interests," and his "Hammer or Anvil" speech, delivered in front of the Reichstag in 1899, invoked the language of rights and status to justify overseas expansion: "If the British speak of Greater Britain, if the French speak of Nouvelle France, if the Russians move into Asia, we too have the right to a Greater Germany."[31]

German reactions to colonial negotiations during the late 1890s are shot through with worries about whether German rights were being respected. During the 1898 negotiation over the future of Portugal's colonial territory in Africa and the Pacific, Bülow wrote to Germany's ambassador in London that if England, "seeing that she is once again getting ready to seize silently a considerable portion of the African continent, is really disregarding the German claim for reciprocity, damage is involved not only to German interests but also to the prestige of the Government of His Majesty the German Emperor both at home and abroad."[32] Negotiations between the United States and the British over the future of Samoa prompted a similar response from the kaiser: "The way certain other nations try to cut Germany out in every way does not seem overly friendly."[33] Bülow admitted that "the entire Samoan question has absolutely no material, but an ideal and patriotic interest for us," and that Germany's primary concern during the crisis over the small Pacific islands was "to maintain our prestige in the world intact."[34] In an 1899 letter to Queen Victoria, the Kaiser expressed his frustration that the British seemed not to have treated Germany as an equal in the negotiations over Samoa and the Portuguese colonies:

As a "rendu" for all this Lord Salisbury has treated Germany in the Samoan Question in a way which was utterly at variance with the manners which regulate the relations between great Powers according to European rules of civility ... This way of treating Germany's feelings & interests has come upon the People like an electric shock & has evoked the impression that Lord Salisbury cares for us no more than for Portugal, Chili [sic], or the Patagonians ... Lord Salisbury's Government must learn to respect & treat us as equals.[35]

---

[30] Quoted in Röhl (2001), p. 935.

[31] Bülow's "place in the sun" speech is quoted in Röhl (2014), p. 235; for Bülow's Hammer or Anvil speech (delivered on December 11, 1899), see http://germanhistorydocs.ghi-dc
.org/pdf/eng/602_Buelows%20Dynamic%20For%20Policy_106.pdf.

[32] Bülow to Hatzfeldt, June 22, 1898, in *German Diplomatic Documents* (Dugdale 1930), vol. III, pp. 32–33.

[33] Quoted in Röhl (2001), p. 964.   [34] Quoted in Kennedy (1980), p. 238.

[35] Quoted in Röhl (2001), p. 996.

The kaiser's complaints should be taken not as evidence that the British were *actually* behaving inappropriately, but that German leaders believed that as a world power Germany had a right to a greater degree of consideration from other powers in the realm of extra-European colonial management. The reference to Portugal, Chile, and Argentina is particularly notable because it strongly suggests that the right to privileged treatment that the kaiser claimed was linked to standing – as one of the most powerful and most civilizationally and technologically advanced states in Europe, Wilhelm evidently believed that Germany deserved to be treated with greater regard.

A similar logic runs through the record of German foreign policy in the first decade and a half of the new century. According to Kennedy, Germany provoked the 1905 Morocco crisis "to satisfy the general dissatisfaction in nationalist circles that the Reich's interests were being disregarded and her world position undermined."[36] Baron von Holstein, a high-ranking Foreign Ministry official, wrote after the conclusion of the 1904 Anglo-French Entente that it would be injurious to German prestige "if we sat still whilst German interests were being dealt with without our taking part." German intervention was "intended to prevent injury to its legitimate interests and dignity" and to avoid an outcome that "wounds our dignity as a Great Power."[37] Bülow, in his memoirs, described the 1904 agreement as "an attempt to exclude us from a great international decision," and maintained that "the dignity of our Empire could not allow German rights to be ignored."[38] The 1911 intervention in Morocco was similarly motivated by a concern that German rights were being ignored and that action was necessary to defend German status.[39]

The second right that German leaders associated with world power status was to naval equality. To be sure, Germany's construction of a battle fleet was justified by different actors in diverse ways – in fact, initially Tirpitz and Wilhelm envisioned it in part as a way of forcing the British to accede to their demands for greater deference outside of Europe.[40] But while it may seem odd to think of naval equality as a *right* rather than as a state of affairs that Germany could either achieve or not, it is common for leaders to think and talk this way about military

---

[36] Kennedy (1980), p. 275.

[37] Memorandum by Holstein, June 3, 1904 in *German Diplomatic Documents* (Dugdale 1930), vol. III, pp. 220–221.

[38] Bülow (1931), vol. II, pp. 121, 232.

[39] See Berghahn (1973), p. 94; memorandum by Kiderlen, May 3, 1911, in *German Diplomatic Documents* (Dugdale 1931), vol. IV, p. 4; Bethmann Hollweg to Count Metternich, July 4, 1911, in *German Diplomatic Documents* (Dugdale 1931), vol. IV, p. 8.

[40] See Röhl (2001), pp. 981–982 and 1030–1039.

technology. In today's international system, the legitimate possession of nuclear weapons is restricted to a particular class of states, and conflicts over other states' nuclear programs are not just about the ability to produce and weaponize fissile material but also about the *right* to do so.

This is precisely how the kaiser and other German elites understood the Anglo-German naval race that developed after 1898. One prominent strand of German foreign policy during the prewar years aimed at striking an agreement with Great Britain to break up the Triple Entente. But these efforts failed in part because the British (understandably) demanded as a condition that Germany agree to limitations on its battle fleet, and the kaiser and other nationalists objected to this as an infringement of Germany's right to naval equality.

In 1906, British Foreign Secretary Grey, increasingly concerned about the spiraling Anglo-German naval race, proposed that naval arms limitations be placed on the agenda for the Second Hague Peace Conference. The kaiser saw this, according to Röhl, "as an unacceptable infringement of his rights as Supreme War Lord and of the sovereignty of the Reich." The kaiser "complained bitterly of the British attitude to disarmament. 'So France and America, Japan and Italy may build as many ships as they want! Only we may not!'"[41] Two years later, in a conversation with British Undersecretary of State Charles Hardinge, Wilhelm responded to a request that Germany "stop or build slower" by exclaiming that Germany would rather "fight for it is a question of national honour and dignity."[42] That same summer, the kaiser commented on a memo about Anglo-German relations from his ambassador in London that he had "no desire for a good relationship with England at the price of the development of Germany's Navy. If England will hold out her hand in friendship only on condition that we limit our Navy, it is a boundless impertinence and a gross insult to the German people and their Emperor."[43]

After the 1911 crisis, renewed Anglo-German attempts at rapprochement again ran up against Germany's insistence on naval equality. The Kaiser reacted angrily to a warning from his ambassador in London that a new navy bill would pose an obstacle to détente: "His argument subjects our naval policy to the influence of a foreign Power in a way that I, as Supreme War Lord and Kaiser, cannot and will not accept, now or ever! And which amounts to a *humiliation* for our people."[44] In early 1914, the diplomats tried again, and again the kaiser objected to any agreement that signaled that Germany was not entitled to naval equality: "I have no desire to see the whole endless, dangerous

---

[41] Röhl (2014), p. 492   [42] Quoted in ibid., p. 634.
[43] Quoted in Marder (1961), p. 143.   [44] Quoted in Röhl (2014), p. 840.

chapter concerning arms limitation ... opened up yet again. One way or another it amounts to England's objecting to my right to determine the sea power necessary for Germany, and in the end, to an attempt to undermine the Navy Law."[45]

The kaiser may have been the most vocal and most powerful advocate of protecting Germany's right to naval equality with Great Britain, but he was not alone. In addition to naval enthusiasts within the government (chief among them Naval Secretary Tirpitz), the Navy League, the Pan-German League, and other radical nationalists felt similarly. In 1914, in a less well-known text than his 1911 sensation, Friedrich von Bernhardi argued that accommodating Germany's claims to world power status would have to entail behavior signaling that England "recognises that Germany possesses equal rights, side by side, with her," including a determination to "no longer oppose the development of Germany's sea power."[46]

Denied Rights Claims and Obstructed Status Ambitions While there is no doubt that other concerns played important roles in motivating both colonial expansion and the construction of a battle fleet, it is clear that German leaders and elites believed that the success of Germany's claim to world power status depended on whether or not other states behaved in ways that acknowledged that Germany had these two rights. And in the years between the inauguration of the policy and the July Crisis, evidence seemed to accumulate that the other world powers – especially Great Britain – were unwilling to do so. This is not an indictment of British foreign policy.[47] London had good reasons to oppose German claims to naval equality and the brash interventions that comprised *Weltpolitik*. Far-flung interests and simple geography meant that the British needed a naval advantage for security reasons, and Germany's interventions in Morocco threatened Paris – an important partner in the decade after the 1904 entente was concluded.[48] Thus, in this case, German status claims clashed with British security requirements: Germany's prewar foreign policy was strategically senseless in part because it sought status at the cost of seeming to threaten vital British security interests.

Still, whatever the sources of London's failure to accommodate Berlin, its consequence was a growing belief among German leaders and other elites that Germany's claim to world power status could not be satisfied

[45] Quoted in ibid., p. 993.   [46] Bernhardi (1914a), pp. 153–154.
[47] For an indictment of British foreign policy on the grounds that it needlessly provoked Germany, see Ferguson (1998), Chapter 3. For a similar – if less strident – argument, see Layne (2015).
[48] Kennedy (1980), p. 416.

within the bounds of the status quo order. The last section suggested that German leaders and elites understood *Weltpolitik* as a struggle for equal rights, and that conflicts with other states – especially Great Britain – were interpreted as evidence of an unwillingness to treat Germany fairly. This process began with the colonial disputes of the late 1890s and was one important justification for building a battle fleet: German rights abroad could be safely ignored so long as Germany lacked serious naval power.

According to Paul Kennedy, the notion that Germany "was being repeatedly disappointed by London" in its quest to become a world power was an important cause of the Anglo-German antagonism that developed in the decades prior to World War I.[49] Two of the most significant diplomatic disappointments were the two Moroccan crises.[50] Both contributed to the notion that German status ambitions could not be accommodated without a revolutionary challenge to the European order.

During the first years of the twentieth century, France sought to establish a protectorate over northern Morocco. The Anglo-French Entente, signed on April 8, 1904, guaranteed British acquiescence to French control in Morocco in return for French acquiescence to British control over Egypt. Throughout the remainder of 1904 and early 1905, French influence in Morocco increased until the French finally approached the sultan in Fez, demanding control over the military and police in February 1905.

These developments may have threatened German economic interests, but the latter were too paltry to have provoked intervention on their own. The entente also threatened Germany's status ambitions. As the evidence presented above suggests, the Anglo-French agreement was inconsistent with what German leaders understood to be their rights as a world power. It also undermined the strategic path (to the extent that there was one) to world power status, which was premised on the idea that Great Britain could be cajoled into supporting or acceding to German claims.[51] This would be difficult in the face of an Anglo-French alliance.

It was these two objectives – defending German rights abroad and splitting the entente, both linked to German status ambitions – that

---

[49] Kennedy (1980), p. 210.

[50] My account of the significance of the Morocco crises is similar to Murray's (2016) in that I focus on the role of perceived failure to achieve recognition on Germany's subsequent foreign policy orientation. Where I differ from Murray is in my contention that the consequence was not just an attempt to ground the aspirational status identity in material practices but rather a deep dissatisfaction with and drive to challenge and overthrow the status quo order.

[51] This was the initial path to achieving world power status that the Kaiser and some others hoped would bear fruit. Even as late as 1913, Bethmann Hollweg and his advisor Riezler apparently hoped to achieve world power status without war. See Röhl (2001, Chapters 30 and 31); and Strachan (2001, p. 34).

motivated the kaiser's landing in Tangier in March.[52] The move succeeded initially: the French offered a private settlement, and the crisis caused the resignation of anti-German foreign minister Théophile Delcassé.[53] But the nature of their aims led Germany to push for an international conference at which they might publicly validate their rights and humiliate France. The conference, held at Algeciras in 1906, turned out to be a fiasco. London supported the French position, and the Algeciras Act effectively confirmed France's status in Morocco. Geiss notes that this was a "resounding defeat for Germany, which attained none of its aims, short-term or long-term, because it had overreached itself."[54] Algeciras strengthened beliefs among German elites that world power status could not be achieved via cooperation with Great Britain. Berghahn notes that the First Morocco Crisis seemed "clear proof that Germany was 'encircled' by her enemies," and suggested that a more radical policy was needed for Germany to achieve its "place in the sun."[55] In *Germany and the Next War*, Bernhardi wrote of Germany's yielding "to the unjustifiable pretensions of France" in a way "unworthy alike of the dignity and the interests of Germany" in the course of arguing that it was impossible to "secure to German nationality and German spirit throughout the globe that high esteem which is due to them" because of "the hostile intentions of the other World Powers."[56] More concretely, German leaders became convinced after Algeciras that consultative conferences held little value as a means of advancing their interests.[57]

The Second Morocco Crisis was just as consequential. In 1911, a rebellion prompted France to send troops to Fez. Germany responded, again more for reasons having to do with status and its influence on domestic politics than with economics or security, by sending the gunboat *Panther* to Agadir. The sting of the defeat of 1906 played an important role. Foreign Minister Kiderlen argued to the kaiser that "by seizing a [territorial] pawn, the Imperial Government will be placed in position to give the Moroccan affair a turn which could cause the earlier [1905] setbacks to pass into oblivion."[58] Kiderlen apparently hoped to force compensation from the French in the form of territorial concessions

---

[52] See Strachan (2004), p. 20; and Kennedy (1980), p. 275.
[53] Kennedy (1980), p. 277; Geiss (1976), p. 103.   [54] Geiss (1976), p. 105.
[55] Berghahn (1973), p. 56.   [56] Bernhardi (1914b), pp. 81, 85.
[57] Fischer (1961), p. 22. Renshon (2017) argues that German intervention in Morocco actually succeeded in raising German status, since it "force[ed] other powers to take account of Germany" (p. 201). But he offers no evidence that the crisis raised German status, that it provided any concrete benefits due to that increase in status, or that German elites understood the result of the crisis as anything but a humiliation and evidence of an obstacle to the eventual satisfaction of German status ambitions.
[58] Quoted in Berghahn (1973), p. 94.

elsewhere "as a gesture of respect and a gain in prestige."[59] But this was not how the intervention's stakes were understood domestically. Much of the nationalist press and public believed the aim of the German government to be achieving territorial concessions in Morocco.[60]

The arrival of the *Panther* off Morocco initially played well in Germany. The *Kreuzzeitung*, a conservative newspaper, commented that "the entire nation breathed a sigh of relief as if a bad dream had ended, as if a nightmare of resigned uneasiness was being dispelled by the rays of the morning sun."[61] A nationalist paper wrote that up until that point, Germany had behaved and been treated "as though we were not the most populous nation in Europe, as though we could not base our justified claims to power on an army of five million men and on a fleet that is not to be despised."[62] The leader of the National Liberal party wrote to Kiderlen that "he welcomed the new 'active policy' which acted 'like a liberation.'"[63] These sentiments were widespread: the only group that actively opposed the Moroccan intervention was the Social Democrats.[64]

In the end, the *Panzersprung* turned into another debacle. On July 21, David Lloyd George delivered the "Mansion House Address," reiterating in no uncertain terms British support for France. This forced Germany to settle for a compromise in which it affirmed French control over Morocco in return for territory along the Congo River. Although this was close to the outcome Kiderlen had hoped for, it failed to meet the raised expectations of nationalist audiences at home, and was seen as yet another humiliation.[65] After the Morocco Treaty was signed on November 4, German papers, politicians, and nationalist pressure groups drew comparisons between Germany's latest defeat and the Treaty of Olmütz, which had reestablished Austrian primacy in the German Confederation after the uprisings of 1848. Even the left-wing Liberal paper *Vossische Zeitung* suggested the parallel as a way of underlining Germany's humiliation.[66]

The lesson of Agadir, though, was more specific than the idea that Germany had once again been humiliated.[67] The more significant conclusion that many in Germany drew was that London's intransigent

---

[59] Kagan (1995), p. 170; see also Fischer (1969), p. 72.   [60] Fischer (1969), p. 80.
[61] Quoted in ibid., p. 74.   [62] Quoted in ibid., p. 74.
[63] Quoted in Berghahn (1973), p. 95.   [64] Fischer (1969), p. 75.
[65] Strachan (2001), p. 25; MacMillan (2013), pp. 455–456.   [66] Fischer (1969), p. 89.
[67] Renshon (2017) again suggests that the second Morocco crisis actually resulted in an increase in German status and that "objectively, this was no humiliation at all" (pp. 205–206). It is, again, difficult to identify any evidence that German status had actually improved. In any event, what matters to the analysis here is not the judgment of future analysts about whether Germans *should* have felt humiliated, but rather evidence that they *did* and that they interpreted the result as yet more support for the notion that they faced an impenetrable obstacle to the satisfaction of their status ambitions.

opposition meant that *Weltpolitik* could not succeed within the constraints of the European status quo – in short, that Germany faced a condition of status immobility. According to Strachan, "the frustration at diplomacy's failure to gain for Germany the status its power warranted grew apace."[68] Kennedy notes that one of the most important consequences of the 1911 crisis was "the identification of Britain as the chief obstacle to German aims."[69] The crisis solidified beliefs among many on the right that the British would not allow Germany to take her "place in the sun" without a "fundamental regrouping of the contractual and sentimental relations" in Europe. Ernst von Heydebrand, the leader of the Conservative party in the Reichstag, announced in the wake of the disaster that (in reference to Great Britain): "now the German people knows that if it wants to spread in the world, if it wants to find its place in the sun to which it is entitled by right and by destiny – now it knows who it is who claims the right to decide whether to allow this or not."[70]

In the epilogue to *Germany and the Next War* (completed just after the Second Morocco Crisis), Bernhardi complained that the outcome "means a lowering of our prestige in the world," worried about the growing "rift" between the government and the dissatisfied nationalists, and argued that the outcome was evidence "that we are confronted by a firm phalanx of foes who, at the very least, are determined to hinder any further expansion of Germany's power."[71] Three years later, in a version of his argument meant for a broader audience, he painted even more clearly the picture of an insurmountable obstacle to German status ambitions: Germany was "prevented from expanding, and at the same time she is a world-Power which is able and entitled to give to Germanism that position in the world which, by right, is her due"; Germany "cannot act as a world-Power anywhere except in those few colonies which we possess and which Germany was able to acquire in agreement with England," a reality driven home by the Morocco crisis, which showed "clearly Germany's deplorable position as a world-Power."[72] British foreign policy "proves that England has not the slightest intention of coming to a peaceful agreement with Germany, treating Germany as an equal."[73] The attempt to achieve world power status seemed, to Bernhardi as to many others, to have proven incompatible with the European status quo order by the end of 1911.[74]

It is worth highlighting the important difference between these sentiments and those expressed during the late 1890s, which had articulated

---

[68] Strachan (2004), p. 32.   [69] Kennedy (1980), p. 447.
[70] Quoted in Fischer (1961), p. 91.   [71] Bernhardi (1914b), p. 286.
[72] Bernhardi (1914a), pp. 17, 53, 55.   [73] Ibid., p. 157.
[74] Kennedy (1980), pp. 351, 367; Strachan (2004), p. 32.

a desire for and determination to achieve world power status. The "place in the sun" address, for instance, is clear evidence of German ambitions for higher status. But the sentiments discussed above – especially those expressed in the wake of the Second Morocco Crisis – articulate a distinct pessimism in the face of what seemed to be a fundamental obstacle to achieving world power status: British intransigence, rooted in part in London's determination to defend the balance of power on the continent. German elites still cared about world power status – but they were no longer optimistic about achieving it, absent a radical change in the European order.

Status Immobility and German Foreign Policy

The increasing prevalence of this belief influenced German foreign policy in two ways that together contributed to the outcome of the July Crisis. First, the belief that Germany faced a status "glass ceiling" fostered preferences for policies aimed at protesting or removing the obstacle to German status ambitions. Demands for policies that sought to overthrow the European balance of power were rooted in many cases in the conclusion that world power status could not be achieved otherwise, and that taking a chance on major war was more consistent with German dignity than remaining a continental power. Similarly, preferences opposed to the use of consultative conferences were rooted in the belief that participation in the institutions that helped maintain the European status quo was antithetical to German interests and inconsistent with German dignity. Second, while this belief was by no means universal, developments that seemed to confirm it had the effect of weakening moderates and strengthening hardliners, which helps explain why Bethmann Hollweg did not go further toward an agreement with Great Britain in the years before the July Crisis, and why the German government was unwilling to take steps that might have held some promise of resolving the crisis short of war.

Status Immobility and Preferences for Rejection

One striking feature of prewar Germany was the increasingly loud chorus of voices demanding a policy that would overthrow the European order. These calls came from inside government (from some military leaders) and outside government (from pan-Germans and other radical nationalists), and reflected multiple logics. There is no doubt that some individuals favored hegemonic war because of fears about the security implications of the rise of Russia. But to focus exclusively on materialist logics ignores an important part of the story: links between beliefs about obstructed status claims, concerns about national esteem and dignity, and support for policies that rejected the status quo order in the thought of those Germans with the most aggressively revisionist preferences. In short, demands for provocative policies both inside and outside the government can be understood in part as calls for rejectionist responses to status immobility.

Among actors outside the government, the Pan-German League was one of the most rabidly revisionist groups in Germany. Throughout the period between its founding in the 1890s and World War I, the League advocated an aggressive, anti-British foreign policy, including support for naval building, imperial expansion, support for the Boers, continental expansion, and an expansion in the size of the army.[75] Identifying the sources of pan-German preferences is difficult, but according to Chickering, the League's ideology was rooted in the idea of a racial hierarchy in which Germans were at the top, combined with a sense that other peoples refused "to acknowledge the superiority of German culture and the respect and authority to which this superiority entitled the German *volk*."[76] In other words, the Pan-German League's aggressive preferences originated in the perception that German superiority had gone unrecognized too long.

This helps explain why members of the Pan-German League grew resentful in the face of evidence that Germany's government was behaving moderately, or that other states continued to block Germany's rise to world power.[77] It also helps explain why the Pan-German League – along with its patron, the crown prince – became increasingly radical as German diplomatic defeats accumulated, and in particular in the wake of the 1911 Morocco Crisis. According to Chickering, the pan-Germans called the Morocco Treaty "'an intolerable humiliation of our Fatherland,' a 'shameful debasement of the international political prestige [*Geltung*] of the German Empire,' a Jena without war."[78] They, along with other nationalist groups, were willing to risk war in order to reverse the humiliation. In 1912, Pan-German leader Heinrich Class published the pseudonymously authored "If I Were Kaiser," in which he "called for a holy war to gain command of the world."[79]

The writings of retired general Friedrich von Bernhardi present even more clearly the logic that linked obstructed status claims to a policy aimed at overthrowing the status quo order in the minds of some German

---

[75] On radical nationalism in pre–World War I Germany, see McGowan (2003), Chapter 2; and Chickering (1984).
[76] Chickering (1984), p. 88.   [77] Ibid., p. 96.   [78] Ibid., p. 265.
[79] Röhl (2014), p. 874.

nationalists. We have already seen that Bernhardi demanded equal rights as a world power for Germany on the basis of arguments rooted at least in part on the demands of German esteem and dignity, but was pessimistic that the British would accommodate German claims. This presented a dilemma: Germany was "entitled to claim an important increase of her sway, corresponding to her economic and cultural importance," but this ambition was "one of the reasons of the present tension." The British could accommodate Germany by conceding "a position of absolute equality," and sharing "with Germany her predominant position," but this seemed unlikely. Instead, it seemed that the "rise of Germany [was] irreconcilable with the old idea of a European balance of power."[80]

One solution to the dilemma was to accept that Germany would remain a continental power. But, for Bernhardi, this would have been "unbearable. Our feeling of exasperation must become all the greater when we remember Germany's importance as a civilising factor and as a trading Power, if we remember our claim upon the world's territories in consequence of the increase of Germany's population."[81] The alternative was to reject and fight to overthrow the European status quo order, as it seemed to be incompatible with Germany's rise to world power status. The logic here is not based on the material requirements of German security, but on an intolerable sense that Germany's aspirational status – which, to Bernhardi, it fully deserved to act out and have recognized – could not be satisfied without a European revolution.

Bernhardi also expressed preferences in line with the expectations of status immobility theory with respect to the other component of prewar European order: consultative conferences and the arbitration treaties that emerged from them. "General treaties of arbitration," he wrote, "must be particularly pernicious to an ambitious and rising nation, such as Germany ... which is compelled to increase its power in order to do justice to its civilisation."[82] These kinds of "courts" were inherently biased in favor of states that had already satisfied their ambitions, and that meant they were hopelessly anti-German. This helps explain why Bernhardi opposed the renewal of the Concert of Europe during the Balkan Wars: "The proposal to settle the affairs of the Balkan Peninsula by the Concert of all the Great Powers would ... be merely a cloak under which the Powers of the Triple Entente would play their own game while keeping Germany and Austria-Hungary in a state of inactivity."[83]

J.A. Cramb, Professor of Modern History at Queen's College, echoed this analysis of German radical nationalism in a series of lectures delivered

---

[80] Bernhardi (1914a), pp. 136–148.   [81] Ibid., p. 56.   [82] Ibid., pp. 127–128.
[83] Ibid., p. 161.

in early 1913. Cramb argued that Germans analyzed the state of world politics and concluded that:

Germany has one enemy. One nation blocks the way. That nation is England ... German indignation then takes the place of German analysis ... can we or ought we, it is asked, to acquiesce in England's possession of one-fifth of the globe? Ought a patriotic German to submit to seeing his nation depleted year by year? Can he, on those conditions, retain his manhood or be true to the religion of valour, the birthright of the Teutonic kindred?[84]

This colorful analysis from abroad should be taken as evidence of German thinking only with caution, but it is consistent with the way the Pan-Germans and Bernhardi seem to have thought about world power status, and it underlines the point that the logic linking beliefs in obstructed status claims and support for overthrowing the status quo order was in significant measure based on concerns about identity and esteem.

It was not only elites outside government who thought this way. While the kaiser's attitude toward major war is complicated, there is little doubt that between 1896 and 1914, he developed suspicions that the European status quo order was incompatible with Germany's claim to world power status. This showed up in a growing willingness to consider (if not a determination to employ) major war as a way forward, and in a dispositional opposition to participating in consultative conferences. During the Bosnian annexation crisis of 1908–1909, Wilhelm made a telling reference to a past failure in rejecting out of hand the possibility that the great powers might collectively manage the outcome: "Heavens!!! The British want to smuggle a whole lot of other questions into the conference, to make it a sort of Algeciras II ... An unreliable pack, totally under *London's* influence!"[85]

The kaiser may not have completely given up on the possibility of cajoling the British into accommodating German claims. But evidence of British obstructionism produced fits of anger that made him particularly belligerent, especially in the wake of the Second Morocco Crisis.[86] The most consequential example is the War Council of December 8, 1912. The War Council is not, as some scholars suggest, evidence that German leaders were coolly plotting an opportunistic bid for hegemony or a well-timed preventive strike on Russia.[87] The kaiser had not just become aware of any particular military-strategic factor that prompted preparations for major war. Rather, he called the meeting after being told of a conversation that British War Minister Haldane had with Germany's ambassador in London, during which Haldane expressed England's

[84] Cramb (1914), pp. 13–14.   [85] Röhl (2014), p. 724.   [86] See ibid., Chapter 33.
[87] Copeland (2000), pp. 65–67.

determination to intervene against Germany in any conflict involving France.[88] This was, crucially, not new information, as Bethmann Hollweg noted later: "Haldane's communication ... only affirmed what we have long known: *now as before England follows a policy of balance of power and therefore will stand up for France if the latter is in danger of being annihilated by us.*"[89] What motivated the kaiser to call the meeting was, instead, resentment at a reminder of British obstructionism. Wilhelm wrote that England "was so deeply envious and hateful of us, for that reason other powers may not defend their interests with the sword," and that it was "jealousy, fear of our incipient greatness" that motivated Britain's intervention.[90] This was no calculated response to a change in the strategic environment.

Tirpitz responded similarly when confronted with evidence of obstacles to German status ambitions. In October 1913, he acknowledged that the battle fleet had failed to secure equality with London. This led not – as might have been reasonable – to a call for the abandonment of the naval race in order to work toward better relations with England, but rather to a call for world war:

The question, generally speaking, of whether Germany should fight against England, if necessary, for her world position – with the enormous effort that such a struggle would involve – or confine herself in advance to the position of a European continental Power of the second rank, this question is in the last resort a matter of political conviction. In the end it would seem more worthy of a great nation to fight for the highest objective and perhaps to perish with honour, than ignobly to renounce the future.[91]

Status Immobility and Constraints on Moderates Demands to overthrow the European status quo order were prominent but hardly universal in prewar Germany. In addition to domestic groups – especially the Social Democrats – who opposed both *Weltpolitik* and fighting to achieve it, there were also moderates within the government. The most important of these was the man who had been chancellor since 1909: Theobald von Bethmann Hollweg. Bethmann Hollweg took a more cautious approach to European order than did the kaiser, Tirpitz, the German military, or the radical nationalists. Bethmann Hollweg was – like the rest of the government – committed to pursuing *Weltpolitik*. But up until July 1914, he thought it was possible to do so without risking hegemonic war, and he preferred more moderate means. His foreign policy sought to improve relations with Great Britain in order to loosen

---

[88] Jarausch (1972), p. 134.   [89] Ibid., p. 134.
[90] Quoted in MacDonogh (2000), p. 335.   [91] Quoted in Röhl (2014), pp. 994–995.

Germany's continental isolation.[92] Accordingly, he tried to limit Germany's naval building, and also worked for better relations with France and Russia.[93] Some analysts suggest that Bethmann Hollweg wanted to break up the Triple Entente in order to *prepare* for major war, but this is controversial. He thought major war was an "incalculable" risk, because it would fundamentally unsettle Germany's fragile socio-political balance.[94] He was also more amenable to using consultative conferences than were German hardliners – he supported Germany's participation, in the face of hostility from the Kaiser, in the revival of the "Concert" that met in London to manage the Balkans crisis in 1913, at least in part because he hoped that this would improve Anglo-German relations.[95] In fact, Wilhelm himself acknowledged that Bethmann Hollweg's apparent moderation was advantageous, because his "honest policy inspires confidence abroad."[96]

But Bethmann Hollweg was constrained in the years before the war by two constituencies who had increasingly radically revisionist preferences. The first of these was the radical nationalist groups. The government's position had declined domestically in the years after 1911, largely as a result of the rise of the Social Democrats as the largest party in the Reichstag. This increased the chancellor's reliance on "external pressure groups" for legitimacy.[97] These groups were increasingly vocal about their disdain for Bethmann Hollweg's moderate policy, especially in the wake of the humiliation of 1911–1912. Foreign Minister Jagow worried that another foreign debacle would topple Bethmann Hollweg and be "another step towards a parliamentary regime."[98] He was right to worry: in 1913 the Pan-German League conspired with Crown Prince Wilhelm to try to depose the chancellor and install the more aggressive Tirpitz in his place.[99]

Still, Bethmann Hollweg was not subject to electoral accountability, and the Reichstag had only a limited ability to interfere with foreign policy. Accordingly, he was far less constrained by public opinion or the legislature than he was by his other constituency: the kaiser. The kaiser had the power to dismiss Bethmann Hollweg and had the final say on all matters of policy. Thus, according to one official, Bethmann Hollweg's "primary concern was not what he should do, but what he was *not* allowed

---

[92] Mommsen (1995), p. 94; Geiss (1976), p. 130; Jarausch (1972), p. 116; Thompson (1980), p. 22; Strachan (2004), p. 38; Watson (2014), p. 32.
[93] Jarausch (1972), p. 118.
[94] See Riezler's diary entry from July 7, 1914 translated in Mombauer (2013), p. 220; Jarausch (1972), p. 146; Thompson (1980), pp. 43, 55; Otte (2014b), p. 108.
[95] Röhl (2014), p. 935.   [96] Ibid., p. 966.
[97] See Chong and Hall (2014), pp. 26–30; Strachan (2001), p. 22.
[98] Otte (2014b), p. 108.   [99] Mommsen (1995), p. 98; Scheck (1998), p. 16.

to do … The moment he was afraid of giving offence somehow, all attempts to move him were in vain. His position with the Kaiser preoccupied him above all else. It was the bedrock of his own authority."[100] Yet the kaiser was more easily managed and manipulated than was public opinion, and as a result Bethmann Hollweg did have significant freedom of action during his time as chancellor.

Nonetheless, there is substantial evidence that these two constraints made the pursuit of his more moderate agenda difficult – if not impossible – as evidence accumulated that world power could not be achieved in the face of British obstructionism. First, the increasingly loud and resonant calls for hegemonic war after the Second Morocco Crisis undercut Bethmann Hollweg's policy by empowering military leaders who had aggressive preferences. The chancellor was not invited to the December 1912 War Council – which, as I argued above, the kaiser called in a fit of rage and an "openly war-like mood" after being reminded that London was committed to maintaining the balance of power in Europe.[101] Bethmann Hollweg understood the War Council as "an impetuous creation of fear" that might "make the [Anglo-French] bond unbreakable."[102] On December 9 – the day after the meeting – the kaiser ordered War Minister Falkenhayn and Naval Secretary Tirpitz to begin the process of pushing new Army and Navy bills through the Reichstag.[103] Bethmann Hollweg derided these decisions as "nervous jumping-jack policies" that Germany should avoid lest foreign actors "lose patience."[104] He urged the kaiser to reverse the new military spending in order to avoid provoking belligerent responses from abroad. Bethmann Hollweg was partially successful but only after surprising the kaiser by deciding to throw his support behind new spending on the army in order to bolster the argument against naval spending.[105] In late 1913, the chancellor protested against increasing belligerence in the Reichstag by arguing that "to rattle our sword every time there is a diplomatic crisis which does not threaten Germany's honor, safety, and future is more than foolhardy, it is criminal."[106] While Bethmann Hollweg may well have thought major war was inevitable at some point, and may even have come around by July 1914 to the position that it was better to fight now than later, there is no doubt that his effort to avoid provoking Germany's neighbors in the years leading up to the July Crisis was made more difficult by increasingly loud and resonant demands for policies that would lash out in protest at the European order.

[100] Quoted in Röhl (2014), p. 967.
[101] Bavarian General von Wenninger, quoted in Röhl (2014), p. 910.
[102] Jarausch (1972), p. 134.   [103] Röhl (2014), p. 910; Jarausch (1972), p. 135.
[104] Röhl (2014), p. 913.   [105] Ibid., pp. 913–915.   [106] Quoted in Hull (2015).

It also seems that accumulating evidence of status immobility prevented him from working to improve relations with the British and especially from using consultative conferences to do so. It is no surprise that the chancellor would work for an Anglo-German détente after the Second Moroccan crisis. But his efforts were hampered by concerns about the reactions of his increasingly anti-British domestic audiences. Berlin and London did negotiate a revision – which was quite favorable to Germany – of a secret 1898 agreement over territorial concessions in Angola and Mozambique. But the effort failed in the end because Bethmann Hollweg – fearing that the German right would think the British had "duped" the government – could not agree to the British requirement that the agreement and its secret predecessor be published.[107] Jagow worried that in the event of publication, "there is no security that a storm of anger may not burst forth in Germany, which will scarcely contribute to our relations with England or to strengthen the Government's prestige."[108]

The kaiser's – and the nationalist public's – obsession with defending Germany's equal rights at all costs continued to make it difficult for Bethmann Hollweg to make concessions to the British on naval building. This complicated the 1912 Haldane mission and a series of subsequent attempts at a settlement.[109] Even at the height of the July Crisis, Bethmann Hollweg – according to two accounts of the July 29 Potsdam Crown Council – suggested that an "understanding with England over the naval question" might help keep the British out of the war. The kaiser, according to Tirpitz, refused: "To make such a promise at this moment would mean going on one's knees to England, and His majesty could not answer for it before History and his own Person."[110]

The kaiser had also decided that consultative conferences were useless because they were simply tools of British obstruction. While he did not prevent German participation in the London ambassadors' conference in 1913, he did, according to Röhl, undermine the chancellor's effort to use the forum as a way to work toward rapprochement with the British by repeatedly "threaten[ing] to abandon the 'Concern of Europe'. 'I am not going along with these embarrassing farces of Europ[ean] Concern – not Concert – any more, and shall from now on go my own way in dealing with the belligerents, as is best for us and without regard for others!"[111] The same attitude took a European conference off the table as a way of managing the July Crisis.[112]

---

[107] Mommsen (1995), p. 202. See also Langhorne (1973), p. 387.

[108] Jagow to Prince von Lichnowsky, July 27, 1914, in *German Diplomatic Documents* (1931), vol. IV, p. 233.

[109] See Carroll (1966), p. 705.   [110] Röhl (2014), pp. 1063–1064.

[111] Röhl (2014), pp. 935–936.   [112] See Röhl (2014), pp. 1037, 1045, 1051, 1057.

Conclusion

Did German leaders manipulate the July Crisis to intentionally provoke World War I? Or did they simply pursue a reckless foreign policy that led to Germany's isolation and contributed to a willingness to risk world war? The answer depends largely upon what one thinks Bethmann Hollweg expected and wanted to happen in July 1914, and that question is unlikely to be settled soon.

The evidence and analytical narrative presented in this chapter – summarized in Figure 3.1 – is consistent with both mainstream interpretations. On one hand, beliefs about the incompatibility of "world power" with the European status quo order contributed to preferences for policies that would protest, delegitimate, and ultimately overthrow that order. Given the centrality of *Weltpolitik* and equal rights to the way so many Germans (including the Kaiser) thought about international politics, status has to be part of any convincing story about the intentional provocation of World War I by decisionmakers in Berlin. And indeed, there is evidence (albeit from after August 1914) that Bethmann Hollweg, too, thought about the European war as a response to obstructed ambitions for world power status.[113]

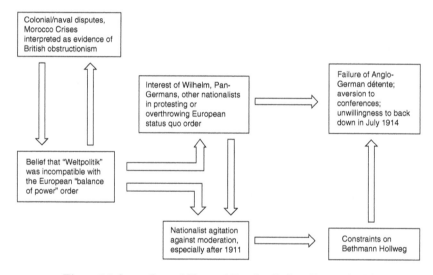

Figure 3.1 Status Immobility and Foreign Policy Change in Wilhelmine Germany

[113] See Hull (2015); and Röhl (2014), pp. 1137–1138.

What this means is that my interpretation of Wilhelmine Germany's foreign policy functions as a complement to prominent realist accounts. Both offensive realism and stories about preventive war have trouble explaining why German leaders would calculate that it made sense to risk disaster in 1914. Germany (and earlier Prussia) had survived without European hegemony for centuries; why should it now become worth putting the survival of the German state on the line? The rise of Russia raises similar questions: did it really threaten Germany's survival to such an extent that preventive war seemed to make sense? Levy has recently suggested that the answer may be no. Preventive motivations may only work as an explanation for World War I in the sense that German leaders worried that changing international conditions might prevent them from achieving some revisionist ambition in the future.[114]

This is where status immobility provides explanatory leverage: by helping to explain deeply revisionist elite preferences. Many Germans did frame foreign policy as a choice between world power and decline, but it is impossible to make sense of this formulation without understanding that remaining a continental great power was intolerable for reasons related to national esteem and dignity. Focusing on physical security alone is insufficient to understand why people like Bernhardi, Wilhelm, and Tirpitz were willing to fight for European hegemony by 1914.

On the other hand, even if one does not believe German leaders intentionally provoked World War I, status immobility still played an important role in the development of a reckless German foreign policy by imposing constraints on German decisionmakers. It contributed to a willingness to risk major war among some and strengthened leaders who preferred more provocative policies; it prevented Bethmann Hollweg from doing more to bring about an Anglo-German rapprochement by agreeing to naval limitations; and it contributed to skepticism among German leaders – especially the kaiser – about the value of Concert-style great power management. While none of these factors alone caused the July Crisis to end the way it did, each made it less likely that Germany would be willing to back down when faced with a choice between war and humiliation.

---

[114] Levy (2014), pp. 145–146.

4   Japan Joins the "Community of the Damned"

In his memoirs, former American ambassador to Japan Joseph Grew noted the importance of Tokyo's withdrawal from the League of Nations in early 1933: "Nobody could miss the political significance of Japan's decision to quit the League of Nations. It marked a clear break with the Western powers and prepared the way for Japan's later adherence to the Axis."[1] Yet political scientists have ignored Japan's withdrawal from the League. Much more attention has been paid to the logic that drove expansion in Manchuria or the decision to bomb Pearl Harbor.[2] The episode has been largely passed over as an insignificant part of the story of Japan's attempt to take over East Asia and the Western Pacific.

But this is not how things appeared to Japanese at the time. On the contrary, withdrawal from the League was a controversial, meaningful, and – for some – painful move that symbolized the failure of Japanese moderates to keep Japan inside the Western order. I argue in this chapter that it constituted a significant step in the direction of a radical revisionist foreign policy combination and that it deserves attention for two reasons. The first is that it was needlessly provocative and therefore puzzling. Japan stood to lose nothing in terms of security or economics from remaining inside the League, and stood to gain nothing from leaving. Japanese moderates understood these incentives and worked for eighteen months after the Mukden Incident to prevent that crisis from leading to Japan's isolation. That they were unable to avoid withdrawal is a puzzle that deserves scrutiny.

The second reason withdrawal deserves attention is that it facilitated subsequent moves toward even more provocative and destabilizing policies. By producing a sense of isolation and removing an important justification for moderation, withdrawal from the League played into the hands of Japan's hardliners, who invoked the heightened threat of conflict with Western great powers to argue for abrogation of the Washington Treaty

---

[1] Grew (1944), p. 75.
[2] See, for instance, Copeland (2011); (2014), Chapter 4; Snyder (1991), Chapter 4; and Sagan (1988).

and departure from the Second London Naval Conference. These moves, in turn, set the stage for the naval race that would end at Pearl Harbor.

I argue that withdrawal from the League – a clear shift toward radical revisionism – was the consequence of developments that seemed to confirm that Japan's ambition to join the Western great power club faced a "glass ceiling" in the form of racial discrimination. A history of race-based slights played an important role in the rise of the militant form of pan-Asianism that motivated the critics of long-time foreign minister Kijurō Shidehara's moderate policy. It also produced fodder for the construction of a narrative about the incompatibility of Japan's interests, dignity, and honor with the Western institutional order. When the League of Nations condemned the Japanese invasion of Manchuria, it was widely interpreted – within the preexisting discourse of racial discrimination – as a hypocritical and unjust denial that Japan had the rights of a great power. This led to loud and widespread demands for withdrawal that Japanese moderates were unable to resist. In short, racial discrimination contributed to status immobility, which influenced Japanese foreign policy both by motivating militant pan-Asianists to promote policies aimed at protesting and overthrowing the Western order, and by producing political conditions favoring such policies that were eventually too much for moderates to resist.

The chapter proceeds as follows. The next section describes the interwar order in East Asia and shows that Japanese foreign policy evolved from a distributive revisionist effort to increase economic influence in Manchuria during the 1920s to a radical revisionist one that increasingly expressed protest and rejected the legitimacy of the status quo order after 1933. The rest of the chapter documents the rise of status immobility in Japan between the Meiji restoration and the Mukden Incident, establishes its link to the ideology and rejectionist policy preferences of prominent pan-Asianists, and shows that it contributed to changes in Japan's domestic political environment that help explain withdrawal from the League and, in turn, the rejection of the naval arms limitation framework that signaled the start of the race to Pearl Harbor.[3]

Japanese Foreign Policy and the Interwar Order

The order that Japan eventually challenged beginning early in the 1930s was forged in the aftermath of World War I. Like all orders, it had both a distributive element and a normative element. The most important facets of the distributive element – for Japan – were the distributions of naval power, economic influence in East Asia, and status as reflected in

---

[3] Material from this chapter appeared previously in Ward (2013).

the rights that Japan was accorded within multilateral institutions and through the behavior of other states. Japanese foreign policy consistently sought to maintain a favorable balance of naval power, to protect and enhance its economic interests in Manchuria, and to satisfy its ambition for acceptance as a member in the Western great power club.

Other states – especially Great Britain and the United States – also had interests in East Asia's economic resources and in the region's naval balance. In the wake of the collapse of Germany's colonial empire, chaos in Russia, and suspicions aroused by increasing Japanese penetration in China, American, British, and Japanese leaders recognized that distributive competition in the region might lead to costly arms-racing, conflict, and another war. In response, they constructed an elaborate normative and institutional order to manage conflicts over distributive resources like naval power and economic influence. The core of this effort was global – the collective security institution of the League of Nations – but the new order in East Asia was buttressed by a series of regional treaties that were negotiated at the Washington Naval Conference between 1921 and 1922. These included the Four Power Treaty, which ratified the distribution of territory in East Asia, prohibited the construction of new naval bases in the Western Pacific, and called for consultation in the case of conflicting claims; the Five Power Treaty (also known as the Washington Naval Treaty), which limited naval building by setting a naval arms ratio of 5:5:3 between Great Britain, the United States, and Japan; and the Nine Power Treaty, which affirmed the principle of the "Open Door" in China.[4]

Japanese Approaches to the New Order

The new order was not universally accepted by Japanese elites – militarists within the navy objected to naval inequality, and others were skeptical of the League of Nations and Washington Conference system more broadly from the start.[5] Nonetheless, Japan's foreign policy throughout the 1920s aimed at improving its economic position in Manchuria by cooperating with the Western great powers and respecting the normative and institutional foundation of the new order – in other words, Japan sought to make limited revisions to the distributive status quo while playing by the rules in order to avoid provocation. This approach – which has come to be known as Shidehara diplomacy, after long-time foreign minister Kijuro

---

[4] See Crowley (1974), pp. 40–41.
[5] On the attitudes of naval hardliners toward the Washington Treaty, see Pelz (1974), p. 14. On the debate over joining the League of Nations, see Burkman (2008), Chapter 3.

Shidehara – was initially adopted in part because Japanese expansion during and just after World War I had made Great Britain and the United States suspicious.[6] Japanese leaders were hardly enthusiastic about the idea of a new multilateral framework that would be dominated by Western states, but calculated that not participating would lead to diplomatic isolation and was therefore not an option.[7]

The commitment to Shidehara diplomacy – to distributive revisionism without challenging the normative and institutional order – lasted through the 1920s and into the early 1930s. It persisted in the face of an increasingly serious threat to Japanese interests in Manchuria from Chinese nationalists and in spite of growing dissatisfaction from militarists within the navy and other proponents of overthrowing the East Asian order. The effort to remain within the normative and institutional order even continued for over a year after a rogue element of the Japanese military provoked a serious crisis – the Mukden Incident – by invading Manchuria in September 1931. It was not until March 1933 that Japan symbolically abandoned Shidehara diplomacy by announcing its withdrawal from the League of Nations. Japanese support for the Washington Conference system subsequently disintegrated: Japan announced its abrogation of the Washington Naval Treaty in December 1934, and by 1936 had withdrawn from an effort to negotiate a replacement.

By the middle of the 1930s, Japan's orientation toward the status quo order had shifted dramatically from an effort to secure its interests while playing by the rules to one aimed at protesting and overthrowing the order itself. This made Japanese foreign policy less inhibited and more dangerous. Crowley notes that the Washington Conference system "had confirmed the viewpoint that cooperation with the Western powers ... was the better method of preserving Japan's leadership in East Asia."[8] The abandonment of the Washington Conference system accordingly empowered advocates of unilateral expansion and unrestrained naval arms-racing. In the absence of this development, it is difficult to imagine the later, more explosive ones – like the conflict in China that started in 1937, Japan's advance into Southeast Asia, and, ultimately, the surprise offensive in the winter of 1941 – that brought world war to East Asia.

The Puzzle of Japanese Revisionism

The distributive element of Japanese revisionism is not difficult to understand. While concerns about a future shortage of natural resources were

---

[6] Nish (2002), p. 177; Beasley (1963), p. 204; Burkman (2008), pp. 17–24.
[7] Burkman (2008), Chapter 3.   [8] Crowley (1974), p. 42.

probably overblown, it is reasonable that the leaders of a small island state would want to secure an economic sphere of influence abroad.[9] But for over a decade, Japanese leaders pursued this interest while simultaneously working to minimize the costs of doing so by signaling that they accepted the basic rules of the new East Asian order. What is puzzling is that by 1933, Japan's foreign policy paired the effort to maintain control over Manchuria with moves that signaled a *rejection* of the normative and institutional order. What was the point of leaving the League of Nations and announcing the abrogation of the Washington Treaty? Neither move makes much strategic sense. Withdrawal from the League came in response to the Lytton Commission's condemnation of the Japanese military's activity in Manchuria during and after the Mukden Incident, but the League at no point threatened to impose economic or military sanctions. Condemnation was purely symbolic. Similarly, Japan announced the abrogation of the Washington Treaty over a year *before* the government had decided on a policy that would require Japan to violate its terms.[10]

There are two prominent explanations for the increasingly anti-status quo orientation that came to characterize Japan's foreign policy during the early 1930s. The first focuses on the effects of the global economic crisis that struck in 1929. Shidehara diplomacy was premised on the idea that avoiding economic isolation was critical to Japanese security. In the wake of the Great Depression and the adoption of increasingly protectionist policies by Western powers, trade with the West no longer seemed like a viable lifeline, which increased the attractiveness of seizing Manchuria regardless of the diplomatic consequences. The reduced value of cooperation with the West might have similarly weakened the justification for remaining within the league and the broader Washington Conference system.[11]

The importance of the economic crisis for the course of interwar Japanese foreign policy is undeniable. Many radical nationalists thought that Japan should expand abroad for reasons of economic security, and the crisis certainly weakened support for Shidehara's moderate approach. Yet there are at least two problems with this explanation. First, the value of cooperation with the West went far beyond economic development. Japan's growth was never particularly dependent on

---

[9] Yasukichi Yasuba (1996) argues that Japan's resource shortage did not cause but was caused by military mobilization during the 1930s.
[10] Copeland (2014), p. 167.
[11] See Copeland (2014), Chapter 4, for a recent explication of this logic. For similar arguments, see Iriye (1965); Peatte (1984), p. 9; Berger (1977), p. 354; Crowley (1966), p. 389; Samuels (2007), pp. 20–21; Barnhart (1987), p. 18.

exports to the West, which undermines the argument that the imposition of Western tariffs alone would have changed the minds of Japanese moderates about the value of cooperation.[12] Imports of natural resources from Western territories, for instance, remained critically important throughout the 1930s – signalling a deep opposition to the Western order can only have put these at further risk. In fact, Japanese moderates remained opposed to unrestrained expansion because they feared the consequences of diplomatic and economic isolation, costly arms races, and war. This is why Shidehara and others worked throughout the Mukden Incident to rein in the military and settle the crisis without a serious break with the Western order.

Second, it is difficult to explain withdrawal from the League as a response to the economic crisis. Moderates strenuously opposed withdrawal as unnecessarily provocative and isolating.[13] It promised no economic or security benefit; the only purpose withdrawal served was to protest against the status quo order. Moreover, Japanese moderates worried not only about diplomatic isolation, but also about the future of Japan's League-mandated territories in the event of withdrawal. It is, in other words, clear that the expected costs of withdrawal outweighed the expected benefits of withdrawal (which were basically nothing), at least in the eyes of Japanese moderates.

In short, the critical question that the economic security perspective leaves unanswered is why Japanese policy did not continue attempting to reduce the costs of its expansion in Manchuria by signalling satisfaction with the normative and institutional foundation of the status quo order. Why provoke when there was nothing to be gained from doing so?

The other prominent explanation for Japan's increasing revisionism during the 1930s involves the pathologies of its prewar domestic politics. The Japanese military had organizational and ideological incentives to pursue unrestrained expansion and unrestrained naval building, and policy ultimately reflected these preferences because the state was constructed in a way that allowed the military to hijack the decisionmaking apparatus. This process was facilitated by the propagation of expansionist "myths" or the creation of a "domestic milieu" that helped the militarists gain public support and defeat the moderates.[14] By the time of the Mukden Incident, the militarist position had grown so popular and resonant that moderates could no longer sustainably resist. They became increasingly marginalized, and Japanese policy was increasingly responsive to pressure from expansionists.

---

[12] See Boltho (1996). [13] See Burkman (2008), pp. 177–181.
[14] See Snyder (1991), pp. 112–152; and Kupchan (1996), pp. 315–323.

There is much to recommend this narrative of Japanese revisionism. The role of military interests and autonomy was certainly central to Japan's conquest of Manchuria after September 18, 1931, and also to the withdrawal from the Washington Treaty and the Second London Naval Conference. Still, domestic explanations raise two unanswered questions. First, why did Japan's militarists want to withdraw from the League, if it promised no strategic benefit? Perhaps they calculated that withdrawing from the League might further weaken moderates, but this would mean that Japanese moderates were not as powerless by 1933 as "domestic hijacking" explanations imply. It would also mean that the story of withdrawal from the League deserves more attention than it gets in most accounts.

Second, why were the militarists so much more successful after 1931 than before 1931? Why did the expansionist "myths" and "domestic milieu" constrain moderates in the 1930s but not before? The economic crisis is one part of the answer, but it does not tell the whole story. Dissatisfaction with economic conditions surely helps explain why the weakened moderates were unable to rein in the Kwantung Army after the Mukden Incident. But Japan's economy had started to rebound by 1933, and the militarists were no less agitated, no less bent on withdrawal from the League, and their rhetoric was no less effective than it had been eighteen months earlier.[15]

The debate over withdrawal from the league was not won by militarists deploying the rhetoric of economic crisis: after all, the economic crisis had begun to abate, and leaving the League promised no plausible macro-economic benefit. Nor was it the case that moderates had by this point already been either coopted or replaced. They remained, as I show below, in positions of power and fought to keep Japan within the League. Explaining why they lost involves interrogating the meaning that the Western order and the League had acquired in Japanese society, and this requires looking beyond the politics of the Great Depression.

Status, Racial Discrimination, and Japanese Revisionism

Hugh Wilson – the American minister to Switzerland between 1927 and 1937 – was observing the meeting of the League of Nations Assembly on February 24, 1933 when Japanese representative Yōsuke Matsuoka delivered his infamous "Japan Crucified" address and led the Tokyo delegation out of the hall. Matsuoka's speech struck Wilson:

---

[15] See Kirshner (2007), pp. 76–81; and Nanto and Takagi (1985) on Japan's early recovery from the Depression.

[W]hen I listened to Matsuoka, for the first time the gravest doubts arose as to the wisdom of the course which the Assembly and my country were pursuing. I began to have a conception of the rancor and resentment that public condemnation could bring upon a proud and powerful people.

Wilson worried that "[c]ondemnation creates a community of the damned who are forced outside the pale, who have nothing to lose by the violation of all laws of order and international good faith."[16]

Wilson's analysis was insightful – it was, in the end, the "rancor and resentment" produced by the League's condemnation of Japan's invasion of Manchuria that prompted withdrawal. Yet the League's condemnation – in the form of the Lytton Commission Report – was actually mild, and there was significant agitation against the League even before its findings became known. The League, in other words, was already unpopular in Japan, and it was easy for its opponents – whose preferences for withdrawal predated the crisis – to argue against continued membership. Wilson's analysis must be supplemented by an account of why some Japanese elites preferred withdrawal even before late 1932, and of the origins of the discursive resources out of which these actors constructed the narrative that effectively silenced defenses of continued participation in the League.

I argue that one of the most important sources of Japanese elite preferences opposed to participation in the institutions of the status quo order was the belief – based in large part on a history of racial discrimination – that Japan's ambitions for equality of status and rights alongside Western great powers were out of reach. Developments that seemed to confirm this belief had produced in Japanese society a prominent – if not dominant – discourse about racial inequality and unfair treatment. The Lytton Commission report fit neatly into this narrative – it seemed to be the final straw, salient evidence that Japan would always be treated as a second-class great power. It was this rhetoric – about racial discrimination, injustice, denied rights, and the incompatibility of participation with Japanese dignity – that Japan's hardliners invoked to publicly oppose remaining within the League after the condemnation of the Manchurian occupation. This proved impossible for moderates – already weakened by the Mukden Incident – to resist, and they were forced to accede to Japan's withdrawal. A similar contest preceded the decision to abrogate the Washington Treaty, only this time the hardliners were able to invoke not just arguments about the injustice of the naval building ratio enshrined in the agreement but also arguments about the new, seemingly

---

[16] Quoted in Burkman (2008), p. 173.

more threatening international environment that had arisen in the wake of Tokyo's withdrawal from the League.

I develop this argument in three parts. First, I establish that Japanese foreign policy prior to 1933 was aimed at – among other objectives – achieving the status of a Western great power, and I delineate the particular rights that Japanese leaders sought as a great power. I also document the rise of race-based status immobility in Japan – with particular attention to the way the failure of the 1919 racial equality proposal and Western anti-Asian immigration restrictions were interpreted. Second, I show that many pan-Asianists opposed integration with the Western order and preferred a policy aimed at leadership in Asia in large part because they believed that racial difference would prevent Japan from being treated as an equal by Western powers. In terms of the conceptual vocabulary introduced in Chapter 2, militant pan-Asianism expressed preferences for policies aimed at rejection in part as a response to the belief that Japan faced a racial status "glass ceiling" and could never be a Western great power.

Third, I explore the influence of status immobility on Japan's shift toward radical revisionism in the early 1930s. I show that withdrawal from the League was facilitated by the way in which the Lytton Report interacted with a preexisting discourse about racial discrimination and Japanese subordination to the West. This produced loud, resonant demands for withdrawal as a form of protest, and moderates were unable to resist. I then argue that withdrawal contributed to the further victory of hardliners in the 1934 conflict over the abrogation of the Washington Treaty.

Status, Rights, and Race in Japanese Foreign Policy

Japan's drive for status began as soon as seclusion ended in the 1850s. The forced opening to Western trade and the imposition of unequal treaties constituted a national trauma for Meiji leaders, and they responded by implementing a program to ensure that Japan would never again suffer such humiliation.[17] This meant emulating Western great powers, not just in order to become militarily and economically powerful, but also to achieve recognition that Japan belonged in their ranks.

At first, Japanese leaders accepted that the problem was internal. Japan had not been treated unfairly by Western powers; rather, Japan was backward and did not deserve to be taken seriously. Yukichi Fukuzawa (an influential writer and the founder of Keio University) wrote in 1875 that "if we compare the knowledge of the Japanese and Westerners, in

---

[17] See Nariaki Tokugawa quoted in Beasley (1955), p. 102; Shozan Sakuma in Tsunoda, de Bary, and Kenne (1958), p. 608; and Tomomi Iwakura quoted Mayo (1966), p. 339.

letters, in techniques, in commerce, or in industry, from the largest to the smallest matter ... there is not one thing in which we excel ... In Japan's present condition there is nothing in which we may take pride vis-à-vis the West. All that Japan has to be proud of ... is its scenery."[18]

Accordingly, a major objective of Japanese foreign policy after the Meiji restoration was catching up: emulating Western practices in order to enhance Japan's international status and eventually be recognized by Western states as a great power with concomitant rights and privileges. Of course, emulation is partially attributable to Japanese security concerns: faced with the threat of being extorted and potentially overrun by the British, the Russians, or the Americans, Japan sensibly chose to copy Western technology and modes of industrial production.[19]

Yet emulation cannot entirely be understood without an appreciation for the importance of status. Beasley notes that "some changes stemmed from a desire to achieve respectability in Western eyes, this being a step on the road to full equality."[20] These included reforms to Japan's legal system (intended to pave the path toward lifting the unequal treaties); the institution of Western dress in the Imperial Court; the hosting of Western-style diplomatic balls; attempts to impose bans on mixed-gender bathhouses and pornographic art; and a prohibition on women's participation in politics.[21] None of this had any obvious connection to material power or security; instead it constituted a program intended to "provide an atmosphere which Victorians might find congenial," thereby making Japan seem less foreign and gaining Western respect.[22]

Equality and the Rights of a Great Power   The objective of gaining equal status with Western great powers was explicit. Fukuzawa reported that Japan's sights were set on "elevating Japanese civilization to parity with the West, or even surpassing it."[23] Professor Korekiyo Takahashi, who would later become prime minister and hold the office of finance minister five times, spoke in 1889 of his students' "duty to advance the status of Japan, bring her to a position of equality with the civilized powers and then carry on to build a foundation from which we shall surpass them all."[24] According to four-time Prime Minister Hirobumi Itō,

---

[18] Quoted in Craig (1968), pp. 120–121.   [19] Taliaferro (2009).

[20] Beasley (1963), p. 138; see also Zarakol (2011), pp. 160–174 on Japan's effort to undo the unequal treaties and achieve the Western standard of civilization.

[21] Beasley (1963), p. 139; Towns (2010), p. 79.

[22] Beasley (1963), p. 139. See also Suzuki (2005) on Japan's attempt to join Western civilization.

[23] Quoted in Strikwerda (2013), p. 17.   [24] Quoted in Duus (1989), p. 389.

The aim of our country has been from the very beginning, to attain among the nations of the world the status of a civilized nation and to become a member of the comity of the European and American nations which occupy the position of civilized countries. To join this comity of nations means to become one of them.[25]

Becoming a member of the Western great power club meant acquiring the markers of that status – for instance, Fukuzawa suggested that Japan would raise its esteem in the eyes of Western powers if it behaved like a Western power by imposing unequal treaties on the less "civilized" states of China and Korea.[26] Reactions to Japan's victory in the First Sino-Japanese War and the Russo-Japanese War reveal that Japanese elites believed they were now approaching a position in which they could demand equal status. After the victory over China, Sohō Tokutomi wrote: "we are no longer ashamed to stand before the world as Japanese ... Before, we did not know ourselves, and the world did not yet know us. But now that we have tested our strength, we know ourselves and we are known by the world. Moreover, we *know* that we are known by the world!"[27] In 1910, five years after the victory over Russia and in the wake of the annexation of Korea, future diplomat Inazō Nitobe wrote that "Our nation has become more of a Great Power than many European countries ... Japan of a month ago and Japan of today are completely different."[28]

But securing equal status alongside the Western great powers meant more than acquiring the trappings of Western civilization and emulating the behavior of Great Britain, the United States, France, Germany, and Russia. It also meant achieving recognition from these states that Japan belonged in the club and had a legitimate claim to the rights that went along with membership. The language of rights and equality of treatment was prominent in the way Japanese leaders thought and spoke about three particular issues: a sphere of influence in East Asia, naval arms limitations, and immigration policy. While Japanese interests in each of these areas surely had multiple sources, these issues were linked to Japanese status because they constituted claims to what Japanese leaders understood as rights that Western great powers already enjoyed. They thus served as measuring sticks against which Japanese elites assessed whether or not Japan was actually being treated as a legitimate great power.

---

[25] Quoted in Tsunoda et al. (1958), p. 678.

[26] Narsimhan (1999), p. 207. See also Suzuki (2005), who notes that "the Japanese saw the adoption of coercive policies towards 'uncivilized' states as an inherent part of a 'civilized' state's identity, and sought to attain such status by engaging in imperialist behaviour towards its Asian neighbours" (p. 139).

[27] Quoted in de Bary et al. (2005), p. 805.   [28] Dudden (1975), pp. 135–136.

The first right that Japan claimed as a great power was to an exclusive sphere of influence in northern mainland Asia. This is not to say that status is what *motivated* Japanese expansion in Korea and Manchuria. There were surely many factors that made controlling territory on the mainland look attractive. But whatever the source of Japan's drive to acquire a sphere of influence, many Japanese leaders and elites understood and spoke about it as one of the rights of a great power. This idea originated both in the "treaty rights" system that Japan had itself been subjected to by Western powers, and in the observation that the United States maintained a claim to an exclusive zone of economic and military influence in its near abroad.[29] The notion that Japan had the right to an "Asian Monroe Doctrine" became prominent throughout the first decades of the twentieth century and was an important public justification for the occupation of Manchuria after September 1931.[30]

The second right that many Japanese elites cared about was to institutional equality in naval arms agreements. This only became salient during the debate over the Washington Treaty in 1921–1922, and there is little doubt that those who objected to the 5:5:3 ratio (which limited Japan to 60% of the capital ship tonnage of the United States and Great Britain) enshrined in that agreement did so for many reasons. Yet historians agree that the opponents of the ratio felt that it was a violation of Japan's right to equality and thus a threat to its honor.[31] Kanji Katō – the most important figure in the so-called fleet faction that opposed the Washington Treaty – thought anything less than a 1:1 ratio would imply "inferiority to the Anglo-American powers."[32] Katō and others in the fleet faction sought a "common international standard for the five great powers."[33] There was no compelling strategic justification for this principle, especially since Great Britain and the United States both had more productive economies and more geographically diffuse interests than did Japan. But the idea that Japan, if it were a legitimate great power, should have the same rights as the other great powers to build capital ships was appealing.

The third right that Japanese elites associated with great power status was to the equal treatment of Japan's people by other great powers. Immigration restrictions imposed by Western powers on Asian populations troubled Japanese leaders, not because of their economic consequences but because they constituted evidence that Japanese were not ranked alongside British, Americans, and French but rather alongside lower status nationalities like Chinese, Indians, or Egyptians. Japanese

---

[29] For an early articulation of this argument, see K. Asakawa (1908).
[30] See for instance Yasaka Takaki (1932), and the discussion in Conroy (1951), pp. 36–37.
[31] Asada (2014), p. 98; Pelz (1974), pp. 27–29.   [32] Asada (2014), p. 99.
[33] Pelz (1974), p. 27.

leaders became sensitive to immigration restrictions as early as 1897, and the racial equality clause that they proposed attaching to the League of Nations Charter was in part an attempt to have the right to equal treatment enshrined in international law. Naoko Shimazu argues that this effort was motivated by a drive to secure Japan's status and rights as a racially different great power.[34]

Racial Discrimination and Obstructed Status Ambitions Japan's quest for great power status was hardly a complete failure. Economic development, military success, and political and social reform increasingly led the Western powers to recognize Japan's rising status. The unequal treaties were ended in 1894, and eight years later the Anglo-Japanese alliance confirmed Japan's worth as a partner, rather than a vassal.[35] After World War I, Japan participated in the Paris Peace Conference as one of the five recognized great powers and joined the League of Nations as a permanent member of the League Council. Japanese leaders celebrated this milestone as a sign of the "concrete attainment of Japan's great power status."[36] At the end of the war, the Western powers even seemed, first through the Lansing-Ishii agreement and then at the Washington Conference, to have recognized Japan's rights in Manchuria.[37]

Yet great power status did not appear secure to many Japanese because these official acts of recognition existed alongside other behaviors that signaled that Japan – because it was not populated by white people – could never achieve equality of treatment from Western powers. The idea that Western great powers discriminated against Asian states on the basis of race originated with Japan's forced entry into international society in the 1850s.

The humiliation of subjugation to the United States and other Western powers produced two responses. The first, discussed above, was emulation in an attempt to gain recognition of equal status. The second was resentment toward Western great powers along with the development of an understanding that unequal treatment was premised, in part, on racial differences. Race began to feature as a potential obstacle to Japanese status enhancement in discourse about international order as early as the 1890s. In 1891, *Kokumin no tomo* – an influential magazine – reviewed Japan's rapid technological and economic advancement and concluded that "if one impartially compares our country with European countries, we are above Spain and abreast Italy."[38] The problem, as the same publication noted two years later, was that Western powers did not compare countries impartially, but through a lens that diminished the

[34] Shimazu (1998), Chapter 4.   [35] Pyle (2007), p. 115.   [36] Burkman (2008), p. 95.
[37] Crowley (1974), p. 41.   [38] Quoted in Pyle (2007), p. 111.

achievements of non-white peoples. Westerners regarded Japan "as only a step above Fiji or Hawaii," because they could not see past the fact that Japan was Asian: "The most progressive, developed, civilized, intelligent, and powerful nation in the Orient still cannot escape the scorn of white people."[39] This sort of sentiment became increasingly common as Japanese encountered Western theories about racial hierarchies, and was a standard interpretation when Japan suffered foreign policy defeats at the hands of Western powers.

During the First Sino-Japanese War, Kaiser Wilhelm II began referring to the "Yellow Peril," the rise of a racial threat from Asia in the form of a powerful Japanese state. Naoko Shimazu notes that Japan's sensitivity to racial difference increased markedly from that point. The idea of Western race-based threat perceptions became common in debates over Japan's foreign policy and contributed to perceptions among many of a "rising world trend towards racial confrontation" which meant that "racial war" was inevitable.[40]

The emergent discourse of racial discrimination influenced and was simultaneously reinforced by Japan's reaction to the 1895 Triple Intervention. In the wake of Japan's victory in the First Sino-Japanese War, Germany, France, and Russia conspired to demand that Japan return the Liaotung Peninsula to China. Soon after, Russia acquired the rights to some of the retroceded territory and established the Port Arthur naval base. Reaction in Japan was predictably furious and marked by intense anti-Western sentiment and the notion that Japan had been "bullied."[41]

The treatment of Japanese immigrants was particularly important for the development of beliefs about international racial discrimination. Interestingly, Western leaders understood this dynamic and in many instances opposed offensive legislation precisely because they feared its diplomatic consequences. As president, for instance, Theodore Roosevelt worked to block a 1906 order by the San Francisco school board that segregated Japanese students from white students because he thought that it would "insult the Japanese recklessly" and perhaps provoke a war; Presidents Taft and Wilson both worked to block statewide legislation in California (the latter unsuccessfully); and Secretary of State Charles Evans Hughes and President Coolidge (ineffectively) opposed the 1924 Alien Immigration Act.[42] This case thus stands as an important example

---

[39] Quoted in Ibid., p. 111.   [40] Shimazu (1998), pp. 95–96; see also Buzas (2013).
[41] Storry (1979), pp. 29–30.
[42] On Roosevelt and the San Francisco crisis, see Neu (1967); and for the Roosevelt quote, see Theodore Roosevelt to Kermit Roosevelt (October 27, 1906). On Taft and the California legislation, see Neu (1975), p. 75; Minohara (2014), pp. 30–32; and Taft to Roosevelt (January 17, 1911). On Wilson and the 1913 California Alien Land Law, see

of unintentional status denial. Immigration restrictions imposed by Western states on the basis of national origin were mostly a function of domestic political incentives and institutions, and ran contrary to the preferences of national leaders who understood the value of accommodating Tokyo. Nonetheless, they were interpreted as violations of the right to equal treatment and as indications that Japan might face an obstacle to securing equal status alongside other powers.

And it is clear that immigration politics – especially the restrictions that the British Dominions and the United States imposed beginning in the late nineteenth century – were sensitive in Japan primarily for reasons related to rights and standing, rather than economics.[43] The economic consequences of immigration were largely insignificant because the supply of potential Japanese immigrants was more trickle than flood. In fact, Japanese leaders were happy to restrict immigration voluntarily. By the terms of the 1904 Passport Agreement, the 1907 "Gentlemen's Agreement," and the 1908 Lemieux Agreement, Tokyo willingly limited the number of immigrants entering Australia, the United States, and Canada respectively. These deals did not provoke resentment among Japanese leaders; on the contrary, voluntary immigration restrictions were a relatively favorable means of dealing with immigration disputes.[44]

Rather, what made immigration politics so explosive in Japan were the implications of formally imposed restrictions for Japan's claim to equal status and the right to equal treatment. Japanese leaders tried to avoid – and resented when they could not – restrictions that implied that Japanese were undesirable or inferior by explicitly placing them in the same category as other Asian immigrants. In 1897, in response to debates over Australian restrictions, Japan's ambassador in London wrote to Prime Minister Salisbury:

The point which caused a painful feeling in Japan was not that the operation of the prohibition would be such as to exclude a certain number of Japanese from immigration to Australia, but that Japan should be spoken of in formal documents, such as Colonial Acts, as if the Japanese were on the same level of morality and civilization as Chinese and other less advanced populations of Asia.[45]

The 1906 San Francisco segregation crisis provoked a similar reaction. The Japanese Association of America wrote that "the Japanese people in San Francisco ... are being subjected to such insult as no other nation

---

Pash (2014), p. 31; and Cooper (2009), pp. 211–212. On Hughes' and Coolidge's opposition to the Alien Immigration Act, see Neu (1975), pp. 123–124; Greenberg (2006), pp. 82–84; and Shlaes (2014), pp. 268, 285.

[43] Shimazu (1998), Chapter 3.

[44] Yarwood (1964), pp. 98–99; Daniels (1988), p. 115; Shimazu (1998), pp. 71–76.

[45] Katō to Salisbury, quoted in Sissons (1971), p. 38.

except the Chinese has been subjected to since the founding of the United States ... If Japan remains humiliated her prestige will be lost forever."[46] The American ambassador in Tokyo reported a "marked feeling of irritation against the United States," which might bring about a "total change of sentiment" and "result in a boycott or some other form of retaliation."[47] The *London Times* reported during the crisis that "the insult was felt very keenly in Japan, whose people justly consider that they have abundantly proved their right to equal treatment among civilized nations."[48] Iriye notes that the crisis promoted in Japan "the notion of fundamental incompatibility among races and cultures."[49]

In 1913, California's legislature passed the Alien Land Law, explicitly prohibiting Japanese immigrants from buying land in the state. The response in Japan, which President Woodrow Wilson anticipated and tried to head off by pressuring California's governor to block the bill, was so severe that Wilson and his cabinet considered preventive naval measures in the Western Pacific.[50] Japan's ambassador Sutemi Chinda wrote to Secretary of State William Jennings Bryan that the law was "mortifying to the Government and people of Japan, since the racial distinction inferable from those provisions is hurtful to their just national susceptibility."[51] This was, to be clear, not a principled objection to racism but an objection to what the restrictions implied about Japan's place in the global hierarchy, and about its ability to secure the status that its leaders felt it deserved. In 1915, Katō (now foreign minister) explained that the problem with the California law was the "discrimination made against our people in distinction from some other nations ... we thought ourselves ahead of any other Asiatic people and as good as some of the European nations."[52] Immigration restrictions, in short, constituted evidence of a race-based obstruction to the satisfaction of Japan's aspiration for equal status alongside the Western great powers.

The racial and status implications of the immigration disputes and other evidence of apparent discrimination made many Japanese leaders wary of the Paris Peace Conference and the construction of a postwar order on Western terms. Burkman notes that during and after World War I, "Japan was made conscious in numerous insulting ways that material power did not grant commensurate status and convey admittance to the Euro-

[46] Quoted in Neu (1967), p. 29.   [47] Quoted in ibid., pp. 29–30.
[48] Quoted in Bailey (1934), pp. 48–49.   [49] Iriye (1972), p. 139.
[50] Shimazu (1998), p. 76; see also the Cabinet Diaries of Josephus Daniels (Cronon 1963), entries from May 13 to May 16, 1913 (pp. 52–67).
[51] Chinda to Bryan, June 4, 1913, in FRUS (1920), p. 635 (available at http://digital.library .wisc.edu/1711.dl/FRUS.FRUS1913)).
[52] Quoted in Pyle (2007), p. 133.

American club."[53] President Wilson's proposed new order "seemed designed to circumscribe Japan's legitimate national development and perpetuate the nation's secondary status."[54] Home Minister Shinpei Gotō, who later became foreign minister, wrote in 1916 that "the racial prejudice of the white race is so strong that even when they make an offensive and defensive alliance with a yellow race they cannot divest themselves of the prejudice ... if you probe their feelings you will find that the white races are displeased at the participation of the yellow races."[55] Legal scholar Sakutaro Tachi wrote skeptically before the conference that "Even in peacetime there are nations which monopolize vast natural resources and deny others a place in the sun. They act to dominate and oppress peoples of different race, language, ideas, and culture."[56] Foreign Minister Kōsai Uchida feared that "the persistence of narrow racial attitudes among nations casts doubt upon the feasibility of the League's goals and creates the possibility that its establishment will be disadvantageous to the Empire."[57]

Fears about racial discrimination were so serious that Japan's conference delegation was instructed to push for the inclusion of a racial equality clause in the League charter. Shimazu argues that this move was intended to accomplish two tasks: to silence racial inferiority-based domestic opposition to participation in the league and to formally eradicate race as a marker of great power status.[58] The racial equality proposal, in other words, was an effort to solidify Japan's status as a great power through the strategy of social creativity.

The attempt to remove the obstacle to Japanese great power status failed due to opposition from the Australian delegation and from anti-immigration groups in the United States.[59] That Japan nonetheless joined the League is attributable to the fact that moderates – who were optimistic and emphasized the status and material benefits of membership – remained in control and were not yet as vulnerable to pressure from hardliners as they would be a decade later.[60]

Still, the rejection of the racial equality clause strengthened the already prominent discourse of race discrimination and deepened skepticism about Japan's place in the Western order. Burkman notes that "public indignation over the rejection of the race equality provision gave rise to demands for a national policy defying the Western powers."[61] These demands did not, at this point, influence policy; but "racial equality" became a rallying cry for opponents of the Western order, who drew on it

---

[53] Burkman (2008), p. 4.   [54] Ibid., p. 10.   [55] Quoted in Ibid., p. 27.
[56] Quoted in Ibid., pp. 37–38.   [57] Quoted in Ibid., p. 45.
[58] Shimazu (1998), Chapter 2 and pp. 112–113.   [59] Ibid., Chapters 5 and 6.
[60] See Burkman (2008), pp. 94–103.   [61] Ibid., pp. 85–86.

throughout the next decade as a rhetorical resource. Hardliners wove subsequent policy setbacks into this narrative – the Washington Treaty's unequal naval building ratio and the 1924 Alien Immigration Act were both interpreted as further evidence that Western powers were unable to see past racial difference and treat Japan as it deserved to be treated.[62] In sum, by the middle of the 1920s, the idea that Japan faced an insurmountable obstacle to the satisfaction of its status ambitions was a prominent and widespread feature of Japanese foreign policy discourse.

Status Immobility and Japanese Foreign Policy

Status immobility remained a background condition throughout the 1920s, but it played an important – and underappreciated – role in Japan's turn against the interwar order in the early 1930s. It mattered in two ways. First, racial discrimination and its implications for Japan's place in the interwar order figured prominently in the thinking of the militant pan-Asianists whose agitation against the restrained foreign policy of Japanese moderates ultimately destroyed Shidehara diplomacy. These groups advocated withdrawal from the League and the rest of the Washington Conference system and the construction of a Japan-led order in Asia in part because they were convinced that the racist Western powers would never treat Japan fairly. This called for, if not revolution against the West, then at least a policy that would protect Japan's dignity by protesting and withdrawing from the order. Second, the prominent narrative of racial discrimination made withdrawal from the League easy for hardliners to sell – and made continued participation hard for moderates to justify – in the wake of the Lytton Commission's condemnation of the occupation of Manchuria. The Lytton Report seemed to confirm the critique that the pan-Asianists had been lodging against the League since its founding, thereby making arguments for withdrawal hard to sustainably rebut. Withdrawal, in turn, removed an important justification for remaining within the other institutions of the Washington Conference framework, which facilitated the victory of the proponents of unrestrained naval arms-racing in the fight over the abrogation of the Washington Treaty.

Racial Discrimination, Militant Pan-Asianism, and Rejection   A major cause of Japan's drift toward radical revisionism was the influence of ultra-nationalist and militarist pan-Asianists. These individuals and groups advocated withdrawal from the Washington Conference system

---

[62] Aydin (2007), pp. 142–143; Hotta (2007), 68; Hirobe (2001), Chapter 1.

and the construction of a Japanese-led order in East Asia, and they influenced policy by making life difficult for moderates through rhetorical and political agitation, assassinations and coup attempts, and the execution of plots that embarrassed the government and caused tension between Japan and the West.

The preferences of militant pan-Asianists had many sources, including straightforward material concerns about Japan's security and economic prospects. But their demands that Japan reject the Western order and construct a Japan-led regional order in East Asia were at least partially driven by the belief that Western racial discrimination meant that Japan would never be able to gain equal status alongside other great powers. They advocated withdrawal from the interwar order and the project of Japanese hegemony in East Asia both for reasons related to the preservation of Japanese dignity and in order to prepare for an inevitable racial war between East and West.

Japanese pan-Asianism – which developed as a coherent set of ideas about Japanese identity and international order during the second half of the nineteenth century – was, at root, concerned with Japan's status in international society. According to Hotta, pan-Asianism's "foremost objective was to assert a positive Asian distinctiveness," to "instill an Asian identity in Asians themselves in order to attain parity with the West, which had placed Asia in a humiliating secondary position in the politics of nation-states."[63] There were multiple streams of pan-Asianist thought, and not all were militant. In fact, one prominent strand saw the solution to Japan's low status in the promotion of a new set of valued characteristics – in other words, through the pursuit of a form of social creativity. Japan could achieve "external recognition by asserting itself as a nonmaterialist pan-nation, which was nonetheless comparable, even possibly superior, to Europe in its cultural and philosophical substance."[64]

But other pan-Asianists – those whose ideas ultimately became influential among the young military officers who agitated against "weak-kneed" diplomacy throughout the 1920s – thought that the solution to the problem of Western disrespect was the *rejection* of the unjust Western order and the construction of an Asian alternative.

The political thought of Shūmei Ōkawa is a useful illustration of the way in which racial discrimination and the rejection of the Western order were linked in the minds of militant pan-Asianists. Ōkawa was a scholar of Islam whose influence on prewar Japanese militarism was so great that he was arrested as a Class-A war criminal after Japan's surrender.[65] Ōkawa's ideas about pan-Asianism developed through his interest in British

---

[63] Hotta (2007), pp. 21–23.   [64] Ibid., p. 31.   [65] On Ōkawa, see Szpilman (2011b).

colonial policy in India. The "contrast between the greatness of ancient Indian civilization that he had studied and the tragic condition of contemporary India" angered Ōkawa and motivated him to dedicate "his life to the revival of Asia."[66]

Ōkawa worked closely in Japan with a number of Indian nationalists to develop the tenets of a militant and rejectionist version of pan-Asianism that implied that the West's racial discrimination rendered working with Western powers both futile and humiliating. Ōkawa thought that, "given its yellow race identity, Japan would gain more by becoming the 'elder brother' and leader of a free Asia than by remaining an isolated member in the club of great powers."[67] In 1917, Ōkawa helped Indian revolutionary Taraknath Das to write *The Isolation of Japan in World Politics*, which objected to the Anglo-Japanese alliance and argued that "since Japan would never be treated equally by the Western powers, it should try to initiate a different regional order in Asia to break its international isolation."[68]

Ōkawa opposed Japan's entry into the League and saw the rejection of the racial equality proposal as an "opportunity to call for an end to the pro-Western diplomatic framework."[69] When the US congress passed the 1924 Immigration Act, Ōkawa criticized "pro-American liberals for 'shaming' themselves by seeking a cooperative diplomacy with a nation that clearly saw the Japanese as members of a second-class race."[70] The idea that racial discrimination rendered cooperation with Western powers both fruitless and humiliating led Ōkawa to the conclusion that an apocalyptic racial conflict between the United States – the representative of the white race – and Japan – the champion of Asia – was inevitable. Remaining within the Western institutional framework was inconsistent both with Japan's dignity and its responsibility to prepare for the war that was coming.[71]

Ōkawa's was hardly the only voice demanding policies rejecting the Western order as a response to the West's apparent unwillingness to treat Japan equally on account of its racial characteristics. Ikki Kita was another influential pan-Asianist militant – indeed, Kita was thought to be so influential with young officers in the army that he was executed after the failed 1936 military coup against the government.[72] While Kita eventually became a rival of Ōkawa's, their ideas about the injustice of the Western order and what it implied for foreign policy were similar. In his most famous work – *An Outline Plan for the Reorganization of Japan*

---

[66] Aydin (2007), p. 113.   [67] Ibid., p. 114   [68] Ibid., pp. 117–118.
[69] Ibid., pp. 141–142.   [70] Ibid., p. 152.   [71] Ibid., pp. 152–153.
[72] Hotta (2007), p. 63.

(1928) – Kita advocated the reordering of Japanese society in preparation for a war to liberate Asia from European imperial influence. He invoked the injustice of the Western order to help make his case:

Britain, astride the whole world, is like a very rich man and Russia is landlord of half the northern world. Doesn't Japan, which is like a propertyless person in international society confined to these small islands, have the right to go to war to overthrow their domination in the name of justice?[73]

Fumimaro Konoe – another pan-Asianist and a future architect of the new order that Japan built in East Asia during the late 1930s – wrote a telling prospective critique of the League before the Paris Peace Conference. Konoe equated the position of Japan with that of Germany before World War I. Japan, like Germany before it, "should be desiring the destruction of the *status quo*."[74] Yet Japan's "opinionmakers" had adopted a "fawning" attitude toward the "Anglo-American-centered pacifism" and the League which, Konoe thought, "from the standpoint of justice and humanity ... should be detested."[75] Konoe was not committed to opposing the League, but would demand equality through the prohibition of "economic imperialism" and "racial discrimination against the yellow race."[76] If these were not forthcoming, Konoe worried that the League would be a tool to perpetuate an unjust status quo. Hotta has identified in this text two themes that underline the relationship between militant pan-Asianism and anxiety about Japan's status in world politics. These were a "fixed and hostile view of the outside world as being dominated by the Anglo-American powers," alongside a deep "craving [for] their recognition."[77] Effectively, what Konoe articulated in "Reject the Anglo-American Peace" was that his support for Japan's participation in the Western order was contingent upon Western recognition that Japan had the same status and rights in world politics as a Western power. Advocating participation in the absence of recognition of equality – as Konoe accused moderates of doing – was shameful "fawning."

These radical ideas about foreign policy became more popular throughout the 1920s, especially in response to events that seemed to confirm the Western powers' unwillingness to treat Japan as an equal. The number of militant pressure groups operating in Japan exploded in the decade after World War I, which Shimazu attributes partially to the influence of the rejection of the racial equality clause at the Paris Peace Conference.[78] Similarly, the 1924 Immigration Act produced conditions conducive to militant pan-Asianism's critique of the Western order,

---

[73] Quoted in Tankha (2006), p. 282.　[74] Quoted in Hotta (2011), p. 316.
[75] Ibid., p. 316.　[76] Ibid., p. 317.　[77] Ibid., p. 314.
[78] See Shimazu (1998), p. 177; Storry (1957), Chapters 2 and 3; and Ito (1973), p. 488.

which supported the contention that "challenging the 'white peril' was Japan's global mission" and resulted in a "wave of literature" predicting a racial war between the United States and Japan.[79] This sort of thinking permeated the Japanese military, parts of which played a critical role in challenging moderate control of foreign policy.[80] For instance, Kanji Ishiwara – one of the orchestrators of the Mukden Incident – shared the views of Ōkawa and Kita about an inevitable racial war between East and West, which was why expanding in Manchuria was critical.[81]

Status Immobility, Constraints on Moderates, and Rejection of the Interwar Order   While militant pan-Asianism's critique of the interwar order became increasingly prominent in Japan's foreign policy discourse during the decade after World War I, it remained in opposition to the official line. The government was committed to participation in the League and the rest of the Washington Conference system – and to distancing itself from talk about racial discrimination and an Asian regional order – in order to avoid provoking the Western powers.[82]

This changed during the first years of the 1930s. By the end of 1934, Japan had invaded and occupied Manchuria, withdrawn from the League of Nations, and abrogated the Washington Naval Treaty. These moves were part of the "process by which pan-Asianist ideas and projects became part of Japan's official foreign policy rhetoric."[83] Why did this new vision of order supplant the moderate vision of the 1920s?

Two important parts of the story are mostly exogenous to status dynamics – both increased the political vulnerability of leaders in Tokyo, but for reasons that had little to do with status anxiety. These are the Mukden Incident and the economic crisis linked to the Great Depression. On September 18, 1931, members of the Kwantung Army (the Japanese military force stationed in Japan's Manchurian economic zone) detonated a section of the Japanese-controlled South Manchurian Railway near Mukden. Using the explosion as a pretext, the Kwantung Army proceeded to occupy most of Manchuria over the protests of Japan's central government. Japanese moderates proved unable to control the military in part because Shidehara diplomacy had been undermined at home by the advance of Chinese nationalist influence in Manchuria and by the economic crisis that had struck after 1929.[84]

---

[79] Aydin (2007), pp. 151–153.   [80] Ibid., p. 163.   [81] Peattie (1975), pp. 81, 141.

[82] Aydin (2007), pp. 156–158; Saaler and Szpilman (2011), vol. II, pp. 15–18.

[83] Aydin (2007), p. 161.

[84] See Copeland (2014), pp. 156–160; and Kirshner (2007), pp. 70–76, for two different versions of this argument.

Yet the occupation of Manchuria did not mean that Japan's rejection of the interwar order – its withdrawal from the League and then the rest of the Washington Conference system – was inevitable. On the contrary, Japanese moderates – who remained in power throughout the crisis leading up to withdrawal from the League – continued to prefer not to provoke Western powers or isolate Japan any more than was necessary.[85] Similarly, both civilians and some army leaders opposed early abrogation of the Washington Treaty. While economic and civil-military crisis had increased the vulnerability of Japan's moderate political leadership to opposition from outside its ranks, the future of Japanese foreign policy remained open and was still the object of domestic contests in the years after 1931.

I argue in the rest of this section that proponents of rejecting the Western interwar order had an important political advantage in these contests because of the prominent pan-Asianist discourse about racial inequality and the injustice of the status quo. The Lytton Report fit neatly within this narrative, which made for a political environment favorable to arguments for withdrawal. Withdrawal in turn made it easier to argue for abrogating the Washington Treaty. In short, hardliners were able to argue persuasively that the pan-Asianist critique of the interwar order – which asserted that Japan could not overcome the barrier of Western discrimination to achieve equality of status – was valid. In combination with the exogenous crises that had already made moderates vulnerable, this was enough to push Japanese foreign policy toward radical revisionism.

Japan Leaves the League   Throughout the Mukden Incident, Japan's moderate leadership consistently hoped for a solution that would allow them to remain within the League and reestablish control over the military. In the wake of the explosion and subsequent invasion, Prime Minister Reijirō Wakatsuki told the emperor that the Mukden Incident was "regrettable" and that he had "decided to prevent [it] from spreading."[86] The day after the crisis began, Foreign Minister Shidehara sought to extract a guarantee from War Minister Jirō Minami that the Kwantung Army would go no further than it already had. After Minami agreed, Shidehara noted that "[w]e were all relieved."[87] Takemoto suggests that Shidehara, aware that the Manchurian Incident had been perpetrated by Japanese soldiers, agreed to endorse the Kwantung Army's version of events – that the culprits were Chinese nationalists – as a quid pro quo for this guarantee.[88]

[85] Schlichtmann (2009), p. 99.   [86] Harada (1978), p. 77.
[87] Quoted in Takemoto (1978), p. 126.   [88] Ibid., p. 127.

In October, Wakatsuki rejected a demand from radical nationalists to withdraw from the League, saying that "If Japan does not act with due consideration of her international position, Japan in the end will be isolated, and this will bring an unexpected misfortune upon the nation."[89] In November, the Kwantung Army (in spite of Minami's guarantee) advanced on Chinchow. Shidehara and Wakatsuki, fearing the consequences for relations with the West, urged Chief of the General Staff Hanzō Kanaya to call off the operation. Kanaya, apparently conceding the point, agreed.[90]

Even after Shidehara and the rest of the Wakatsuki cabinet fell in late 1931, Japan's central leadership continued to hope for a resolution that would not alienate them from international society. In mid-November, Minami warned against a plot to establish a puppet state in Manchuria because doing so might "rapidly bring about a situation extremely disadvantageous to our national policy with regard to the powers."[91] Tsuyoshi Inukai, Wakatsuki's successor as prime minister, worried that "a head-on collision with the Nine Power Treaty would be inevitable," and aimed "to terminate the present crisis as soon as possible."[92]

The Kwantung Army proclaimed Manchukuo – the Manchurian puppet state – in March 1932, yet Inukai refused to grant recognition in the hope of avoiding "world-wide condemnation."[93] Sadako Ogata suggests that this policy – a serious risk, considering growing popular support for the military and the danger of assassination – was one of the last expressions of "traditional Japanese foreign policy, which considered cooperation with the powers as vital to the execution of an expansionist program on the Asian continent."[94] Inukai paid a heavy price for his restraint, as he was killed by a group of young military officers in May.

As late as early 1933 Japanese leaders were still struggling to avoid unnecessary provocation. Kumao Harada (genrō Kinmochi Saionji's secretary) reports that in early February, Saionji's opinion was that "withdrawal [from the League] will be disadvantageous to Japan" and that Prime Minister Makoto Saitō agreed.[95] Of course, many voices advocated withdrawal by this point, but it is significant that two of the most influential leaders thought it unwise. Far from seeing leaving the League as a beneficial move – or even as one without significant downside – Japanese moderates feared its consequences.

But they faced overwhelming pressure for withdrawal that emerged with the Lytton Report's condemnation of Japan's activity in Manchuria. Even

---

[89] Harada (1978), p. 107.   [90] Ibid., p. 116; Ogata (1964), p. 114; Nish (1993), p. 55.
[91] Quoted in Ogata (1964), p. 121.   [92] Quoted in ibid., p. 139.   [93] Ibid., p. 145.
[94] Ibid., p. 156.   [95] Harada (1978), p. 522.

before the Lytton Commission arrived in Japan, there was intense opposition to League demands for a halt to operations. One paper published an editorial criticizing the League's intervention as an "attempt to deprive the rising nation of Japan of her natural rights."[96] Press coverage of the Commission's second visit to Tokyo – by which point it was clear that the report would reject Japan's claim that the occupation was an act of self-defense – was "generally hostile."[97] Chief Cabinet Secretary and militant pan-Asianist Kaku Mori demanded at a Seiyūkai party convention that Japan cease "fawning at the League of Nations ... hesitating before the prestige of a great nation and being startled or dazzled by the name of the sacred covenant of the League or the Kellogg-Briand Anti-War Pact," which were "nothing more than expediencies to help a few influential nations maintain the status quo."[98] In August 1932, after Tokyo announced that it would recognize Manchukuo after all, Mori celebrated as "Japan now defiantly rose from her traditional diplomacy characterized by servility."[99]

While the record of Japanese public discourse is uncertain, this evidence does suggest that the Lytton Commission's rejection of Japan's occupation of Manchuria elicited such a strong response because it resonated with extant beliefs about status immobility – this is the meaning of references to "fawning," "servility," and concerns about Japan's rights being trampled. It is also notable that moderates – while opposing withdrawal – were unable to make much of a public case for remaining in the League. Public defenses of continued participation came from a small group of internationalists who had staunchly supported the League throughout the 1920s. They invoked concepts like "international duty" – which would have had little chance against the militant pan-Asianist argument that the interwar order was a cover for the perpetuation of a global hierarchy whose purpose was to keep Japan down. One internationalist stressed the material costs of withdrawal and warned that Tokyo might have to "show deference to others and compromise" in order to avoid isolation. He had an increasingly difficult time finding a mainstream platform for these ideas.[100]

Anti-League sentiment created incentives that punished restraint. Sandra Wilson notes that one important consequence of anti-Western agitation was to cause an outbidding process in which members of whichever major party (Seiyūkai or Minseito) was currently out of power could gain popularity by criticizing the opposition for not acting strongly

[96] Quoted in Ogata (1964), p. 89.   [97] Nish (1993), p. 157.
[98] Quoted in Wilson (2002), p. 87; on Mori's pan-Asianism, see Szpilman (2011a).
[99] Quoted in Ogata (1964), p. 160.   [100] Burkman (2008), pp. 178–179.

enough to "establish an independent foreign policy."[101] For instance, in March 1932 Minseito, generally the more moderate party, pressed the Seiyūkai cabinet to recognize Manchukuo immediately.[102] What emerged from this process was a political space in which there was little room for integration with the Western order.

In February 1933, the League Assembly voted 42–1 to adopt the Lytton Report. The next month, Japan formally withdrew. The Lytton Report had not recommended any material sanction against Japan, nor had the League threatened any. What pushed the government to withdraw was sensitivity to the status implications of the League's actions and to public opinion, which was primed to believe that Japan would be treated unfairly and denied the rights of a Western great power (especially the right to intervene abroad to ensure stability in its backyard). These fears seemed to be confirmed by the League's response to the Manchurian crisis. The Lytton Commission's finding that Japan's actions in Manchuria were not justified by claims of self-defense was interpreted as a condemnation and evidence of the inability of the West to accommodate Japan's claim to great power status.[103] Bix notes that the League's "resolutions on the Sino-Japanese dispute were likened to the Triple intervention of 1895," which was a reminder of unfair treatment at the hands of Western powers.[104] Prior to withdrawal, Yōsuke Matsuoka (the man who went to Geneva to lead Japan out of the League) told Setsuzō Sawada that "if we do not take steps to leave the League, we shall inevitably invite the ridicule of the world."[105] Afterward, Matsuoka drew a parallel between Japan and Germany, which "also fights for recognition and its place in the eyes of the world."[106] Inazō Nitobe – a defender of moderate foreign policy – warned an American audience a year before Japan's withdrawal that the West must "recognize the justice of our claim which involves our honor and our very existence as a nation."[107]

Burkman notes that the decision "to withdraw was made under tense circumstances of public and press clamor against the League and rumors of assassination plots."[108] Nish suggests that the "hostility of the army ... and other right-wing organizations was formidable and commanded much public support" and that "the Foreign Ministry was receiving hundreds of letters daily calling for Japan to pull out" of the League.[109] Cabinet members felt the pressure, as an account of a February 1933 meeting suggests. Harada notes that there was discussion that "the newspapers were too hasty in advocating withdrawal," and Finance Minister Korekiyo Takahashi

---

[101] Wilson (2002), p. 89.   [102] Ibid., p. 88.   [103] Burkman (2008), p. 143.
[104] Bix (2000), p. 256.   [105] Quoted in Nish (1993), p. 210.
[106] Quoted in Presseisen (1969), p. 99.   [107] Quoted in Burkman (2008), p. 183.
[108] Burkman (2008), p. 174.   [109] Nish (1993), p. 184; see also Bix (2000), p. 262.

"attacked the army savagely" for not quieting the anti-League press.[110] Nobuaki Makino, a member of the emperor's Privy Council, complained that the press was pushing for withdrawal "as an end in itself," without considering the consequences.[111]

Although Prime Minister Saitō believed that "no matter what the contents [of the Lytton Report] are, we should remain in the League and contend that Japan's claims are just," Saionji thought that "withdrawal is inevitable."[112] Bix suggests that while the emperor could have prevented withdrawal, his entourage – the so-called court group, many of whom were critical of the moderate Saionji – came down on the side of the radicals, in part because they "tended to see international affairs in antagonistic racial terms."[113] In the end, moderates had no choice but to accede to the demands of the hardliners for withdrawal.

Kiyoshi Kiyosawa notes that "the overwhelming majority of the Japanese people were genuinely relieved when the government decided to cast off the restrictions of the League covenant and other international treaties."[114] Writer Kameo Ito complained after withdrawal of the League's "betrayal" and noted that "the League's anti-Japanese attitude was consistent from beginning to end. This is only to be expected of the League, which is controlled by whites."[115]

Japan Abrogates the Washington Treaty   Leaving the League was not a point of no return for Japanese foreign policy. In the wake of the decision to withdraw, Japanese moderates made a significant effort to assure the world that they had not isolated themselves.[116] Yet the fact of withdrawal made it harder to avoid subsequent provocative steps, as the story of the abrogation of the Washington Treaty shows.

The Washington Treaty, which established the 5:5:3 capital ship tonnage ratio in 1922, had been revised in London in 1930 and was due for another revision in 1935–1936. The 1930 extension had been violently opposed by hardliners in the Japanese navy on the grounds that it violated Japan's right to equality and ability to secure itself. In May 1934, the fleet faction launched a campaign insisting that the government abrogate the treaty and demand equality at the Second London Naval Conference. Its reasons for doing so are difficult to understand from the perspective of Japan's security. The ratio arrived at in Washington and then revised in Japan's favor in London actually benefited Japan, since – as moderates (including those in the navy) understood – the United States had

---

[110] Harada (1978), p. 519.   [111] Quoted in Burkman (2008), p. 191.
[112] Harada (1978), pp. 521, 537; and Ogata (1964), p. 174.   [113] Bix (2000), p. 264.
[114] Quoted in Kakegawa (1973), p. 541.   [115] Quoted in Wilson (2002), p. 144.
[116] Burkman (2008), p. 195.

a massive advantage in industrial capacity.[117] And if the point of rejecting the London ratio was to allow Japan to build above these institutional limits, we would expect abrogation to have been preceded by a decision to implement a massive naval buildup. But that decision came only in August 1936, almost two years *after* Japan announced that it was no longer bound by the Washington Treaty.[118] Instead, it seems that the fleet faction was motivated by two considerations: first, that the unequal ratios were insulting to Japan's honor; second, that abrogating the treaty might make it easier to win approval later for a larger navy.[119]

But moderate civilian leaders and parts of the army leadership opposed abrogation because they understood that it was unnecessarily provocative. So how did the fleet faction prevail? Pelz suggests that they ran an effective "press campaign" that made it impossible for opponents to object to abrogation. Proponents of the fleet-faction position stressed two points in making the case for leaving the Washington Treaty: the injustice of inequality, and Japan's isolation in the wake of withdrawal from the League. These arguments proved effective, but not necessarily persuasive: the army minister, the treasury minister, and the foreign minister fell into line not because they thought abrogation was a good idea but because they were unable to offer a sustainable public counterargument.[120] By the middle of August, Prime Minister Okada "came out against continuance of the ratio system because it injured Japan's self-respect," and by the end of the month the government had decided to abrogate the Washington Treaty.[121]

This episode nicely illustrates the way in which status immobility and its consequences can empower hardliners no matter where their preferences come from. The navy's "fleet faction" sought abrogation for a variety of reasons; but it succeeded because arguments about the injustice of inequality and the danger associated with isolation – isolation that Japan had imposed on itself eighteen months before – resonated in a way that leaders with moderate preferences found impossible to resist.

Conclusion

Racial discrimination alone did not cause the Mukden Incident, the Marco Polo Bridge Incident, or Pearl Harbor. Neither did economic deprivation, insecurity, or dysfunctional domestic politics. These were complex events that cannot be adequately explained by a single variable or process.

[117] See Snyder (1991), p. 120; Asada (1973), pp. 227–237.
[118] Copeland (2014), p. 167.   [119] Asada (2014), p. 98; and Pelz (1974), p. 27.
[120] For this account, see Pelz (1974), especially Chapters 3 and 4.   [121] Ibid., pp. 60, 62.

Yet perceived racial discrimination – as an apparently permanent obstruction to Japanese status ambitions – played a critical role in producing conditions favorable to policies that put Japan on the road to the Pacific War. Status does not account for all of the variation in Japan's foreign policy before World War II. There are convincing non-status explanations for Japan's interest in expanding in Manchuria, for its increasing willingness to use force to do so, and for its gamble in December 1941.

But status immobility theory does help to explain some particularly significant and puzzling aspects of Imperial Japan's foreign policy: why, during the early 1930s, did it aim not just at material expansion in Manchuria but also, simultaneously, at a challenge to the normative and institutional foundations of the interwar order itself? Why did militant pan-Asianists oppose the Washington Conference system when there was no material reason to? And why did Japan withdraw from the League of Nations and abrogate the Washington Treaty when influential moderates opposed doing so? Status immobility theory provides answers to these questions. In the terms of the conceptual framework developed in Chapter 2, the understanding that Japan faced a status "glass ceiling" contributed to militant pan-Asianist preferences for rejectionist policies, and increasingly prominent beliefs about and discourses of status immobility imposed constraints on moderates that translated into concrete policy change. Figure 4.1 summarizes the relationship that this chapter

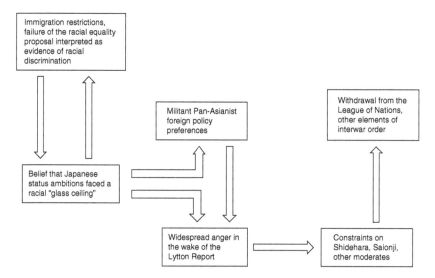

Figure 4.1 Status Immobility and Foreign Policy Change in Imperial Japan

has established between status immobility, the development of radical revisionist foreign policy preferences, and Japan's withdrawal from the institutions of the interwar order.

These elements – militant pan-Asianist revisionist preferences; withdrawal from the League; and abrogation of the Washington Treaty – played critical roles in the story of Japan's later violent challenge to the Western interwar order by unnecessarily provoking Western powers, contributing to Japanese diplomatic isolation, and further empowering Japanese hardliners. None can be fully understood without an appreciation for the social psychological and political dynamics of obstructed status ambitions – by inquiring not into the material costs and benefits of challenging the order, but rather into what the order meant within early 1930s Japanese society.

5   A Peace "Incompatible with Our Honor"
Status and the Genesis of Revisionism in Interwar
Germany

Unlike the war that began in August 1914, there is little controversy about
the origins of the one that started in September 1939. World War II was
Adolf Hitler's war – Germany's invasion of Poland was part of an attempt to
destroy the interwar status quo and establish a new order in Europe based on
German hegemony. This was a deeply radically revisionist project to which
Hitler had been committed since well before becoming chancellor in 1933.

This complicates efforts to theorize German foreign policy during this
period. Hitler was a singular character, and there is little use in attempting
to locate the key source of his drive to destroy the interwar status quo. His
motives were partially racial, partially ideological, and partially based on
a conception of the future of world politics that demanded German
hegemony over Europe.[1]

Status immobility does not explain why Hitler wanted to overthrow the
status quo any better than do concerns about German security. But there is
another puzzle that is central to this case: how did someone relegated to the
margins of Weimar politics through the end of the 1920s suddenly emerge
as the standard-bearer of the German right by 1930? This is a critical
juncture. Other German leaders had substantially more moderate ideas
about German foreign policy, and had they remained in charge, history
would have been fundamentally different. In becoming Germany's largest
right-wing party after the September 1930 federal election, the NSDAP
(the Nationalsozialistiche Deutsche Arbeiterpartei – better known as the
Nazis) created the conditions that made possible Hitler's rise to the chancellorship twenty-eight months later and set the stage for the emergence of
the most deeply revisionist foreign policy in modern history.

Status immobility theory provides a compelling account of how this
happened. While Hitler himself was not primarily concerned with the
injustice of the interwar order, this was a central theme of the NSDAP's
rhetoric from the time of the party's founding. The Nazis consistently

[1] On Hitler's foreign policy vision, see Jackel (1972), pp. 27–46; Hilgruber (1981),
pp. 49–55; Thies (2012).

opposed the moderate policy of "fulfillment" on the grounds that it acknowledged the legitimacy of the Treaty of Versailles and thus debased German dignity. Versailles had unjustly removed Germany from the ranks of the great powers, and to fulfill its terms was to accede to its implications for German status. The NSDAP critique of fulfillment, in terms of the conceptual vocabulary developed in Chapter 2, was informed by a rejectionist logic – playing by the rules of the Versailles settlement would only strengthen the foundations of an order whose primary purpose was to deny Germany its rightful place in the world. That order had to be opposed and destroyed, both in order to uphold German dignity and as a precursor to the return of German greatness.

Other German leaders had different ideas. Gustav Stresemann – the most important German statesman during the 1920s – was no more a fan of Versailles than were the Nazis. But, especially after the 1923 Ruhr Crisis, Stresemann realized the dangers of outright opposition and instead sought to improve Germany's position in Europe by working within the terms of the Versailles settlement. Part of this policy involved an effort to restore Germany's rights as a European great power through cooperation with the allied powers as a way of silencing domestic critics of moderation. Stresemann's policy, in other words, was partially informed by a logic of recognition. He hoped to secure Western acquiescence in Germany's return to equal status by fulfilling Versailles' terms.

Stresemann's moderation did not deliver quickly enough. The NSDAP remained consistently opposed to anything that smelled like kowtowing to Great Britain, France, and the United States; this position made the party increasingly popular as developments appeared to vindicate the view that the Allies would never restore German rights. It was, in fact, the furor over the Young Plan – which promised concrete material benefits but was widely seen as confirmation that Germany would remain subservient to the Allies for decades – that provided Hitler's NSDAP with the opportunity to move into the mainstream of the German right wing. In the federal election the next year, the NSDAP harnessed growing dissatisfaction with Versailles and Weimar foreign policy to supplant the more moderate DNVP (the Deutschenationale Volkspartei – or the German National People's Party) as the German nationalist standard-bearer. This put pressure on German leaders to adopt more provocative policies and positioned Hitler to take over the government in early 1933.

In sum, my core claim in this chapter is that status immobility created conditions by the late 1920s that were favorable to elites promising to reject and lash out at the interwar status quo order and unfavorable to those counseling moderation. This contributed to changes in German foreign policy through the second and third causal pathways developed in

Chapter 2: Hitler's emergence in 1930 as the standard-bearer of the German right pressured the Brüning government to move further away from fulfillment than it preferred; and, more consequentially, the NSDAP took control of German decisionmaking in January 1933, which finally ended without question any debate about whether Germany would integrate within or try to overthrow the interwar order.

The chapter proceeds as follows. The next section describes the interwar European order and traces variation in Germany's approaches to revising the terms of Versailles. I then show that Stresemann's foreign policy aimed to reestablish German rights as a great power through cooperation with the allied powers, and document the rise of the belief that this course was untenable because Western powers were committed to keeping Germany down. The rest of the chapter establishes a link between status immobility and the abandonment of German moderation, with a particular focus on Hitler's rise to prominence in 1929–1930.

German Foreign Policy and the Interwar European Order

The interwar European order – like the interwar East Asian order – was founded upon the peace settlement that ended World War I. The Versailles settlement had serious consequences for the distribution of resources in Europe. Germany – already weakened by four years of fighting and domestic unrest – ceded Eupen-Malmedy, Alsace-Lorraine, Upper Silesia, the Polish Corridor, and Memel, lost its overseas colonies, and was made financially responsible for the damages incurred by the war's victors.

But the interwar order also had a clear normative and institutional component. The Versailles settlement did not just weaken Germany; it also set out a process through which Germany could eventually gain relief from its sanctions, and an institution – the League of Nations – through which future distributive disputes could be settled pacifically. This institutional order evolved over the course of the next decade through conferences held at Genoa, Locarno, Lausanne, and Geneva.

German Approaches to the Interwar Order

The fundamental question that confronted German leaders in the aftermath of the imposition of the Versailles settlement was whether it was better to normalize relations with the Allies through fulfillment – accepting the terms of the treaty and playing by the new order's rules – or to reject the settlement entirely and either restart the war or ally with the system's other major pariah (the Soviet Union). German policy flirted with the latter path. The Germans dragged their feet on reparations and signed the Rapallo Treaty – a "gesture of national resistance" against the new order – with the Soviet Union in 1922.[2]

This course ultimately prompted the French and Belgians to invade the Ruhr valley in January 1923 to extract reparations payments themselves. The Ruhr crisis was a fiasco for Germany. The initial German response was passive resistance (military resistance was out of the question, given French dominance). The result was a humanitarian disaster in the Ruhr and an economic disaster in the rest of Germany. The French invasion of the Ruhr called Berlin's bluff, and eventually convinced the new German chancellor – Gustav Stresemann of the national liberal German Peoples Party (the Deutsche Volkspartei, or DVP) – that German foreign policy would have to change course. In September 1923 Germany agreed to fulfill French demands for reparations payments.

For the rest of the decade, German policy was directed by Stresemann and aimed at improving Germany's position in Europe by fulfilling the terms of the Versailles settlement as a way of convincing the Allies to lift Versailles' sanctions. Stresemann's objectives – lightening the reparations bill, ending the occupation of the Rhineland, and lifting restrictions on the military, all as a way of restoring Germany to the position it had occupied before the war – were consonant with those of the most strident German nationalists. In fact, Stresemann had been one of the foremost proponents of *Weltpolitik* and of annexation before November 1918.

What distinguished Stresemann from his critics on the far right was that he sought to restore Germany's great power status by working within the normative and institutional boundaries of the interwar order. While others demanded rejection of the settlement, Stresemann counseled fulfillment of Versailles' terms, participation in the institutions of the interwar order, and a piecemeal bargaining process through which Germany used economic leverage and exploited divisions among France, Great Britain, and the United States to secure concessions. Stresemann, in other words, pursued a form of distributive revisionism, which bore fruit in the form of the Dawes agreement of 1924, the Locarno Treaties of 1925, and the Young Plan in 1929. Each of these achievements improved Germany's security, economic position, or status in Europe, and each was possible only because Stresemann continued to signal that Germany remained committed to fulfilling the terms of the Versailles settlement and playing by the rules of the interwar order. Germany, for instance, continued to make reparations payments and in 1926 joined the League of Nations – a controversial move among German nationalists

---

[2] Tooze (2014), p. 436.

because it acknowledged the validity of the interwar order. Nonetheless, League membership was central to Stresemann's project because it would help clear the path for future gains.[3]

Germany abandoned Stresemann's distributive revisionist approach in the years after his death in 1929. There was no decisive break, but a series of developments over the course of the next four years signaled that German foreign policy would no longer be committed to playing by interwar rules. In 1931, Heinrich Brüning announced the creation of an Austro-German customs union (directly violating the terms of the Treaty of Versailles) and a unilateral end to reparations payments. In January 1933, Adolf Hitler – who had been stridently and sometimes violently opposed to fulfillment since 1920 – became chancellor. In short order, Hitler completed Germany's rejection of the interwar order by withdrawing from the League of Nations, openly rearming, and remilitarizing the Rhineland. Thus in the years between 1929 and 1933, German foreign policy experienced a rapid shift from Stresemann's pragmatic distributive approach to a radical revisionism that rejected the rules, norms, and institutions of the interwar order. This process culminated in the rise to power of a leader with the most deeply aggressive grand strategic vision in modern history.

The Puzzle of German Revisionism

IR scholarship on interwar German foreign policy has mostly focused on the period after 1933, and on the question of why Hitler sought European hegemony. Realists argue that this was a case of expansion for the sake of security maximization or a response to fears about the rise of the Soviet Union. Others have suggested the ideological distance between fascist Germany, on one hand, and the communist Soviet Union and democratic Allies, on the other, as the key to understanding Hitler's aggression.[4]

Both answers paint valuable but incomplete portraits of what happened between 1919 and 1939. Any story about German foreign policy that proposes a single key variable to explain why Hitler tried to take over the world lacks credibility. To argue that Hitler was merely the vessel through

---

[3] See Cohrs (2006), p. 352. Rathbun (2014), p. 88, describes Stresemann's approach to foreign policy as being influenced by his "realism" and "pragmatism," as well as by the consciousness of German weakness and an appreciation for French insecurity, all of which is consistent with the account I develop in the rest of this chapter.

[4] See Mearsheimer (2001), p. 189; Copeland (2000), Chapter 5; Haas (2005), pp. 106–120. It is worth noting that processes of domestic dysfunction do not provide a plausible account in this case. As Snyder (1991, Kindle locations 2456–2517) notes, stories about the logrolled interests of sub-state actors are not absent from interpretations of the rise of Nazi revisionism, but they are less compelling in this case than in those examined in Chapters 3 and 4.

which some structural stimulus – like growing power, impending decline, or ideological distance – was translated into an expansionist German foreign policy inappropriately minimizes his importance, as this implies that the broad contours of German grand strategy would have been basically the same had Hitler never come to power. While faith in German strength, fear of the Soviet Union, and hatred of communism each played an important role, they worked in combination with each other and other factors – especially the racial element of Hitler's ideology – to motivate what was a singularly aggressive and destabilizing vision.

Unlike other accounts of Nazi Germany's foreign policy, I do not attempt to unravel the puzzle of Hitler's motives. Instead, I address a different puzzle. Hitler operated at the margins of Weimar politics for most of the 1920s, both because his radical racist rhetoric put off some more mainstream conservatives and because of his role in the 1923 Beer Hall Putsch. And throughout the 1920s, Germany had very good strategic reasons to follow exactly the course that Stresemann pursued: seeking piecemeal revisions to the Versailles settlement while signaling limited ambitions through compliance with its terms. Germany's ability to militarily resist a French attack remained non-existent until the mid to late 1930s, which meant that provoking the French or any of the other Allies was to be avoided.

Yet by 1929, German foreign policy had begun to shift in the direction of radical revisionism, and by 1930 Hitler had emerged from obscurity to become the leader of the largest party on the German right. Why did Germany abandon Stresemann's moderate foreign policy? And how did a leader who had been demanding the rejection of the interwar order since its founding come to occupy such a prominent place in Weimar politics that he was only a crisis away from the chancellorship?

One common answer is that this story is really about the collapse of the Weimar Republic and cannot be understood apart from the German government's bungled response to the Great Depression.[5] This is undoubtedly true: the economic crisis that began in 1930 is an important part of the explanation for the abandonment of Stresemann's moderate approach to the interwar order and for the rise of Hitler. But it is also, on its own, unsatisfying. The economic crisis did not hit Germany with full force until at the earliest 1932. Yet the initial NSDAP breakthrough came in local elections in 1929 (which preceded the stock market crash) and in the 1930 federal election. The Brüning government's initial shift away from fulfillment came in 1931. Before 1932, Marks notes, the crisis

---

[5] See, for instance, Nicholls (1968), p. 126; Taylor (2013), p. 343; Evans (2004), pp. 208–209; Tooze (2014), Chapter 26.

mostly affected workers, which is significant because they had been before the crisis and remained after mostly supporters of the communist and socialist parties, not of the Nazis.[6]

In addition to these timing issues, focusing exclusively on the economic crisis of the late 1920s and early 1930s misses – as in the case examined in Chapter 4 – the important influence on Weimar domestic politics of the meaning Germans attached to the interwar order. Most prominent histories of the Weimar Republic mention the deep resentment that German nationalists felt toward the Versailles settlement, yet this element has not made its way into the IR literature on interwar European politics.[7] In the rest of the chapter, I explore the influence of the meaning of Versailles in Germany through the lens of status immobility theory and argue that it accounts for important elements of this case that a focus on power, security, ideology, or the economic crisis does not capture.

Great Power Status and Weimar Foreign Policy

Between the signing of the armistice that ended the fighting on the Western front and the delivery of the terms of the Treaty of Versailles in May 1919, Walter Rathenau composed a letter to Woodrow Wilson:

Our offer of an armistice was not made with the aim of gaining time or altering the existing balance of forces or preparing in any way for an extension of the war. We are prepared to offer guarantees for that, but they must not violate the honour of the army and the people ... Nobody can or may demand that our people accept conditions which are beyond the limits of justice and violate its honour.[8]

Rathenau never sent the letter, but the warning it contained was apt. The Treaty of Versailles threw the German people (especially the nationalists on the right) into a rage, and it has been cited as one of the causes of the downfall of the Weimar Republic.[9] The treaty immediately weakened the government that signed it in the eyes of its own people. As Tooze

---

[6] Marks (1976), p. 112; for others who maintain that economic crisis is an indispensable but inadequate explanation for the rise of Hitler, see Welch (1993), p. 137; Mitcham (1996), p. 133; Allen (1965), pp. 12, 24, 34; Eyck (1962b), pp. 278–298; Burleigh (2000), p. 124; Evans (2004), pp. 230, 263. The consensus among historians is that support for the NSDAP was not class-based (as one might expect had it been driven primarily by economic distress), but that the Nazis were rather a "catchall party of protest" (Childers, foreword in Abel [1986], p. xvii). See also Orlow (1969), pp. 154–155; Fritz (1987); Abel (1986); Kater (1983); Childers (1983); Hamilton (1982); Merkl (1975); Fischer (1996).

[7] See Marks (1976); Feuchtwanger (1993); Kimmich (1976); Kissinger (1994); Kennan (1996), p. 21; Hurd (1997); Evans (2004), p. 445; Andelman (2008); Sharp (2010); Tooze (2014), p. 314.

[8] Cited in Pogge von Strandman (1985), p. 236.

[9] See especially Graebner and Bennett (2011).

notes, the "peculiar agony of Versailles was that it forced the vanquished to will their own defeat as a conscious choice."[10] And it was not just defeat that signing seemed to acknowledge, but also the demotion of Germany from the ranks of the great powers. The terms of the Versailles settlement imposed on Germany obligations that seemed inconsistent with the rights of a great power, or even of a sovereign state, and thus signaled that Germany had been excluded from a status club to which many Germans continued to believe it had a legitimate claim.[11]

Resentful Germans were willing to let Stresemann try to improve Germany's position through "fulfillment," but support for that approach began to disintegrate by the end of the decade in response to developments that – while beneficial to Germany's economic and security position – seemed like symbols of persistent German subservience. I argue that the story of the abandonment of German moderation and the rise of Hitler cannot be understood without an appreciation for the way in which the increasingly prominent notion that Germany could not regain its rights as a great power through fulfillment undercut support for moderation and produced an opportunity for a leader who promised to reject the status quo.

This does not necessarily imply that the peace settlement was too punitive. The claim that the rise of Hitler was the consequence of a *toothless* peace is also compelling. If the Allies had been willing to return Germany to its pre-1871 status as a loose federation, there might have been no powerful state to challenge the status quo two decades later.

Yet, as Machiavelli wrote, "men should be either caressed or eliminated," and the Versailles settlement did neither.[12] The Allies were unwilling to eliminate Germany, but were also unwilling (or unable) to construct an order that would reintegrate Germany and restore its rights as a great power. The idea that the interwar order was designed to create and maintain Germany as a state subservient to the victors of World War I poisoned Weimar politics from the start and played a critical role in producing the conditions that led to the abandonment of Stresemann's moderate foreign policy and the rise of Hitler.

I develop this argument in four parts. First, I establish that German foreign policy under Stresemann was aimed at recovering German rights and German status. Second, I show that the radical nationalist critique of Stresemann's foreign policy – most stridently expressed by the Nazis – linked the status implications of the settlement and the demand that Germany stop participating in its own humiliation in a way consistent with the expectations of status immobility theory. Third, I show that the

---

[10] Tooze (2014), p. 314.   [11] Evans (2004), p. 66.   [12] Machiavelli (1998), p. 10.

prominence in late Weimar nationalist political discourse of the idea that German rights could not be restored through fulfillment made this critique resonate and produced the opening that Hitler jumped through to become the leader of the German right by 1930. His success in turn put pressure on the Brüning government to adopt more provocative policies, and set the stage for his rise to power in January 1933. Finally, I argue that Germany's withdrawal from the League of Nations that fall was driven by status-based demands for protest against the interwar order that continued to impose constraints on German foreign policy even after Hitler became chancellor.

Stresemann and the Restoration of German Status

Gustav Stresemann was no pacifist. He was an ardent expansionist during World War I and opposed the armistice of November 1918. He also voted against the acceptance of the terms of the Treaty of Versailles, which he saw as his "patriotic duty."[13] But Stresemann was also a realist.[14] He realized that rejecting the Allies' terms would have resulted in a renewal of the war, and Germany was not prepared for that fight. As a result, he voted "no" in the Reichstag only because he knew that this would not affect the outcome.[15]

After the war, Stresemann remained committed to restoring German power, but German weakness and the lessons of the crisis of 1923 meant that this had to be done gradually, without provoking a repeat of the Ruhr occupation. Thus – as chancellor and then foreign minister from late 1923 until late 1929 – he was committed to normalizing relations with the Allies first in order to end the French occupation of the Ruhr, and later to relax the restrictions that Germany faced under the Versailles settlement and lay the groundwork for the return of ceded territory in the east.[16]

This was a difficult task. Normalizing relations with the Allies involved a period of fulfillment – acknowledging and abiding by the terms of the Versailles settlement – which was politically unpopular. Even before the Ruhr occupation, Stresemann had trouble keeping the DVP within the Weimar governing coalition, because governing meant being associated with official support for the peace settlement, while remaining in opposition provided a political buffer between the party and the shame of Versailles.[17] Opposition to the treaty remained

---

[13] Wright (2002), p. 131.   [14] See Rathbun (2014), p. 88.   [15] Ibid., p. 131.
[16] Rubarth (1939), pp. 276–277; Bretton (1953), Chapters 3 and 4; Grathwol (1980), p. 4; Cohrs (2006), p. 277; Wright (2002), p. 152.
[17] Wright (2002), p. 163.

a salient feature of German domestic politics throughout the 1920s, and complicated efforts to negotiate with the Allies, because negotiation implied acceptance of the interwar order, and acceptance implied acknowledging the legitimacy of what the order had done to Germany's status.[18]

This meant that, to build support for revision by fulfillment, Stresemann had to work to undo Germany's demotion from the ranks of the great powers. The idea that a return to equal status and rights was possible through compromise was a key part of Stresemann's public justification for developments like the Dawes Plan, the Locarno Treaties, accession to the League of Nations, and the Young Plan. The focus on restoring German status forced Stresemann to push France and Britain harder than he preferred on issues related to German honor, like war guilt and the early end of the occupation of the Rhineland. It also helps explain why economic and security victories (like the Dawes Plan and the Young Plan) were so controversial.

Versailles and the Rights of a Great Power   Convincing skeptical German nationalists that fulfillment was a bearable approach to the interwar order could only be done by persuading the Allies to reverse the elements of the Versailles settlement that signaled that Germany no longer had the same rights as other great powers. In other words, Stresemann needed the Allies to recognize the restoration of German status in order to maintain enough support in the Reichstag to remain in power. The specific form that the claim to equality took varied. It included opposition to the War Guilt Clause of the Versailles Treaty, concern that Germany would enter the League of Nations in a position that befitted its aspirational status, a drive to end the occupation of the Rhineland early (since military occupation was inconsistent with the rights of a great power), and even a half-hearted claim to colonial mandates concomitant with membership in the League. The point of all of this was not to satisfy Stresemann's own ambitions – which were more concerned with tangible achievements and avoiding provocation than with issues related to status and rights – but to keep the nationalists on board, or at least out of open opposition. As Wright notes, Stresemann "could not claim less than equal rights, if he was to maintain domestic support."[19]

The negotiation over the Dawes Plan nicely illustrates the conflict between the tangible benefits that Stresemann sought and his need to

---

[18] See Evans (2004), p. 66; Burleigh (2000), p. 47.
[19] Wright (2002), pp. 155–156; see also Taylor (1973), p. 9.

make progress on restoring German rights for domestic reasons. The Dawes Plan was meant to stabilize Europe's economic and political relations after the Ruhr Crisis by reformulating Germany's reparations liabilities. While the plan was by no means unambiguously favorable to Germany, it carried significant advantages that Stresemann and others expected to improve Germany's position. Reparations payments would now be conditional on an American expert's assessment of Germany's ability to pay; Germany would be given an 800 million mark loan to revive its economy; and the plan would facilitate the French withdrawal from the Ruhr and prevent the future use of reparations as a political "lever."[20] The upshot was that Germany gained a measure of political independence that it had not enjoyed since the end of the war.

Stresemann and his allies understood these advantages very well: "A millard more or less does not matter if what we buy with it is freedom."[21] Moreover, the foreign minister worried that rejecting the plan or making excessive demands would abort the nascent détente that was developing in Western Europe, and perhaps "lead to the triumph of right-wing nationalism in neighboring France."[22] But the more radical nationalists – especially the DNVP, but also more marginal groups – were uncomfortable with the Dawes Plan because it seemed to legitimize the Versailles settlement. The president of the Pan-German League, for instance, thought "the Dawes Plan would do nothing but further weaken and humiliate Germany in relation to the Allied powers."[23] In response to this sort of opposition, the DNVP leadership published a list of demands that Stresemann and the Western powers would have to meet before they would fall in line. These clearly show that what concerned the National People's Party was restoring German status and rights. The DNVP demanded that Germany be recognized as an "equal partner" in negotiations, that the government reject "affronts to German dignity," and, most important, that Germany nullify Article 231 – the War Guilt Clause – of the Versailles Treaty.[24]

Stresemann resisted these demands and was able to cajole enough votes from the DNVP to ratify the Dawes Plan anyway. But he was forced to partially give in on the War Guilt Clause, which predictably created suspicion abroad. The episode demonstrates the critical role that the claim to great power status and equal rights played in legitimating German foreign policy and as an obstacle to Stresemann's moderate approach to revision.[25]

---

[20] See Eyck (1962a), pp. 227–323; Feuchtwanger (1993), p. 150.
[21] Quoted in Sutton (1937), p. 251.   [22] Bretton (1953), p. 82.
[23] See Jackisch (2012), p. 105.   [24] Grathwol (1980), pp. 30, 37.
[25] See Wright (2002), p. 294.

The same dynamic affected subsequent negotiations with the Allies. After the ratification of the Dawes Plan, Stresemann's next project was a political settlement that would increase German security and influence in Europe by resolving outstanding issues, especially with France. The result was the Locarno agreement and German accession to the League of Nations, which, Wright suggests, "set the scene for the European détente which followed."[26]

As with the Dawes Plan, this process was hampered by Stresemann's need to demand the restoration of German rights as a great power. Joining the League carried significant advantages from Stresemann's perspective, but he also worried that it would give "the impression that [the government was] voluntarily recognizing the Versailles treaty."[27] So, to weaken this impression, the Germans demanded, as a condition of their accession, that they be given the same rights as the other members of the League Council: a permanent seat on the Council and the right to colonial mandates.[28] This would signal that Germany had regained its place among the great powers. When Poland, Brazil, and Spain also claimed seats on the Council, Stresemann worried that Allied recognition of these "artificial" claims would "discredit his entire Locarno policy" by diminishing the significance of Germany's permanent seat. As a result, he objected and delayed German entry.[29]

One of the most important rights that Stresemann worked for was freedom from occupation. According to the terms of the Versailles settlement, the Rhineland was to be occupied for fifteen years, which meant that – as long as Germany complied with its obligations – evacuation would come by 1935. But starting with the Locarno negotiations in 1925, Stresemann sought to achieve an earlier evacuation. While ending an occupation early seems like a perfectly pragmatic policy, the strategic rationale for doing so is actually deeply questionable, and the evidence suggests that Stresemann cared about early evacuation primarily for reasons related to status, rights, and domestic politics.

For one thing, while control of bridgeheads over the Rhine gave France a military advantage (which the French consistently touted as an argument against early evacuation), foreign troops were slated to leave the Rhineland in 1935 anyway. This meant that occupation would only disadvantage the Germans "in the unlikely eventuality of a Franco-

---

[26] Ibid., p. 330.
[27] Wright (2002), p. 295; see also Gatzke (1954), p. 54; Cohrs (2006), p. 350.
[28] Wright (2002), p. 296. On colonial rights, see Schmokel (1964), pp. 64–65 and Townsend (1938).
[29] Cohrs (2006), p. 350.

German war" before then.[30] Given the state of the military balance between Germany and France during the 1920s and early 1930s, the disposition of the Rhineland would not likely have changed the outcome of such a war – France would have overrun Germany either way.[31]

There were other good reasons for patience. The most obvious was that France might take German demands as a threat, which could strengthen French hardliners and thereby worsen Germany's position. Just as compelling was the argument that time was on Germany's side. The more vigorously Germany demanded early evacuation, the higher the French would estimate Germany's value on that outcome, and the more valuable the concessions France would demand in return. On the other hand, if Germany simply waited for the clock to run out on Versailles, Paris might be "confronted with the possibility of gaining no benefit from evacuation" and might then be willing to negotiate on better terms.[32]

Yet in the face of these compelling reasons not to, Stresemann pushed hard for early evacuation. This was because the occupation was understood as a violation of German rights as a great power, and the German public (especially the nationalists on the right) demanded progress on restoring German status. Germans understood the Versailles settlement as an unjust *diktat* that had humiliated Germany by imposing conditions that were inconsistent with great power status. One of these was the presence of foreign troops on German territory.[33] This inconsistency was an important source of dissatisfaction, especially as Stresemann's foreign policy led to deeper integration with the interwar order. The normalization of relations with the Allies – in the form of the Dawes Plan, the Locarno Treaties, and accession to the League – prompted parts of the German press, the public, and members of the Reichstag to expect early evacuation as a "natural consequence."[34]

The need to deliver on this expectation – to defuse the radical nationalist critique that Stresemann was leading Germany to participate in its own humiliation – prompted the drive for early evacuation. There were two major attempts to secure this concession: the first came just before entry into the League, in order to "popularize the Locarno policy within

---

[30] Jacobson (1972), p. 362. What made war especially unlikely was Paris' renunciation of the right to invade Germany without the approval of the League of Nations Council. See Eden (1962), pp. 382–405; Wolfers (1966), pp. 47–48.

[31] In 1933, after a decade of covert rearmament, Hitler was still confident that France would have no problem defeating the German military (Hilgruber 1981, p. 57). Murray argues that the balance remained so much in France's favor that as late as 1938, a French offensive would have overrun Germany (Murray 1984, pp. 170–177).

[32] Jacobson (1972), p. 172; see also Cohrs (2006), p. 387.

[33] See Fulda (2009), p. 47; Lee and Michalka (1987), pp. 28–29; Collar (2013), p. 252.

[34] Kimmich (1976), p. 117; Grathwol (1980), pp. 160–161.

Germany," and the second came in 1928, "in order to demonstrate the practical benefits of [Stresemann's] policy of understanding."[35] Early evacuation was important because of what it would have meant about Germany's status, and thus for the popularity of Stresemann's moderate approach to the interwar order. It would have been "a symbol of recovery from defeat, of respect regained, and of the restoration of Germany to a position of full equality among the great powers"; it "became the touchstone of the success of [Stresemann's] foreign policy."[36]

Status Immobility and the Failure of Stresemann's Diplomacy   Like Japan's quest for great power status before 1931, Stresemann's attempt to revise Versailles through fulfillment was not a wholesale failure. He managed to secure concessions on Germany's reparations bill, a permanent seat on the League Council, and, eventually (but posthumously) the evacuation of the Rhineland five years early. Still, Stresemann's policy was widely interpreted as a failure, as confirmation that Germany could not return to great power status without completely overthrowing the interwar order. Western concessions seemed to be too little, too late. As in the Japanese case, what were in reality gains (in an economic and strategic sense, but also in the realms of German rights and status) were seen as failures because prominent discourses of injustice and humiliation made it easy to interpret them in those terms.[37]

In the German case, this was because of the shocking influence of the terms of the Versailles settlement. In the period between November 1918 and the delivery of the terms of the peace the following May, German leaders and other elites had hoped for and expected a settlement in line with what they understood to be Wilsonian ideals. These hopes were based primarily on the notion that German aggression had been the fault not of the German people but rather of the Wilhelmine elite, which had been overthrown.[38]

The terms the Allies delivered dashed German hopes. The treaty, many Germans believed, institutionalized subservience. According to Nicholls, Germany "was not given equality of status with the victors" which "strengthened the already widespread feeling in Germany that the League would just be an Association of Victors designed to maintain the supremacy of the Entente Powers."[39] Worse, the Allies appeared to the Germans to have applied the principles of the peace hypocritically: the

---

[35] See Jacobson (1972), pp. 77 and 168. See also Cohrs (2006), p. 486.
[36] Jacobson (1972), p. 364.   [37] Burleigh (2000), p. 49.
[38] See Nicholls (1968), pp. 45–48; Morris (1982), p. 66; Feuchtwanger (1993), p. 47; Mitcham (1996), p. 38; Snyder (1966), p. 36.
[39] Nicholls (1968), p. 48.

principle of self-determination, for instance, had been invoked to justify the creation of Poland and Czechoslovakia, but was "non-existent where it would have ruled in favor of Germany."[40] This apparent inconsistency made it easy for Germans to come to the conclusion that there was now one set of rules for Germany and a separate set for the rest of the world – in other words, that the new interwar order had been set up in a way that would perpetuate German submission.

The response was furious for all these reasons. Newspapers decried the "rape of Germany," and referred to the treaty as "unjust," "unfair," and "degrading."[41] Snyder describes an "explosion of wrath throughout Germany," and newspaper columns "filled with expressions of outrage" when the terms were publicized.[42] Philipp Scheidemann, Germany's first Social Democrat chancellor, decried the treaty as "the *malleus malleficarum* by which the confession of our own unworthiness, the consent to our own merciless dismemberment, the agreement to our own enslavement and bondage, are to be wrung and extorted from a great people," and he resigned in order to avoid signing it.[43] Nationalists and conservatives rallied against what they called the *Schmackfrieden* (shameful peace).[44] On June 28, in anticipation of the signing of the treaty by Gustav Bauer's newly formed government, the Pan-German *Deutsche Zeitung* published a telling rant against Versailles:

Vengeance German nation! Today in the Hall of Mirrors at Versailles a disgraceful treaty is being signed. Do not forget it. In the place where in the glorious year of 1871 the German Empire in all its glory had its origin, German honour is being carried into its grave. Do not forget it! The German people will with unceasing labour press forward to reconquer the place among nations to which it is entitled. Then will come vengeance for the shame of 1919.[45]

The juxtaposition of the glory of 1871 and the shame of 1919, the reference to Germany's deserved "place among nations" and the concern for German honor are clear indications that a central reason for such deep resentment was that Versailles seemed to have removed Germany from the ranks of the great powers and created an institutional obstacle to its return.

This was not a universal conclusion – after all, Stresemann's policy was based on the premise that Versailles did *not* present an insuperable obstacle to Germany's restoration to the ranks of the great powers. But the shock of Versailles' terms left a mark that facilitated interpretations of international politics portraying the Allies and the interwar order as unjustly obstructing Germany's path back to equality. A wide range of

---

[40] Heiber (1993), p. 37; Snyder (1966), p. 37.   [41] Fulda (2009), pp. 46–47.
[42] Snyder (1966), p. 37.   [43] Scheidemann (1929), p. 627.   [44] Kolb (1988), p. 35.
[45] Quoted in Pinson (1966), p. 398.

historians and other analysts conclude that the psychological and political effects of the treaty – which posed serious challenges to any leader who attempted fulfillment rather than outright rejection of its terms – were a critical cause of Germany's weakening commitment to the interwar order because they made unpopular and suspicious any policy or compromise that seemed to strengthen or acknowledge the legitimacy of the settlement.[46]

Fury over Versailles colored interpretations of Stresemann's policy. His accomplishments notwithstanding, throughout the post-Locarno period, concessions from France and Britain came too slowly to avoid confirming in many quarters the suspicion that Germany faced a status "glass ceiling" and could not regain great power status without a total rejection of the interwar order. This was both because Germans were predisposed to see the interwar order as an unjust exercise in status denial and because – in response – Stresemann was forced to make exaggerated claims about the gains that would flow from fulfillment. This only set German opinion up to be further disappointed.

Even before Locarno, Stresemann argued – with an eye toward nationalist opinion – that "the early evacuation of the Rhineland could, and would follow the conclusion of the treaty."[47] It was on the basis of this promise that he was able to justify cooperation with the Allies and, especially, Germany's accession to the League, which was unpopular because it was seen as "nothing but an instrument to maintain the Peace Treaties."[48]

Stresemann could not deliver on this promise. The British and French did not agree to early withdrawal from the Rhineland – which Stresemann had pitched as Germany's "'just' rewards" – and this made the Locarno Treaty unpopular.[49] Jacobson notes that Stresemann's tactics "had the unintended consequence of raising the expectations of the German public," which resulted in "popular disappointment."[50] Although the foreign minister himself was pleased with Locarno, his government, "to maintain pressure on the Allies for further concessions ... assumed an attitude of official disappointment," which publicly confirmed the view that the Allies were dragging their feet.[51]

In the years after Locarno, Stresemann continued to parry charges from the right and other quarters that Germany had been duped by the Allies. According to Cohrs, the

---

[46] See, for instance, Carr (1946), pp. 221–222; Nicholls (1968), p. 50; Matthias (1971), p. 16; Degrelle (1987), pp. 529–530; Welch (1993), pp. 127–139.

[47] See Jacobson (1972), p. 53; for similar evidence, see Sutton (1937), pp. 79, 83, 111, and 247; Turner (1963), pp. 189–190; and Grathwol (1968), pp. 101, 104.

[48] Schwarz (1931), p. 197.   [49] Cohrs (2006), p. 345.   [50] Jacobson (1972), p. 66.

[51] Ibid., p. 66; Sutton (1937), p. 246.

Wilhelmstrass's "policy of small steps" increasingly came under attack in Germany, not just in the right-wing press. The demands of its critics included not only that Stresemann at last present tangible compensations for his Locarno concessions, most of all in the Rhineland, but also that he should finally press for revisions of the Polish-German border; even the "Anschluss" of Austria reappeared on the horizon of public debate.[52]

Trapped by high expectations that he had helped to create and needing a "breakthrough" to "contain inner-German opposition to his policy," Stresemann made a series of attempts to secure early evacuation.[53] He began pitching the claim in terms of entitlement: in 1927, the Conference of Ambassadors certified that Germany had disarmed, which meant that – under Article 431 of the Treaty of Versailles – Germany now deserved an end to the occupation. Evacuation was no longer a subject of negotiation, but rather a right, the denial of which was inconsistent with the terms of the peace settlement itself.[54]

The Allies did not finally agree to withdrawal until 1930, and it came in exchange for Germany's accession to a new formulation of the reparations bill (the Young Plan, to which I return below). Thus while Stresemann had finally succeeded, his achievement seemed to be evidence not of successful fulfillment, but rather of the Allies' continued determination to treat Germany unfairly.[55] The press complained that Chamberlain and Briand had "broken the promise of Locarno to regard Germany as an equal"; Ludwig Kass of the Center Party bemoaned the "undeniable failure of German foreign policy"; even Chancellor Hermann Müller – who ultimately went along with the compromise – "resisted paying a price for what in his eyes should be a natural consequence of Locarno."[56]

Thus, by the end of the decade, fulfillment had been tried and – in spite of some successes – appeared to nationalist German opinion to have failed to restore Germany to equal status alongside Europe's other great powers. This created conditions favorable to leaders promising not patient conciliation but rather policies that would reject the interwar order.

Status Immobility and the End of Fulfillment

One leader whose record and platform fit this bill was Adolf Hitler. Hitler's NSDAP operated on the margins of Weimar politics until 1929, at which point it began a steep upward trajectory that saw the Nazis become the largest right-wing party in the Reichstag in September 1930, the largest

---

[52] Cohrs (2006), p. 440; Wright (2002), pp. 404–405; Jacobson (1972), p. 117; Sutton (1937), p. 421.
[53] Cohrs (2006), p. 383.   [54] Jacobson (1972), pp. 137–168; Wright (2002), p. 412.
[55] Kimmich (1976), p. 124.   [56] Jacobson (1972), p. 229; Cohrs (2006), p. 517.

party in the Reichstag in July 1932, and finally Hitler's ascent to the chancellorship in January 1933.

No theory can, on its own, account for Hitler's rise to power. But status immobility theory provides a critical and underappreciated part of the explanation. Before September 1930, the most important representative of German right-wing nationalism in the Reichstag was the DNVP, the German National People's Party. If this had still been true in 1933, the parliamentary crisis that brought Hitler to power might instead have resulted in the appointment to the chancellorship of a more moderate establishment conservative – someone like Franz von Papen or Kurt von Schleicher. And if history had taken that path, Europe might have avoided the conflagration that erupted in the later 1930s. But because the NSDAP had overtaken the DNVP and become the standard-bearer of the German right in September 1930, Hitler was in a position to demand the chancellorship in the winter of 1932–1933.

The combination of Hitler's foreign policy rhetoric and record along with German disillusionment with the policy of fulfillment constitutes a critical element of any satisfying account of the Nazi breakthrough from marginal rabble-rousers to nationalist standard-bearers. Hitler and the NSDAP had consistently criticized Stresemann's foreign policy as the participation in Germany's own humiliation (an attack that drew on the social psychological urge to protest against perceived obstacles to the satisfaction of status ambitions). And – unlike the DNVP – the Nazis had never themselves acceded to any decision that seemed to acknowledge the legitimacy of the interwar order. This proved an important advantage during 1929 and 1930, when the controversy over the Young Plan and the failure of Stresemann's policy to restore German rights seemed to validate the radical nationalist critique of fulfillment. In sum, a development that seemed to be yet more evidence that the interwar order posed an insuperable obstacle to the return of Germany to equality of status and rights alongside Europe's other great powers helped launch the NSDAP – a party whose foreign policy platform promised open revolt against the status quo – into the mainstream of Weimar politics, and ultimately into a position from which Hitler could become chancellor.

Rejection and the NSDAP's Critique of the Interwar Order   While there is little doubt that Hitler's worldview was colored by a sense of humiliation that emerged from the end of the war and the Versailles settlement, he does not personally seem to have cared so much about the *injustice* of the interwar order as about redressing German *weakness*.

As Welch notes, for "Hitler, neither Versailles nor the borders it established were *unjust* – they were merely *unacceptable*.[57]

But beginning in 1920, Hitler and the newly formed NSDAP developed a critique of fulfillment that revolved around the indignity of participating in an unjust system that had removed Germany from the ranks of the great powers and refused to let it return. In other words, the Nazi foreign policy program was informed in large part by a rejectionist logic: since the interwar order could not accommodate Germany's return to equality of status with its other great powers, it had to be undermined and overthrown – doing otherwise was tantamount to participating in Germany's own humiliation. To be sure, the Nazis were not the only radical nationalist group to develop such a critique – historians agree that "repudiation of Versailles and of the affront to German honour and great power status" played a key role in motivating a wide range of groups (including the Pan-German League, the *Stahlhelm*, the United Societies for the Fatherland, and others) to oppose fulfillment.[58] Because of the party's eventual success and significance, though, the Nazi critique is the most important to investigate.

The earliest statement of the Nazi platform was the Program of the German Workers Party (the DAP – the forerunner of the NSDAP), which was presented in Munich in February 1920. The program covers a great deal of ground, but the first two points clearly indicate opposition to the status implications of the Versailles settlement.

First, the DAP demanded "the union of all Germans in a Greater Germany on the basis of the right of national self-determination," which was a sore point because the apparent failure of the Allies to apply the principles of self-determination consistently suggested unequal treatment. Second, the DAP demanded "equality of rights for the German people in its dealings with other nations, and the revocation of the peace treaties" that had ended World War I."[59] According to Welch, these planks "were designed to play on the widely accepted view both in Germany and in the liberal democracies that Versailles was fundamentally unjust."[60]

Hitler's early rhetoric further developed the claim that Germany had been unjustly placed in a low status category and that anything less than outright opposition to the interwar order would be incompatible with

---

[57] Welch (1993), p. 134.
[58] Feuchtwanger (1993), p. 148; see also Michael Burleigh (2000), p. 47; Evans (2004), p. 76; Grathwol (1980), p. 11.
[59] See the Program of the German Workers' Party, available at http://germanhistorydocs .ghi-dc.org/sub_document.cfm?document_id=3910.
[60] Welch (1993), p. 135.

German dignity and interests. One of his favorite themes during the early 1920s, according to Kershaw, was "the Treaty of Versailles – the 'Peace of shame,' the instrument of Germany's slavery."[61] Germany was "already a colony of the outside world"; by signing the Versailles Treaty, "we humiliated ourselves morally, we positively destroyed our own honour and helped to befoul, to besmirch, and to deny everything which we previously held sacred."[62] Hitler railed against the war guilt clause, and those Germans – guilty of "despicable self-humiliation" – who had signed the treaty.[63] He reminded audiences that before the war, Germany had enjoyed "her honour and the consciousness that the world regarded her as an honourable people," but declared that "with the armistice begins the humiliation of Germany."[64]

The contrast Hitler drew here is worth emphasizing. Before the war, Germany had been highly regarded by other states; after the war, this was no longer true, and German moderates had participated in their own humiliation by signing the treaty and fulfilling its terms. The conclusion Hitler drew about Germany's approach to the interwar order was precisely the opposite of Stresemann's. Whereas Stresemann saw an improvement in Germany's position coming only *through* fulfillment, Hitler argued that Germany could not rise again *until* it had overthrown the treaty: "so long as this Treaty stands there can be no resurrection of the German people"; "to set aside this Treaty is a necessity, it is the condition which must be fulfilled before any later revival is in any way possible."[65]

This rhetoric constituted a clear demand for a policy aimed at protesting, delegitimating, and ultimately overthrowing the interwar order, and it justified this demand by linking it to a critique of the status quo order as an insuperable obstacle to the satisfaction of German status ambitions. And, by all accounts, it resonated well with German nationalists. The anti-Versailles critique was far more effective than Hitler's anti-Semitic rhetoric, which actually did more to marginalize than popularize the NSDAP.[66] As the right-wing *Deutsche Zeitung* wrote in 1921, many Germans turned "red with shame at the sight of a chancellor ... boasting to the world how obediently he has done everything, how punctually he is paying the billion marks ... how conscientiously he is turning us into slaves."[67] This was the sentiment that Hitler's critique of the interwar order tapped into, and in 1929 and 1930, he would use it to help springboard the NSDAP to the forefront of the German right.

---

[61] Kershaw (1998), p. 150.   [62] Baynes (1942), p. 5   [63] Ibid., p. 54.

[64] Ibid., pp. 55–56.   [65] Ibid., pp. 56–57.

[66] See Welch (1993), pp. 135–136; Evans (2004), p. 218; Eatwell (1995), p. 104; Graebner and Bennett (2011), pp. 110–111.

[67] Quoted in Feuchtwanger (1993), p. 95.

The Young Plan and the Nazi Breakthrough   While the more radical parts of the German political spectrum had – like the Nazis – advocated outright rejection of the Versailles settlement from the moment the treaty was signed, moderate voices – like Stresemann's – maintained control of German foreign policy throughout the 1920s. The NSDAP was a fringe party for most of the decade, in part because it was seen as overly radical. Anti-Semitism – a divisive issue within the more mainstream DNVP – and his role in the Beer Hall Putsch combined to discredit and marginalize Hitler. In December 1924, the NSDAP won only four seats in the Reichstag; the party was banned in Bavaria until 1925, and Hitler was not allowed to enter Prussia until 1928.[68]

But in September 1930, in one of the most consequential electoral surprises in modern history, the NSDAP won 107 seats in the Reichstag (a massive increase from the twelve it had held previously). The DNVP, by contrast, won only forty-one, a loss of thirty-two seats. While the Social Democrats held the most seats, the real historical significance of the 1930 election was this shift in the balance of power on the right. The Nazi break-through made possible Hitler's emergence as chancellor in January 1933.

There is no single explanation for the NSDAP's stunning success, but it cannot be understood without an appreciation for the way that Hitler's critique of the interwar order and the policy of fulfillment seemed to match the circumstances of 1929 and 1930. The Nazis took full advantage of conditions that appeared to validate the claim that the moderates – whom Hitler referred to as "illusionists" – had harmed German dignity and interests by participating in the interwar order and had failed to demonstrate that the order could be revised sufficiently from within. In short, apparent evidence that Hitler was right about the futility of fulfillment facilitated the NSDAP's emergence as the most important party on the German right.

The first phase of the Nazi breakthrough was the formation of an alliance between the DNVP and the NSDAP that brought the Nazis into the mainstream. The Nazi/DNVP alliance was made possible by the domestic politics of protest against the interwar order. In early 1929, an international "committee of experts" began devising a revision to the Dawes reparations schedule – eventually named after the commit-tee chair Owen Young – that was meant to be a "definitive reparation-war debt settlement."[69] The Young Plan was advantageous for Germany in many ways. It set the total German reparations bill at 114 billion marks to

---

[68] See Kershaw (1998), p. 234; Evans (2004), pp. 199–201; Hertzman (1963), pp. 124–161.
[69] Jacobson (1972), p. 159.

be paid over fifty-nine years, but it significantly reduced payments – compared to their level under the Dawes Plan – over the first decade. This was especially attractive because German leaders expected to negotiate for yet another decrease within that period. Moreover, in exchange for agreeing to the Young Plan, Germany finally extracted a promise that the Rhineland would be completely evacuated by the middle of 1930.[70]

These gains notwithstanding, the Young Plan was deeply controversial in Germany, especially on the right, because of what it implied about German status and rights. The idea that Germany was being made to haggle for the evacuation of the Rhineland, in addition to what looked like the extension of submission to the Versailles powers for six more decades, appeared to confirm suspicions that fulfillment could never restore Germany to equal status alongside the other great powers. This provoked intense opposition to the plan among nationalists.[71]

It was in this context that the NSDAP broke into the mainstream of Weimar politics. Alfred Hugenberg – the head of the DNVP – saw anger over the Young Plan "as a golden opportunity for rallying the masses" against moderates and republican government more broadly.[72] On June 15, 1929, he announced the creation of a broad nationalist coalition that would lead a campaign against the "Paris Tribute Plan."[73] The National Committee for the German Referendum consisted of the DNVP along with more radical groups, one of which was the NSDAP. It campaigned for the Law Against the Enslavement of the German People, which – among other measures – provided that anyone who voted to ratify the Young Plan would be prosecuted for treason.

The DNVP/NSDAP alliance was a marriage of convenience. The Nazis' enthusiasm and anti-Versailles purity – they had never participated in a governing coalition and thus had never been complicit in any policy that appeared to acknowledge the legitimacy of the interwar order – were assets that the DNVP did not have. Hugenberg's wealth, mainstream respectability, and access to media outlets were assets that the Nazis did not have.

This marriage worked out better for Hitler than for Hugenberg. The campaign did not receive enough votes to block the Young Plan, but it did jumpstart the Nazi breakthrough. Leopold suggests that the campaign transformed "vague hostilities into a rejection of the policy of understanding and the Weimar system."[74] This played to Hitler's advantage, as the Nazis had been firmly opposed to the "policy of

---

[70] Marks (1976), p. 103; Jacobson (1972), p. 273 and Part 7.
[71] Marks (1976), p. 105; Nicholls (1968), pp. 136–139; Bracher (1991), pp. 160–162.
[72] Leopold (1977), p. 56; Wright (2002), p. 489.   [73] Jacobson (1972), p. 354.
[74] Leopold (1977), p. 38.

understanding" – fulfillment – since its inauguration. In addition, Hitler gained a platform and a significant measure of credibility. Jacobson notes that "the Nazi Party was enriched, strengthened, and popularized" and, according to Evans, "now had a respectable face as well as a rough one, and was winning friends among the conservative and nationalist elites."[75]

The NSDAP started making significant gains in local elections – at the DNVP's expense – almost immediately.[76] This set the stage for the second phase of the Nazi breakthrough – its strong performance in the September 1930 federal election. The campaign leading up to the election was in many ways a replay of the Young Plan referendum campaign, only this time Hitler and Hugenberg competed against one another for nationalist votes. The political environment was fertile ground for the NSDAP. In the wake of the Young Plan's ratification, German nationalists were focused on foreign affairs, resentful of the government's cautious policy, and demanded the repeal of the reparations law.[77] The Great Depression – which by now was beginning to cause problems in Germany – exacerbated this dissatisfaction, but its effects were filtered through the already deeply entrenched belief that the interwar order was hopelessly biased against Germany.

The NSDAP flourished in this environment. The Nazi critique of the policy of fulfillment seemed vindicated, and Hitler was able to argue effectively that he – and only he – had understood that the interwar order could not be revised through integration and that Germany should not participate in its own humiliation. As Marks notes, "the Nazis loudly proclaimed that they alone had never endorsed anything done under the Versailles *diktat*."[78] Hitler released a manifesto a few days before the election that exemplifies his rhetorical tack. The document's general argument is that conditions proved the NSDAP's critique of the interwar order to be fundamentally correct: fulfillment had not led to the restoration of Germany's position and prosperity, but rather to humiliation and exploitation. One striking passage consists of a screed against the "illusionists" – the parties of the government and the more moderate nationalists. They had led Germany to ruin by foolishly participating in the exploitative institutions of the interwar order:

As the Armistice began to introduce the most terrible exploitation there has ever been, one lamented once more that with *Wilson's 14 Points* one had fallen for an illusion. And then one illusion was followed by another. *Spa* and *Brussels* and

---

[75] Jacobson (1972), pp. 354–355; Evans (2004), p. 246.   [76] Kolb (1988), p. 105.
[77] Bullock (1971), p. 143; Marks (1976), p. 113; Jacobson (1972), p. 355.
[78] Marks (1976), p. 113.

Versailles and *Geneva* and *Paris* and *London* and *Locarno* and the *League of Nations* and the *Dawes Agreement* and finally the *Young Plan*.[79]

The consequence, according to Hitler, was that Germany "had lost its freedom . . . forfeited its moral credit, had no political honor anymore, and had finally sacrificed its economic reserves."[80] Germany had "humiliated itself," and Hitler called on Germans to vote for change. The election "will only make sense if through it the only reparation which we are duty bound begins, the reparation of our honour, of our freedom, the reparation of our inner guilt."[81]

Historians agree that the NSDAP's advantage as the purest, most strident critic of the interwar order and the policy of fulfillment helps explain the party's stunning success at the ballot box in September 1930.[82] The role of status immobility in this process was critical. Opposition to the Young Plan and the interwar order more broadly – which was based largely on the implications of these for German status – provided, in Welch's words, "the one respectable issue that would allow [the Nazis] to grow from a fringe group to a mass movement."[83] And once the NSDAP had gone mainstream, the resonance of its critique of the interwar order helped propel it into its new position as the preeminent right-wing opposition party.

Hitler's victory threatened Center Party chancellor Heinrich Brüning and prompted the beginnings of a shift in the direction of radical revisionism. Brüning's foreign policy was markedly less concerned with playing by the rules of the interwar order than Stresemann's had been. Brüning worked toward the cancellation of reparations payments completely and the formation of a customs union with Austria – both of which clearly violated the terms of the Treaty of Versailles. Cohrs suggests that this tack is partly explained by the need to "contain the rising NSDAP."[84] Brüning's foreign policy – like Stresemann's – bore fruit in significant ways. He did manage to end reparations, in part because the British were eager to prevent the rise of a German government led by the radical nationalists. But the damage had been done. The NSDAP was the largest right wing party in Germany, which gave Hitler the leverage he needed to demand the chancellorship when the opportunity arose in the winter of 1932–1933.

Germany Withdraws from the League of Nations   Once Hitler became chancellor in January 1933, it was likely nearly inevitable that Germany would eventually seek to overthrow the European interwar

---

[79] See Muhlberger (2004), p. 400.   [80] Ibid., p. 400.   [81] Ibid., p. 400.
[82] See Marks (1976), p. 113; Evans (2004), p. 261; Bendersky (2014), p. 65.
[83] Welch (1993), p. 138.   [84] Cohrs (2006), p. 578; see also Helbich (1959).

order. But this did not mean that Germany's foreign policy immediately reflected his revolutionary objectives. Hitler – while committed to a wildly unrealistic grand strategic vision – was not incapable of strategic thought. He understood German weakness and the importance of appearing conciliatory in order to avoid fostering suspicion among Germany's neighbors.

His immediate aim was to reconstruct Germany's military. The minutes of the Conference of Ministers meeting from February 8, 1933, note that the "Reich Chancellor again stressed that the for the next 4–5 years the main principle must be 'everything for the armed forces.'"[85] At this point, Hitler was clearly wary of German weakness. Five days earlier, he warned that "the most dangerous period is that of rearmament. Then we shall see whether France has statesmen. If she does, she will not grant us time but will jump on us (presumably with eastern satellites)."[86] He and others understood that the implication of vulnerability was that Germany should try not to do anything that would provoke its more powerful neighbors. This included withdrawing from the League of Nations and the Geneva Disarmament Conference. Either move might signal aggressive intentions and raise the risk of premature conflict. On March 17, the head of the German delegation at Geneva reported that Hitler had directed him to avoid sabotaging the Conference and to "work for a positive conclusion," in order to facilitate "further utilization of the League of Nations as a tribune for the German point of view."[87] On April 7, Foreign Minister Konstantin von Neurath told the Conference of Ministers:

Although the accomplishments of the League of Nations are by no means satisfactory, Germany's withdrawal is out of the question. We would gain nothing by a withdrawal but only worsen our position. Withdrawal would be possible only if continued presence in the League were no longer compatible with Germany's dignity and if a direct, actual advantage were connected with the withdrawal. It should be taken into account that if Germany should withdraw, the League might make decisions that could bring us into a dangerous situation (Saar Territory).[88]

Neurath argued further that "foreign policy conflicts are to be avoided until we have completely regained our strength," and that Germany "must therefore avoid any provocatory demonstration."[89] In September, with

---

[85] Extract from the Minutes of the Conference of Ministers, February 8, 1933 (Document no. 16), DGFP (1918–1945), series C, vol. I, p. 37.

[86] Quoted in Hilgruber (1981), p. 57.

[87] The head of the German Delegation at Geneva to the Foreign Minister, March 17, 1933 (Document No. 94), DGFP (1918–1945), series C, vol. I, p. 176.

[88] Extract from the Minutes of the Conference of Ministers, April 7, 1933 (Document No. 142), DGFP (1918–1945), series C, vol. I, p. 260.

[89] Ibid., p. 260.

the Geneva Conference floundering, German leaders still preferred to remain within the League: withdrawal would only make sense once the League had returned the Saar to Germany.[90]

Although the disposition of the Saar was not settled until 1935, Hitler's commitment to avoiding a provocative withdrawal lasted only until early October 1933. It was at this point that the government began considering leaving the League in response to the imminent collapse of arms talks over issues of Allied supervision of German rearmament and temporary bans on military technology.[91] On October 13, Hitler announced to the Conference of Ministers that Germany would withdraw from the League within the week.

This premature withdrawal presents a puzzle. Why, when he and the advisors with whom he surrounded himself understood the benefits of playing along – at least temporarily – with the rules of the status quo order, did Hitler take this potentially provocative step?

The answer seems to have had to do with the domestic politics of status immobility. Hitler had been promising a policy of protest against the inequality of the interwar order for over a decade. He now faced a situation in which the Geneva Disarmament Conference was set to reject German demands for equality. This had the potential to be dangerous domestically. Bennett notes that the conditions offered by the allies at Geneva "would have been an obvious step backward ... discrediting the regime in the eyes of the German nationalist public and particularly of the army," and Kimmich suggests that Hitler "could not afford a spectacular setback."[92]

But the collapse of Geneva could also be turned to the NSDAP's advantage as long as the reaction signaled protest against the interwar order. Leaving the League fit this bill. Kimmich argues that withdrawal functioned as a "patriotic foreign diversion," and the way Hitler justified the move corroborates the interpretation that it was driven by the demand for a defiant response to further evidence that the interwar order was incapable of restoring Germany's rights as a great power:

Equality of rights cannot be granted to present-day Germany ... As a national government we find it incompatible with our honor to take part in the deliberations of a Conference which revokes the requirements which would have enabled us to take part again in the Conference. We shall therefore have to leave both the Disarmament Conference and the League of Nations, since the condition that we be recognized as a nation with equality of rights is not fulfilled.[93]

[90] Minutes of the Conference of Ministers, September 12, 1933 (Document No. 426), DGFP (1918–1945), series C, vol. I, p. 797.
[91] Bennett (1979), p. 466.   [92] Bennett (1979), p. 466; Kimmich (1976), p. 179.
[93] Minutes of the Conference of Ministers, October 13, 1933 (Document No. 499), DGFP (1918–1945), series C, vol. I, p. 924.

Hitler and his cabinet would have preferred to remain in the League in order to avoid unnecessary provocation and to make use of the League as a "tribune" for Germany's perspective. This proved impossible, and the circumstances of Germany's withdrawal strongly suggest that the same kinds of forces that influenced Japanese decisionmakers between 1931 and 1933 also played a role in Hitler's decision to leave the League. The domestic demand for protest against the interwar order was strong enough to make withdrawal an appealing option even though it was strategically unattractive.

Conclusion

Status immobility may not have motivated Hitler, and cannot explain why he tried to conquer Europe. In fact, its most significant role in this story largely ends by the beginning of 1933 – for the rest of the decade, German foreign policy was driven by Hitler's worldview, his objectives, and his beliefs about how to pursue them. Still, status immobility played a central role in Weimar Germany's shift toward radical revisionism, which is summarized in Figure 5.1.

It produced deep dissatisfaction with the interwar order on the German right and is an indispensable part of the explanation for the rise to power of a leader whose foreign policy preferences were as deeply revisionist as any in history. Germany's apparent inability to regain the status and rights of a great power in the decade since Versailles and the indignity and futility of the policy of fulfillment helped bring Hitler into the mainstream of the German right; and the resonance of his demand that Germany stop participating in its own humiliation and exploitation propelled the NSDAP to the forefront of the nationalist opposition in September 1930.

The interpretation in this chapter raises an important set of counter-factual questions: What if the Allies had been more accommodating to Stresemann? What if reparations had ended earlier? What if the Rhineland had been evacuated without being linked to the Young Plan? Could a more visibly successful Stresemann have blocked Hitler's path to the chancellorship? These are difficult questions to answer, but historians argue that had the treaty's terms been less punitive, German democrats would not have been so disadvantaged in the contest against the radical nationalists over the fate of the Republic.[94] Thus, it seems plausible that had the most offensive provisions of the Versailles settlement – those that provided fodder for radical nationalists throughout the 1920s – been lifted earlier than they were, the critique that integration within the interwar order was futile and

[94] See Marks (2013), p. 658.

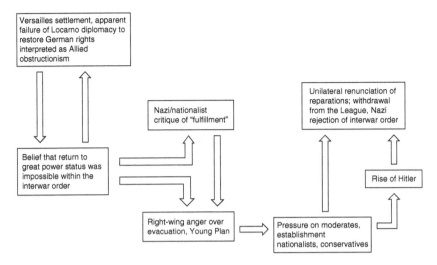

Figure 5.1 Status Immobility and Foreign Policy Change in Weimar
Germany

incompatible with German dignity might not have been so resonant by the
end of the decade. And, since timing was so significant in this case, small
counterfactual changes might have produced important differences.
If reparations had been lifted in, say, 1927 or 1928 rather than 1930,
there would have been no Young Plan, no campaign against the Young
Plan, and no opportunity for the NSDAP to become demarginalized.

Still, history was not completely open. The Allies *did* make significant
concessions to Stresemann between 1924 and 1929, and there were very
good reasons for them – especially for France – to stand firm on the
occupation of the Rhineland and reparations. Allied concessions, though,
did not seem to German nationalists to be evidence that the interwar order
could be transformed from within. Rather, because Versailles had already
produced such firmly held and widespread beliefs that the status quo was
fundamentally anti-German, Allied concessions were derided as too little,
too late, or were opposed because they were linked to further German
integration in an institutional order that was incompatible with Germany's
honor. The role of path-dependence was especially important in this case.

This suggests that the key Allied mistake – at least from the perspective of
status immobility theory – may have been the imposition of the Versailles
Treaty itself. This is not to say that it was necessarily too punitive. Rather,
the problem was that the settlement was simultaneously weak and provocative. The Allies were unwilling to destroy the bases of German power, or

even to occupy Germany so as to disabuse Germans of the notion that they could plausibly claim the rights of a great power. Yet they were also unwilling to – in Machiavelli's words – "caress" Germany, to treat it as if it were a normal European great power. The middle path that the Versailles settlement followed eventually produced a powerful, humiliated state that could not easily be reconciled to the status quo order.

6   Status and the Anglo-American Power Transition

The previous three chapters have connected status immobility to shifts toward radical revisionism in rising states. In this chapter, I investigate a case in which the rising power did not challenge the system presided over by the dominant power: the Anglo-American power transition of the late nineteenth and early twentieth centuries. This chapter provides additional evidence that status immobility matters for the foreign policies of rising powers by showing that its *absence* was a critical – but largely silent – part of the explanation for the United States' disinterest in challenging the Pax Britannica during the decades before World War I.

Assessing the contribution of status immobility theory in a negative case is tricky. The theory does *not* suggest that rising states behave in moderate, pragmatic ways *because* they are satisfied with the status they have been accorded in the international system. Moderate, pragmatic behavior can often be explained by reasoning that has nothing to do with status. So, for instance, the answer to the question "Why did the United States support British interests during the Second Boer War?" or "Why did the United States not oppose the British during World War I?" is, in a sense, simple: the United States benefited from the role the British played in European and global politics and had no good reason to work to undermine it.[1]

Yet this answer is incomplete, in light of the cases examined in Chapters 3, 4, and 5. Wilhelmine Germany had no good strategic reason to challenge British naval dominance; Imperial Japan had no good strategic reason to leave the League of Nations; and Weimar Germany's leaders had no good strategic reason to abandon Stresemann's moderation in the early 1930s. Yet in all three cases, status concerns interfered with the pursuit of pragmatic policies based on realist thinking and contributed to deep challenges to the status quo order. The question at the heart of this chapter is how the rising United States avoided that fate: why was the United States – no less

---

[1] See, for instance, Lewis Einstein (1918) and Alfred Thayer Mahan (2009 [1910]) for evidence that contemporary American elites understood this.

a status-obsessed rising power than Germany or Japan – not subject to forces that interfered with the pursuit of a foreign policy that in important ways buttressed the dominance of the incumbent hegemon?

I demonstrate in this chapter that status immobility *could have* produced forces that might have interfered with American foreign policy if the British had not accommodated American status claims beginning with the resolution of the 1895–1896 Venezuela Crisis. I make this argument in three steps. First, I establish that during the last decades of the nineteenth century, the United States was anxious to achieve recognition of world power status, and I delineate the rights Washington sought and the ways in which status anxiety inflected American foreign policy. Second, I investigate the sources of British accommodation in 1895–1896 and after. I do this for three reasons: to demonstrate that the British retreat was in part the result of contingent factors that make it possible to imagine a different future; to establish that the British understood that status and rights were at stake in the Venezuela Crisis and that backing down was not costless; and to investigate the manner in which the British managed the status anxiety associated with ceding dominance in the Western Hemisphere. Third, I employ counterfactual analysis to show that if the British had *not* accommodated American status claims, it is possible to imagine American foreign policy evolving in ways that would have more directly challenged Britain's global position in the years after 1896.

A note on this chapter's limitations is in order before proceeding. This case is different in salient ways from those analyzed in the previous three chapters. These differences – which include, most importantly, geography, political institutions, and the degree to which the rising power's status ambitions seemed incompatible with the established power's interests and role identity – make it difficult to draw inferences by comparison. This is precisely the problem that makes explicit counterfactual analysis valuable. Counterfactual analysis proceeds by comparing the Anglo-American case against a plausible alternative version of *itself*. Of course, this comes with its own set of limitations. The most significant is a high degree of uncertainty about the downstream consequences of the concrete shifts in policy that I posit as results of small changes in the history of Anglo-American conflict over status. The analysis below shows only that Washington's foreign policy orientation could have been markedly *more* opposed to the British-dominated order than it was during the decades around the turn of the twentieth century. This does not mean that the United States would eventually have turned into a revisionist on the order of Imperial Japan or Nazi Germany. That outcome – though possible – remains difficult to imagine because contextual differences (including those cited above) might have mitigated or changed the manner in which the drive to reject the status quo order manifested itself. My claim in this chapter is simply that the dynamics highlighted by status immobility theory could have functioned in the American context, and that they would likely have pushed US foreign policy in the same direction – even if not as far – as they pushed the foreign policies of other rising states.

Status and American Foreign Policy

The rise of the United States as an economic powerhouse over the course of the nineteenth century raised expectations among many Americans that the United States should become a world power. This was by no means a universal concern, but as early as the Gilded Age, Herring notes, "younger Americans, especially offspring of the elite, shared a growing sense of the nation's rising power and status in the world."[2] The link between social identity and the performance of the state abroad was, according to Rhodes, a new development in the late nineteenth century United States: for a variety of reasons the "traditional construction of 'America'" as a weak, isolationist state no longer worked to bind "the nation together into a single civil society."[3] In its place, the state and its "ability to represent the American people against an external 'them'" became "central to social identity."[4] As a result, status anxiety began to inflect discourse about a wide range of substantive issues in foreign policy, from objections to European import restrictions to diplomatic representation. Americans increasingly demanded that their government act as a world power, and that their status be *recognized* abroad.

Acting as a world power meant doing the kinds of things that are familiar from the discussion of *Weltpolitik* in Chapter 3. The demand for the construction of a larger navy is the most obvious parallel. In 1890, the US Navy – which had until then been relegated to the roles of coastal defense and commerce raiding – began the construction of a battleship fleet that could "operate offensively as a unit."[5] By 1905, the United States had twenty-four battleships, and by 1921, it had thirty-three (with another thirteen under construction).[6] It is more difficult, given differences in geography, to establish that the American naval program was strategically unnecessary than it is to make that argument about Germany's *Flottenpolitik*. If one believes that colonial and economic expansion abroad were critical to American security, then building a battle fleet to protect these interests is sensible.

---

[2] Herring (2008), p. 277. Others (Perkins 1994; Freeman 2001) have argued that status and honor (though not necessarily at the national level) were central concerns of American politics and foreign policy since the founding of the Republic.
[3] Rhodes (1999), p. 62.   [4] Ibid., p. 63.   [5] Rhodes (1995), p. 68.   [6] Ibid., p. 68.

Still, the rise of the American battle fleet cannot be completely attributed to concerns about physical security. The way that Americans – and even the Navy – wrote and spoke about the need for the fleet suggests that it was *also* seen as a symbol of status. In 1889, the secretary of the Navy's *Annual Report* called for a massive increase in naval armaments, not, according to Zakaria, because new threats had emerged but because fleets of battleships would be "the means by which the United States would assume its rightful place among the world powers."[7] While the secretary of the Navy's Policy Board admitted that the probability of war between the United States and another great power "would seem to be at a minimum," it suggested increased spending because "our navy is insignificant and totally disproportionate to the greatness of the country."[8] The link between naval power and world power status was laid out most influentially in the work of Alfred Thayer Mahan – which in short order became a sensation and "provided a persuasive rationale for the new battleship navy and a more aggressive U.S. foreign policy."[9] Journalists picked up on the call: in 1897, Murat Halstead wrote in the journal *Forum* that "we need to be armed as becomes a great Power."[10] Rhodes attributes the dramatic shift in American naval policy in 1890 most directly to the new salience of the United States' place in the world for the way that Americans understood their identities.[11]

There is a similar story to be told about overseas expansion. The demand that the United States expand abroad – to the point of acquiring territorial possessions – cannot entirely be attributed to concerns about American status. Economic and strategic interests played an important part in debates about the American role in East Asia and Latin America and the Caribbean.[12] And expansion was also controversial – imperialism conflicted with American anti-colonial sensibilities, and also raised fears about the consequences of racial difference for national coherence.[13] Yet it is clear that for the most diehard cheerleaders of the so-called large policy, acting out the status of a world power for reasons of social identity and national pride was a central part of the appeal. Nationalist elites like Henry Cabot Lodge, Albert Beveridge, Brooks Adams, Whitelaw Reid, Albert Shaw, Theodore Roosevelt, Richard Olney and others supported expansion because, according to O'Connell, they "dreamed of the day when the United States would play a role on the world stage commensurate with its

---

[7] Zakaria (1998), p. 128.   [8] Tracy (1890), pp. 3–4.
[9] Herring (2008), p. 303; see Mahan (1890), especially the introduction.
[10] Halstead (September 1897), p. 66.   [11] Rhodes (1999), pp. 63–64.
[12] For these arguments, see Williams (1970); LaFeber (1963); and McCormick (1967).
[13] For a recent overview of the controversy that attended the inauguration of American imperialism, see Kinzer (2017).

size and prosperity."[14] In September 1898, for instance, Senator J.R. Proctor asked "whether this country is to continue in its policy of isolation, or is to take its rightful place among the great World-Powers," reminded readers that "*prestige* is as dear to nations as it is to individuals," and counseled the government to hold onto the newly acquired Philippines.[15]

But becoming a world power did not only mean acquiring overseas territory and a fleet of battleships. It also meant being *recognized* as a world power by other states. And indeed, American leaders and other elites were sensitive to the signals that foreign behavior sent about the United States' status. For instance, Herring notes that American "diplomats had long bristled at the lack of precedence accorded them in foreign courts because of their lowly rank of minister. They viewed the snubs and shabby treatment as an affront to the prestige of a rising power."[16] In 1893, this source of status anxiety was erased – to the diplomats' relief – when Congress agreed to upgrade some American ministers to the rank of ambassador. Great Britain, France, Italy, and Germany reciprocated in short order, thereby sending a signal that the United States belonged in the great power club (which, was, at the time, the only category of states that customarily exchanged ambassadors with one another).[17]

By far the more important test of whether European powers would accept the status role and rights that the United States claimed for itself came in the winter of 1895–1896. There is little question that Americans understood the maintenance of a "sphere of influence" in the Americas as a right linked to the United States' position in the world. Other world powers had exclusive spheres of influence in the form of colonial empires or economic zones in places like China and India; Latin America and the Caribbean – according to the Monroe Doctrine – amounted to an American sphere of influence.[18]

British behavior during the 1890s threatened the American understanding of its rights as the protector of the Western Hemisphere. In early 1895, the British coerced Nicaragua to pay 15,000 pounds for mistreating British residents, including the vice-consul. The response in the United States – "part patriotism, part frustration, part militarism" – prompted president Grover Cleveland to look for an opportunity to assert American rights vis-à-vis Great Britain in order to "stifle this jingoism."[19] The Venezuela Crisis was his chance.

---

[14] Quoted in Rhodes (1999), p. 64.   [15] Proctor (1898), pp. 14, 22.
[16] Herring (2008), p. 300.   [17] See Ilchman (1961), pp. 71–72.
[18] On the Monroe Doctrine as an American claim to the right to a sphere of influence, see Hast (2014), pp. 41–44; see also Vincent (1974) and Kaufman (1976).
[19] Dobson (1978), p. 77.

The crisis arose out of a dispute over the border between Venezuela and British Guiana. A boundary line drawn in 1840 was tacitly accepted by the British, but both parties claimed territory extending on either side. The discovery of gold during the 1880s enhanced the value of the disputed region. Increasing British pressure for an agreement on its terms led Venezuela to request American intervention.[20] Until the middle of the 1890s, American policy was generally to apply gentle pressure, but remain basically uninvolved. In the summer of 1895, though – under the influence of new Secretary of State Richard Olney and in light of domestic frustration related to the Nicaragua crisis – the Cleveland administration invoked the Monroe Doctrine to demand that the British submit to arbitration under American supervision.[21] When British Prime Minister Salisbury refused, Cleveland delivered a message to Congress in which he claimed an American right to be involved in the dispute, and he acknowledged the threat of war that accompanied his words: "I am fully alive to the responsibility incurred and keenly realize all the consequences that may follow."[22]

The evidence suggests that American prestige was implicated in Cleveland's aggressive diplomacy. A note from Olney to Salisbury in July had claimed "not to protest [British behavior toward the Venezuelans] and give warning that the transaction will be regarded as injurious to the interests of the people of the United States as well as oppressive in itself would be to ignore an established policy with which the honor and welfare of this country are closely identified."[23] In other words, just as Germany claimed a right to be consulted and compensated in the wake of the Anglo-French entente by virtue of Germany's position, the United States claimed a right to have its voice heard in the course of negotiations between the British and the Venezuelans.

Cleveland's message to Congress and the public response provide further evidence that American status was at stake in Venezuela. The message ended with the assertion that "there is no calamity which a great nation can invite which equals that which follows a supine submission to wrong and injustice and the consequent loss of national self-respect and honor beneath which are shielded and defended a people's safety and greatness."[24] The response to the address was overwhelmingly positive. According to Dobson, the message elicited a "great emotional outpouring," because it "well suited the American temperament."[25]

---

[20] Campbell (1976), Chapter 11.   [21] Ibid., p. 200; Young (1942).

[22] Cleveland to Congress, December 17, 1895, in FRUS (1895), Part I, p. 545.

[23] Olney to Salisbury, FRUS (1895), Part I, p. 592.

[24] Cleveland to Congress, December 17, 1895, in FRUS (1895), Part I, p. 545.

[25] Dobson (1978), pp. 82–83. Eggert (1974, p. 223) notes that Democrats were pleased because the President's policy had proven so popular.

Responses in the press and among elites from both parties suggested that Americans "cared much more about America's prestige than about Venezuela's boundary."[26] The *New York Times* noted that the sentiments that Cleveland articulated were "at once a surprise and a gratification," and claimed that "never before, following a public utterance by President Cleveland or any other recent President, have the words of a message been received with such prompt and cordial approval." While war did not seem likely to result, the *Times* suggested that if it came, Americans would not flinch: "the American people will stand by the President in making good the assertion that their cause only can be upheld with honor and self-respect by a strict enforcement of the position the President has taken." The paper also reported that there was nearly universal approval in Congress, and published a statement of support from Ohio Governor William McKinley, who thought that Cleveland's defense of the Monroe Doctrine "upholds the honor of the Nation and insures its security."[27]

Other papers also took note of the broad approval inside and outside Washington, and made clear that the stakes seemed to involve American status and rights, rather than any sort of material gain. The *Chicago Daily Tribune* reported that both parties displayed "a sober almost solemn and grim determination to support the President in every step to maintain the dignity of the Nation."[28] The *New York Sun* recorded the enthusiastic approval of congressional Republicans, who thought the "message must be endorsed by every patriotic citizen in the whole country regardless of politics or party"; the paper also noted the determination of Confederate veterans of the Civil War to participate in any armed conflict that might arise as a result. [29] Henry Cabot Lodge, one of Cleveland's political rivals, approved as well. He maintained that the stakes in the crisis were high: the British "do not realize that, while it is a mere question of more or less territory to England, it involves for the United States a principle as vital almost to their rights and interests as a nation as their own independence."[30] Olney received a "flood" of notes from friends and rivals alike complimenting [him] for the vigor and tone of his note, which "stole the Republican party's thunder."[31]

The *Wichita Daily Eagle* approved of the closing lines of the message in a way that highlights the role of status, prestige, and honor in the crisis:

[26] Dobson (1978), p. 82.
[27] "Exciting Scenes in Washington," *The New York Times* (December 18, 1895), pp. 1–2.
[28] "War on Every Lip," *Chicago Daily Tribune* (December 18, 1895), p. 1.
[29] "John Bull Is Angry," *New York Sun* (December 18, 1895), p. 1.
[30] "Lodge Indorses Cleveland," *The San Francisco Call* (December 18, 1895), p. 2.
[31] Dobson (1978), p. 82.

Confessing that there is some supreme guiding power that elevates nations and degrades them, still the potentiality of all nations that history records as great, has rested on national self-respect and honor, and, what Cleveland does not specify, national pride. National honor is more than all else in a nation's fabric. Ambition for commercial supremacy is impossible without it. And without it a nation and its citizens are subject to insult and injustice.[32]

The link the paper drew between the self-esteem of American citizens and their identification with a state that does not allow its rights to be trampled is striking. It is not only consistent with the expectations of status immobility theory, it also echoes the sentiments of pan-Germans, pan-Asians, and interwar German nationalists.

On January 2, Theodore Roosevelt – a Republican – warned in the Harvard *Crimson* that backing down from the position that Cleveland had articulated for economic or financial reasons would lead to disaster. Roosevelt is worth quoting at length because he articulates a fear of the social psychological and political dynamics highlighted by status immobility theory:

By a combination of indifference on the part of most of our people, a spirit of eager servility toward England in another smaller portion, and a base desire to avoid the slightest financial loss even at the cost of the loss of national honor by yet another portion, we may be led into a course of action which will for the moment avoid trouble by the simple process of tame submission to wrong. If this is done it will surely invite a repetition of the wrong; and in the end the American people are certain to resent this ... When our people as a whole finally understand the question they will insist on a course of conduct which will uphold the honor of the American flag; and we can in no way more effectively invite ultimate war than by deceiving foreign powers into taking a position which will make us certain to clash with them once our people have been fully aroused.[33]

In short, Roosevelt worried that if the United States backed down in Venezuela, British insults would continue until finally the American people would grow so resentful of being disrespected (that is, having their rights claims go unrecognized) that Anglo-American conflict would be unavoidable. Thus a policy of standing firm would *avoid* conflict in the long run by preventing the growth of anti-British resentment in American opinion. This reasoning may not have been Roosevelt's primary motivation in promoting a firm response (though there is no reason to doubt that the dynamic he describes genuinely concerned him). But at the very least the fact that he deployed it as a rhetorical tool means that he

---

[32] "National Honor and Pride," *Wichita Daily Eagle* (December 22, 1895), p. 12.

[33] Roosevelt, Letter to the Editor of the Harvard *Crimson*, January 2 1896, in Brands (2001), p. 115.

must have believed it would resonate with his readers, which underlines the significant degree to which status, the Venezuela crisis, and Anglo-American relations seemed to be intertwined in early 1896.

Of course, opinion was hardly universally belligerent. Financial and economic interests and a shared Anglo-Saxon identity pushed many to oppose war at all costs. But it is at the same time clear that some of the most influential American elites were interested in establishing the United States as a world power and saw the Venezuela crisis as a test of whether or not the British would acknowledge the rights that the United States had claimed in the Western Hemisphere. This makes 1895–1896 a critical juncture for Anglo-American relations and for the fate of American status ambitions.

Ultimately, of course, the British stood down and acknowledged the United States' special position and rights in Latin America and the Caribbean – not only during the Venezuela Crisis but also in subsequent acts of accommodation. What if they had not? Is it possible to imagine a denial of American rights claims by Great Britain in 1896 contributing to a more deeply revisionist American foreign policy? If so, then this suggests that status accommodation played a central – if silent – role in the story of Anglo-American rapprochement and strengthens this book's core argument: that obstructed status ambitions can turn rising states against the status quo.

Explaining British Accommodation

Before exploring this question, I first investigate the causes of British accommodation, and specifically of Britain's retreat in 1896. The primary reason to do so is because an effective counterfactual should be based on a *minimal, plausible* alteration to the historical record. In the context of the Anglo-American case, that means showing that it is possible to imagine the British standing firm in 1896 by making a small and realistic change in the conditions that faced British leaders that winter. Thus, this section's primary purpose is to show that British accommodation (at least in 1896) was *not* completely determined by factors like imperial overreach or the rise of the German threat across the North Sea. However, the section has two secondary purposes. One is to establish that the British understood the implications for their own status of acknowledging American claims in 1896. The rise of the United States posed a serious threat to Great Britain's position in the international status hierarchy, and ratifying Cleveland's interpretation of the Monroe Doctrine was a symbolic and concrete retreat from global hegemony. That the British understood these costs strengthens the argument made in the previous section that status seemed to be at stake in Venezuela in 1895–1896. It also raises a puzzle: how did the British manage the status anxiety associated with acknowledging a rising power's claim? Addressing this puzzle is this section's other secondary purpose. I argue that while geostrategic pressure for retrenchment may have pushed the British to accommodate American claims, retrenchment was facilitated by the availability of the identity discourse of *Anglo-Saxonism*. Anglo-Saxonism allowed some British leaders to engage in what social psychologists call *recategorization*: instead of obsessing about losing status to the United States, many British leaders came to understand and talk about themselves as members of a broader Anglo-Saxon "team" engaged in a civilizational struggle for status against Slavs, Teutons, and Asians. In this civilizational game, the Anglo-Saxons were winning, and American gains could be celebrated as successes for the English-speakers, instead of grieved as signposts on the road to British decline.

Was British Accommodation Inevitable?

There is little doubt that perceptions among British leaders that the empire's liabilities exceeded its capabilities played an important role in the determination to retrench during the late nineteenth and early twentieth centuries. The conclusion of the Franco-Russian alliance in the early 1890s worried British policymakers because it posed the most significant threat to British naval dominance. The Venezuela Crisis and the crisis that broke out in the Transvaal around the same time compounded the problem. British policymakers clearly faced pressure to reduce their commitments – and list of potential rivals – abroad.[34]

But this does not mean that accommodation of the United States was inevitable. In fact, the sort of strategic adjustment that the British made is hardly universal. Great powers often refuse to accommodate the claims of rising rivals even when there are compelling strategic reasons to do so – as the record of the rise of Japan discussed in Chapter 4 illustrates. And it is striking that accommodation of the United States began relatively early, at a time when the British still could conceivably have resisted American demands and well before the German threat had emerged in full force and clarity.[35]

Thus it is ahistorical to interpret the Anglo-American détente as the necessary product of ironclad geopolitical forces. There was a great deal of fluidity and uncertainty in the way British leaders thought about their

---

[34] See Kennedy (1981), pp. 108–109. For similar interpretations from political scientists, see Layne (1994), p. 25 and Kupchan (2010), Chapter 3.
[35] Thompson (1999), p. 215.

strategic position in the second half of the nineteenth century. As Bourne notes, the rise of the United States – especially as a seapower – *did* threaten British interests.[36] According to Zakaria, "the British ... were the most concerned about America's rise: a great naval power across the Atlantic could only be a rival."[37] In the aftermath of the *Trent* Affair, Colonial Secretary Newcastle worried about the security of British North America: "Even if peace be for the present preserved, I fear we cannot count upon its safe continuance for any length of time in the present temper of the American people, and it is of great importance that our North American possessions should not again allow themselves to be caught in a state of utter unpreparedness."[38]

By the 1890s, British concern about the Franco-Russian alliance led them initially to seek an alliance not with the Americans but with the Germans.[39] In this context, American expansion was seen "as a major additional strain upon the political and naval foundations of splendid isolation," and it was not obvious at the time that accommodation of the United States would be possible.[40] Salisbury worried during the Venezuela Crisis that "A war with America – not this year but in the not distant future – has become something more than a possibility: and by the light of it we must examine the estimates of the Admiralty. It is much more of a reality than the future Russo-French coalition."[41] The chancellor of the Exchequer and the first lord of the Admiralty agreed: the American threat – not the German threat – prompted the creation of the "flying squadron" whose task was rapid response to challenges against British interests around the world.[42] Lord Dufferin, the former governor general of Canada, suggested replacing the two-power standard with a three-power standard, "for the best way of discouraging American hostility, is to make them feel that they might get the worst of the contest."[43]

It is also significant that Salisbury's initial reaction to American demands during the Venezuela Crisis was to reject them out of hand. Colonial Secretary Joseph Chamberlain agreed.[44] It was not until the second week of January 1896 that the doves in the cabinet overruled Salisbury and the British accommodated the American demand to arbitrate. This outcome

---

[36] Bourne (1967), pp. 251–312.   [37] Zakaria (1998), p. 48.
[38] Newcastle to Monck, private correspondence, January 4, 1862, in Martineau (1908), p. 305.
[39] Elvert (2003), p. 45; Friedberg (1988), p. 293;
[40] Bourne (1967), p. 341; Friedberg (1988), p. 299.
[41] Salisbury to Hicks Beach, January 2, 1896, quoted in Grenville (1955), p. 51.
[42] Marder (1964), p. 256; Bourne (1967), p. 339.
[43] Dufferin and Ava to the Queen, January 1, 1896, in Bourne (1967), p. 341.
[44] Salisbury to Pauncefote, November 26, 1895, in FRUS (1895), Part I, pp. 563–576; Chamberlain to Selborne, December 20, 1895, quoted in Humphreys (1967), p. 156.

was deeply contingent. On December 29, Leander Starr Jameson led a force of British policemen to encourage an insurgency against the Boers in the Transvaal. The Jameson attack failed, and on January 3, Kaiser Wilhelm II cabled a message to Boer President Paul Kruger congratulating him for thwarting the raid. The telegram infuriated the British, and the episode raised fears about instability in South Africa and trouble from Berlin: London could not afford a conflict with the United States in these circumstances. The cabinet met for the first time that year eight days later, and at this meeting Salisbury was overruled. The cabinet voted to open negotiations with the Americans and Venezuelans, and Arthur Balfour voiced full public support for Cleveland's interpretation of the Monroe Doctrine.[45]

While, as Layne suggests, the search for a "smoking gun" is futile, most historians agree that the Jameson Raid and the Kruger telegram – which could just as easily not have happened at that particular time – played a critical role in the cabinet's decision.[46] While geopolitical factors certainly provided good reason for the British to accommodate the United States as a world power, the evidence shows that the decision to do so was more uncertain and contingent than the realist interpretation lets on.

British Status and the Accommodation of the United States

One objection to the contention that British accommodation can be plausibly reimagined is that the British were not giving up much. Their real interests lay elsewhere – in India, in East Asia, in South Africa. This is a misleading depiction of the way the British understood the matter. The rise of the United States threatened London in a way that no other rising power at the time did: the United States was positioned to "usurp Britain as the anointed political leader of the world."[47] In other words, while the rise of Germany or the Franco-Russian combination clearly threatened British interests, the rise of the United States constituted a unique threat to British status. This was the case for two reasons.

First was the United States' sheer size and economic potential. It was obvious to British elites as early as the 1860s that Washington's domination of North America would inevitably lead to a negative shift in the global

---

[45] See Clark (2012), pp. 146–147 on the Kruger Telegram. On the cabinet's decision to accommodate Olney and Cleveland, see Eggert (1974), p. 227; Grenville (1964), pp. 68–69; Boyle (1978), p. 1211.

[46] Layne (1994), p. 25; Humphreys (1967); Gelber (1938), p. 3; Dobson (1978), p. 83; Dobson (1995), p. 20; LaFeber (1963), p. 276; Campbell (1976), p. 212 and (1974), p. 182; Grenville and Young (1966), p. 170.

[47] Bell (2007), p. 239.

status hierarchy unless the British took extraordinary measures. This was one of the most important justifications for the "Greater Britain" project, the attempt to consolidate the British Empire into a coherent state. One proponent worried that if London did not adequately respond to the rise of the United States, "we shall be depressed into a second or third-rate power." Another warned that "If England wishes to maintain the position she has hitherto occupied amongst the nations of the world, she must endeavour to bind together the far-distant portions of her Empire." Only then, argued a third, could the British hope to "in the future stand in a position of equality beside the American Union, or any other great power."[48] The United States, because of its size and rapid economic development, presented a threat to Great Britain's privileged position in the global status hierarchy that was, in some ways, more serious than that posed by any other contemporary power.

Second, the United States made claims to rights in international politics that conflicted with the British understanding of international law and London's role as its defender. This is clear from the response to American assertions about the Monroe Doctrine during the Venezuela Crisis. According to Salisbury:

Mr. Olney's principle that American questions are for American decisions, even if it receive any countenance from the language of President Monroe (which it does not), cannot be sustained by any reasoning drawn from the law of nations. The Government of the United States is not entitled to affirm as a universal proposition, with reference to a number of independent States for whose conduct it assumes no responsibility, that its interests are necessarily concerned in whatever may befall those States, simply because they are situated in the Western Hemisphere.[49]

What Salisbury objected to most strongly was the principle that the United States was entitled to a right that was in conflict with international law, which in turn was both constitutive of and constituted by British leadership. Chamberlain similarly rejected any "unnatural and altogether unprecedented extension" of the Monroe Doctrine, and the foreign secretary (the Earl of Kimberley, who actually supported giving in) understood the significance of backing down as the "recognition of a quasi-U.S. protectorate over the whole of America."[50]

In short, what backing down in Venezuela (and in subsequent accommodations over territorial rights in Alaska and Central America) signified was that the British had shown deference to the United States and

---

[48] All quoted in ibid., p. 239.
[49] Salisbury to Pauncefote, November 26, 1895, in FRUS (1895), Part I, pp. 563–576.
[50] Quoted in Boyle (1978), p. 1210.

acknowledged a dramatic change in both the global status hierarchy and in the rules under which Anglo-American relations would henceforth be conducted. This hardly seemed costless to British leaders at the time.

Anglo-Saxonism, Status, and Decline

This raises an important puzzle: how did the British overcome the status anxiety associated with relative decline and the accommodation of a rising state that they understood would soon overtake them? The simple answer is that geopolitical pressure eventually crowded out or overrode any discomfort that would come from accommodating the United States. This is certainly part of the story. But status concerns can override security concerns or at least inflect and distort policies driven by sound strategic reasoning. In this case, though, British leaders showed very little discomfort at the prospect of ceding status to the United States in the years after 1896. What accounts for this smooth transition?

An important part of the answer is *Anglo-Saxonism*. The claim that the idea of a shared Anglo-American ethnic identity helped facilitate rapprochement is hardly new. What I offer here is a new interpretation of how Anglo-Saxonism mattered. Others have focused on threat perceptions or a normative prohibition against fighting one's kin.[51] These are important elements but they leave out a critical part of the story of Anglo-Saxonism's influence on the Anglo-American power transition: Anglo-Saxonism provided leaders in Great Britain (and in the United States, for that matter) with the social psychological resources necessary to engage in *recategorization*. British leaders were able to identify as members of an Anglo-Saxon civilizational "team" that – along with Americans and other members of the English-speaking world – was competing for status against Teutons, Slavs, and Asians. And, critically, the Anglo-Saxons seemed to be winning because the rising United States was picking up where the British Empire was leaving off. This allowed British leaders to celebrate and derive positive social identity from American achievements.

According to social psychologists, recategorization occurs when an individual in a low status group partially transfers his or her social identity to a group constituted at a higher level of aggregation as a way of alleviating the problem of negative intergroup comparison. One classic example comes from a study on German identities after the end of the Cold War. East Germans perceived that they had lower status in the newly reconstituted Germany than West Germans, and one of the ways that some of them dealt

---

[51] See Buzas (2013); Rock (1989), pp. 24–63; Kupchan (2010), Chapter 3; Vucetic (2011), Chapter 2.

with this problem was by thinking of themselves as simply Germans.[52] Doing so alleviated the social psychological consequences of the negative intra-German social comparison. But recategorization is only open to individuals when a broader identity category is available and salient.

This was one of the roles that Anglo-Saxonism played during the Anglo-American power transition. Although ideas about Anglo-Saxon cultural and institutional distinctiveness predate the late nineteenth century, Anglo-Saxonism as an ideology of racial superiority did not emerge until after a mid-century shift in the Anglo-American intellectual climate toward a particular form of pseudo-scientific racialism.[53] The new Anglo-Saxonism tied natural selection to a hierarchy of races and "blood units:" – it divided the world not only into states but also into language and ethnic groups.[54] And these distinctions were commonly linked to ideas about foreign policy – it is notable that the modern field of international relations originated in the study of global race relations during this period.[55] Racial categories, in short, provided a means of organizing international politics during the late nineteenth and early twentieth centuries.

The existence and salience of racial categories is part of the explanation for British accommodation of the United States. Leaders on both sides of the Atlantic spoke and seem to have thought in ways that indicate that they understood themselves as members of a common Anglo-Saxon civilizational entity competing for status against other civilizational entities. American elites like Theodore Roosevelt, Alfred Thayer Mahan, Andrew Carnegie, and Richard Olney; and British elites like Joseph Chamberlain, Arthur Balfour, and Cecil Spring-Rice made frequent reference to "race patriotism" and seem to have derived positive social identity from comparisons of Anglo-Saxon achievements against the achievements of Slavs and others.[56]

This was particularly important for the British because it allowed them to celebrate American achievements as Anglo-Saxon achievements. During the Venezuela Crisis, British elites issued a memorial calling for peace, noting that Anglo-Saxons had, "we trust, such a future as no other race has yet had in the history of the world" and asking Americans to "join us in helping to protect that future."[57] In 1898, as the United States and Spain

---

[52] Mummenedy et al. (1999); see also Blanz et al. (1998); Crisp et al. (2006); Eller and Abrams (2004); Gaertner and Dovidio (2005) Hornsey and Hogg (2000).

[53] See Vucetic (2011), Kindle locations 574–613; Campbell (2007), pp. 158–159; Stuart Anderson (1981), Chapters 1 and 2; and Rock (1989), pp. 49–50.

[54] Anderson (1981), Chapter 1.   [55] See Vitalis (2010, 2015) on this point.

[56] See, for instance Roosevelt to Spring Rice, December 2, 1899, in Gwynn (1929), vol. 1, p. 307; Mahan to Thursfield, January 19, 1896, in Seager and Maguire (1975), vol. 2, p. 442; Anderson (1981), p. 85; Charles Campbell (1957), p. 10.

[57] Quoted in Anderson (1981), p. 98.

headed for war, the *London Daily Chronicle* lamented the sinking of the Maine because Americans were "'on our side' in the great game of the world."[58] After the American naval victory in Manila, the *Spectator* celebrated: "We rejoice in the efficiency of the American representative of our race, because we believe that, failing the Anglo-Saxon, the wronged of the world will find no defenders; we exult in his skill, his preparedness, his daring." In the next breath, the publication expressed a fervent desire that the Americans would "keep the Philippines," develop a "position in the world equal to their position among nations," and "give up their idea of non-intervention." The reason was that the British needed help "civilizing" the world. Great Britain "cannot undertake to govern the whole dark world," and "it would be a relief if another English-speaking Power would take up a portion of our task." [59] Anderson, following Geoffrey Seed, goes so far as to claim that "the most powerful incentive among the British populace toward support of American imperialism was the assumption of Anglo-American racial affinity."[60]

And it was not just in the media that Anglo-Saxon unity allayed British concerns about the rise of the United States. British elites expressed in private correspondence sentiments that are consistent with the interpretation of Anglo-Saxonism's influence proposed here. Cecil Spring Rice, a longtime British diplomat and close friend of Theodore Roosevelt, understood the world largely in ethno-racial terms. He had resigned himself to the decline of British power, but was heartened by the belief that the United States was "the real fortress of our race."[61] In 1904, he wrote to Roosevelt that "whatever happens to the old establishment there is a new branch on a larger scale, which no Emperor, however splendid, can do any harm to."[62] According to Anderson, "the contemplation of America's growing strength gave [Spring Rice] much satisfaction."[63] Spring Rice was not alone. Arthur Balfour and Joseph Chamberlain – both Conservative nationalists and imperialists – were also noted "race patriots."[64]

This is not to say that Anglo-Saxonism was the *impetus* for accommodation. Accommodation made good sense given the circumstances that faced Great Britain, especially in January 1896. But Anglo-Saxonism *facilitated* continued accommodation afterwards by making it easier to give up status and position to the United States. After all, the rise of the

---

[58] Quoted in Campbell (1957), p. 28.
[59] "The Capture of Manila," and "The Fate of the Philippines," *The Spectator* (May 7, 1898), pp. 645–646.
[60] Anderson (1981), p. 126.
[61] Spring Rice to Henry Cabot Lodge, March 25, 1904, in Gwynn (1929), vol. 1, p. 407.
[62] Spring Rice to Roosevelt, March 1904, in Gwynn (1929), vol. 1, pp. 396–397.
[63] Anderson (1981), p. 93.
[64] See Young (1934), pp. 277–284 and Vucetic (2011), Kindle location 639.

United States meant that, as Roosevelt reassured Spring Rice, "the twentieth century will still be the century of the men who speak English."[65]

The Counterfactual: What If the British Had Stood Firm in January 1896?

The remainder of this chapter uses counterfactual analysis to show that it is not difficult to imagine American foreign policy developing a much more anti-British tone if London had not accommodated American claims in 1896 and after. This is the most appropriate way of assessing the role of the dynamics highlighted by status immobility theory in a case of accommodation. Establishing the potential significance of a set of processes that did *not* operate cannot be done directly; instead it must be done by imagining a plausible alternative world in which they *did* operate and exploring their possible consequences.

While counterfactual analysis may seem like a questionable tool, it is at least implicit whenever a social scientist makes a causal claim.[66] Rather than eschewing counterfactual analysis, scholars should embrace it while ensuring that explicit counterfactuals meet criteria that maximize their utility. First, users should be clear about what is to be explained (the "consequent") and what historical alteration is meant to account for the change (the "antecedent"). Second, users should specify the "connecting principles" or mechanisms by which the antecedent brings about the consequent, and ensure that these are consistent with history and established theoretical understandings about how the social world works. Third, counterfactuals should be based on plausible, minimal alterations to the historical record so that the effects of the antecedent can be identified as cleanly as possible.[67]

In the analysis that follows, I show that a British refusal to accommodate American status claims in 1895–1896 (the antecedent) is easy to imagine by making a minimal, plausible rewrite of that winter's history. This could have resulted in an American foreign policy (the consequent) that more vigorously challenged British dominance and London's efforts to defend the status quo order over the subsequent decades. This might have manifested itself in American opposition to British policy during the Second Boer War and during the period leading up to and following World War I. The "connecting principles" or mechanisms are those at the heart of status immobility theory – status denial might have led to

---

[65] Roosevelt to Spring Rice, March 16, 1901, in Gwynn (1929), vol. 1, pp. 344–345.
[66] See Tetlock and Belkin (1996), p. 6; Lebow (2010a), p. 31; Fearon (1991), p. 180.
[67] Lebow (2010a), pp. 54–56; Tetlock and Belkin (1996), pp. 19–25; see also Grynaviski (2013).

increases in anti-British sentiment and made pro-British policies impossible to sustain. Previous chapters have demonstrated that these mechanisms operated in other cases, and I show here that conditions were ripe for their operation in the United States as well.

Minimal, Plausible Rewrite: Erasing the Jameson Raid

It is relatively easy to imagine an alternate version of the events of winter 1895–1896 in which the British cabinet follows Salisbury's line and stands firm against Washington's demands. Recall from the previous section that Salisbury's initial response was to reject the interpretation of the Monroe Doctrine relayed in the Olney note. But in the wake of an acute degradation in Great Britain's strategic position between December 17 and January 11, the cabinet decided to accommodate American demands. This had to do with the timing and result of the Jameson Raid in South Africa and the German reaction to it. But what if the Jameson Raid had been delayed or postponed indefinitely? This is not difficult to imagine. Jameson's plot could have been blocked by any number of plausible factors, including action by the British colonial office or the government of the Cape Colony, or a change in Jameson's health or state of mind.[68]

Andrew Roberts imagines just such a scenario in his counterfactual analysis of the Venezuela Crisis. While Roberts suggests that the absence of the Kruger telegram might have led to war between the United States and Great Britain, it is not necessary to go this far.[69] For the purposes of this chapter, it is enough to imagine a plausible scenario in which Salisbury and Chamberlain got their way in the January 11 cabinet meeting, and the British maintained their opposition to Olney's version of the Monroe Doctrine. How might US foreign policy over the next two decades have been different under these circumstances?

Alternatives to the Great Rapprochement

The first section of this chapter established that American elites and the public cared about the rising nation's status and saw the Venezuela Crisis as a test of London's willingness to accommodate American claims to the right to a sphere of influence in the Western Hemisphere. The fury at Salisbury's initial dismissal of Olney's note – even if accompanied by an unwillingness to ultimately risk war over the issue – suggests that

---

[68] In fact, Cecil Rhodes had a few days earlier decided against any immediate action in Transvaal. See Garrett (1897), p. 83.

[69] Roberts (2003), p. 168.

a different decision by the British cabinet in January could have produced a significant increase in public and elite resentment against London, as Roosevelt feared that it would. But could this have caused a discernible shift in American foreign policy's orientation toward the British Empire?

Evidence from the *actual* course of the Anglo-American rapprochement suggests that it could have. This is so both because anti-British opinion had a significant influence on foreign policy, and because alternatives to rapprochement remained conceivable at least through the end of World War I.

Rapprochement – beginning with London's Venezuela retreat and culminating in the eventual formation of the "special relationship" in the first half of the twentieth century – is remarkable to scholars of international relations because it emerged out of a century of rivalry.[70] Great Britain and the United States were hardly destined to be friendly – in fact, they seemed from some perspectives "almost destined to be enemies."[71] This was not only because their interests clashed (as detailed in the previous section), but also because of a deep Anglophobia that had characterized American public opinion since the early days of the republic.

As American leaders sought to improve relations with the British after their Civil War–era deterioration, public and elite resentment against Great Britain was a serious obstacle and remained so through the first decades of the twentieth century. During the years after the Civil War ended, for instance, American and British diplomats negotiated over the so-called *Alabama* claims, which arose from London's facilitation of Confederate ship construction during the war. At the end of the Johnson administration, William Henry Seward attempted a settlement in the form of the Johnson-Clarendon Convention, which would have submitted outstanding claims from the Civil War to a mixed commission. The Senate rejected the convention 54–1 because, according to Charles Campbell, it was inconsistent with the "vindictive American attitude after the Civil War."[72] Massachusetts Republican Charles Sumner resented the convention:

The massive grievance under which our country suffered for years is left untouched; the painful sense of wrong planted in the national heart is allowed to remain. For all this there is not one word of regret or even of recognition; nor is there any semblance of compensation.[73]

Even after the *Alabama* claims were settled (favorably for the United States) under President Grant, "there remained resentment ... and accusations were leveled that 'Unconditional Surrender' Grant had capitulated to

---

[70] Kupchan (2010), Chapter 3; Rock (1989), pp. 31–35.   [71] Rock (1989), p. 31.
[72] Charles Campbell (1974), pp. 113–114.   [73] Charles Sumner (1869), p. 21.

the British."[74] According to D.A. Campbell, this sort of anti-British vitriol was a common obstacle for leaders working toward warmer relations.[75]

In 1888, the first Cleveland administration negotiated the Bayard-Chamberlain Treaty, which regulated American fishing rights in Canadian waters. The Gloucester Board of Trade (an American fishing interest group) rejected the treaty as "detrimental to the interests of the United States as a people, and injurious to its honor and dignity as a nation," and the Senate killed it 30–27.[76] In response Cleveland, now worried about being seen as too pro-British, suggested that Congress retaliate by imposing restrictions on the duty free transit of goods between the United States and Canada.[77] Seven years later, during the second Cleveland administration, the United States and Great Britain nearly came to blows over the border between Venezuela and British Guiana, in part because Cleveland needed to satisfy anti-British public and elite sentiment. Five years after the Venezuela Crisis, the McKinley administration concluded the Hay-Pauncefote Treaty with London, which allowed the United States to build a canal through Central America. The treaty was favorable to Washington, but it banned fortifications in the canal zone, and thus provoked a "storm of disapproval" because, as Dobson notes, "the self-assertive American people seldom concealed their indignation over anything they could construe as an affront to their nation's prestige, and this treaty virtually dictated what the United States could and could not do."[78] The Senate rejected the treaty, Hay and Pauncefote went back to the negotiating table, and a year later the British caved once again.

American opinion was clearly engaged, attentive to British slights, and capable of influencing foreign policy. The last task that remains is to show that stronger anti-British resentment – as might have arisen without British accommodation – could have had concrete effects at specific junctures during which historical US policy turned in London's favor but could have gone in the other direction. I focus on two such junctures.

The first is the Second Boer War, which began in 1899. American public opinion was generally pro-Boer, yet the United States – alone among the great powers – maintained a fundamentally if unofficially pro-British orientation.[79] The McKinley and Roosevelt administrations made no attempt to deny the British access to credit or resources. In fact, the British financed about twenty percent of their war-effort with American

---

[74] D.A. Campbell (2007), p. 187.   [75] Ibid., p. 187.
[76] Quoted in Charles Campbell (1974), pp. 159–160.   [77] Ibid., p. 161.
[78] John Dobson (1978), p. 153.
[79] Perkins (1968), pp. 90–93; Beisner (1975), p. 125; Charles Campbell (1974), p. 195; Dobson (1995), p. 23; Gelber (1938), p. 71.

credit.[80] Of course, there were good reasons – both strategic and economic – for the United States to support London between 1899 and 1902. But solid strategic logic does not always prevent states from abandoning conciliatory policies, as Chapters 3, 4, and 5 demonstrated. The point is simply that the Second Boer War constitutes a juncture during which deeper public and elite anti-British resentment might have produced a concretely more confrontational foreign policy.

A similar juncture is the early part of World War I. While today it seems unthinkable that the United States might have opposed the British during the war, there was significant Anglo-American conflict between 1914 and early 1917. When the war began, President Wilson did not agree with the Allied perspective that Germany had to be crushed. To Wilson, the best outcome was a draw: postwar Europe would be most stable if the great powers fought each other to a standstill and neither side were able to impose an "unjust peace."[81] Wilson maintained the commitment to settlement through the beginning of 1917, and the Allied pursuit of total victory caused substantial Anglo-American friction. Americans resented British attempts to stop them from trading with Germany, and the British worried that Wilson would use economic leverage to force London to make peace. In late November 1916 – apparently at Wilson's behest – the Federal Reserve Board did just that by warning American investors to avoid foreign short-term debt, which, predictably, caused the value of Allied war bonds to tank.[82] By that point, Anglo-American tension had developed to the extent that armed conflict – while never likely – became conceivable for leaders on both sides of the Atlantic. Wilson told Edward House on November 15 that "if the Allies wanted war with us we would not shrink from it," and the British General Staff warned the incoming Lloyd George government about "the possibility of trouble arising with the United States."[83]

In the end, Germany's resumption of unrestricted submarine warfare in January and the publication of the Zimmerman telegram in March ended the possibility of any further Anglo-American conflict. But Anglo-American rapprochement was more fragile than it often appears in retrospect, even as late as the winter of 1916. It is not implausible that a British failure to accommodate American status claims in 1895–1896 could have resulted in a political environment in which more aggressive anti-British

[80] Ferguson (1939), p. ix; Perkins (1968), p. 95.
[81] Woodward (1993), p. 9; Cooper (2009), p. 276.
[82] Woodward (1993), pp. 22–28; Burk (1985), pp. 80–88.
[83] Wilson quoted in Doenecke (2011), p. 223; General Staff warning quoted in Yearwood (2009), p. 35.

measures (or just an earlier, more vigorous application) might have seemed natural or politically expedient.

Conclusion

The counterfactual analysis presented above has a limited but important purpose. It cannot establish that the United States rose to power without frontally challenging British global hegemony or the rules, norms, and institutions of the status quo order *because* the British accommodated American status claims. The eventual pro-British orientation of American foreign policy made good sense for military and economic reasons. The United States had no real reason to challenge the Pax Britannica, and American leaders understood the advantages that the United States derived from British dominance.

But strategic expediency is an incomplete explanation for the development of the Anglo-American rapprochement. Rising states *normally* have incentives to avoid directly challenging the dominant state in the system, and yet they sometimes violate that logic. This book's central argument is that status immobility can function as an obstacle to the pursuit of pragmatic, cautious policies. Chapters 3, 4, and 5 provided direct evidence that it had this effect in three positive cases. This chapter, by contrast, has shown that status immobility *could have* worked similarly in the United States around the turn of the twentieth century. Elites and the public cared about international status; elite and public frustration and resentment toward Great Britain (which was linked to disrespect) had in the past influenced policy; and more provocative alternatives to rapprochement remained conceivable through at least 1917. In the absence of British accommodation – which was more contingent than it often seems – it is not difficult to imagine perceived status denial being translated into dissatisfaction with the British-dominated status quo order and from there into pressure for anti-British policies.

Other factors mattered as well – strategic and economic concerns play an indispensable role in explaining the relative smoothness of the Anglo-American power transition. Yet they do not tell the whole story on either side of the Atlantic. Both sides suffered from status anxiety, and status anxiety has the potential to influence foreign policy in disruptive ways. That it did not in this case means that its influence was less visible – but no less important – than in the previous cases. Viewed through the lens of status immobility theory, the story of the rise of the United States is the tale of a dog that could have barked louder than it did.

7 Status, Order, and the Rise of China

The rise of China raises with urgency the question at the center of this book: will China try to delegitimate, overthrow, and replace the contemporary status quo order? This is the $64,000 question of international relations and American grand strategy. Much rides on the answer, and not just for the prospects of direct Sino-American military conflict. As Thomas Christensen has argued, the central challenge associated with the rise of China is securing its cooperation in shouldering the burdens of global governance.[1] This requires getting Chinese leaders to buy into – or at least not reject – the status quo order, along with its rules, norms, and institutions. A China committed to protesting, undermining, and ultimately overthrowing and replacing the US-backed order will hardly be willing to help the United States manage problems like climate change or non-proliferation.

Many analysts – whom I refer to as "rejectionists" – believe that China is destined to challenge the order that the United States built after World War II and has maintained in some form since. For them, there are two options for Washington: become resigned to the demise of what Ikenberry calls the "liberal international order," or prepare to contain the rise of China at great cost and the risk of serious conflict. For others – whom I label "integrationists" – options are less limited and the future is less gloomy: China can be persuaded that the status quo serves its interests and that it should become a defender – not a challenger – of the order's rules, norms, and institutions.

Both rejectionists and integrationists err by ignoring the ways in which status ambitions may matter for China's trajectory. Rejectionists go too far in arguing that a Chinese challenge to the status quo is inevitable. They base this claim on the records of the behavior of rising great powers from history, but my analysis in Chapters 3, 4, and 5 has shown that shifts toward radical revisionism were not structurally determined. In none of these cases was there a consensus about the wisdom of challenging the status quo order, and in each case the ultimate domination of the hardline perspective was to some

---

[1] Christensen (2015), p. 288.

degree a function of the nature of beliefs about the prospects of the rising power's status ambitions, which were in turn influenced by at least partially contingent factors like decisions made by domestic elites, the behavior of foreign actors, and the consequences of exogenous crises.

The integrationists, on the other hand, place too much faith in the idea that integration within the liberal order is in China's material self-interest. As a result they understate the difficulty of keeping China satisfied with the status quo. It is true that China profits from the open economic order that the United States underwrites, that it benefits by free-riding on the other public goods that American hegemony provides, and that its leaders understand how costly a war with the United States might be. Moderate leaders in Wilhelmine Germany, Imperial Japan, and Weimar Germany also appreciated the material benefits of *not* challenging the status quo orders within which their respective states rose to power. The material benefits of patience and integration were outweighed, in these cases, by a set of forces that have mostly been left out of analyses of China's trajectory: the social psychological and political consequences of beliefs about the compatibility of its status ambitions and the liberal order.

The purpose of this chapter is to demonstrate that these same forces are critical for understanding the future of Chinese foreign policy, and thus the future fate of the international order. China – like other rising states – has outstanding status ambitions. As is always the case when status is involved, these ambitions can only be satisfied if they are recognized. And this means that there is a possibility that influential Chinese observers may come to the conclusion that China's status ambitions have been unjustly obstructed and are incompatible with the US-backed order. Obstructed status ambitions might in turn lead to demands for policies that aim to protest, delegitimate, or overthrow elements of the status quo order, and these – if they are resonant and widespread enough – could influence Chinese foreign policy as they did in the German and Japanese cases from the first half of the twentieth century. In short, Western accommodation failure could produce forces that push China toward policies that reject and challenge the norms, rules, and institutions of the liberal international order.[2]

---

[2] This argument is similar in some ways to that made by other analysts of status in world politics. Larson and Shevchenko (2010; 2014a), for instance, have warned that China may adopt a geopolitically competitive form of status-seeking if it is persistently denied recognition (see also Wolf 2014 and Lee 2016). The problem with this claim is that China is *already* pursuing geopolitically competitive policies – like naval arms-racing – as part of a drive for status; and my analysis in the previous chapters suggests that geopolitical competition is neither the consequence of persistent status denial nor a necessarily destabilizing phenomenon. Rather, the danger raised by the prospect of status immobility is

My intention in making this argument is not to advocate that the United States accommodate Chinese status claims. Depending on what these are, accommodating them could be prohibitively costly. But the debate over whether or not to accommodate China should consider not only the costs of accommodation but also the costs of status denial, and these include the possibility of an adverse shift in China's orientation toward the status quo order. I return to the implications of my argument for US grand strategy in the concluding chapter.

This chapter proceeds in three parts. First, I describe the parameters of the "liberal international order," imagine what a Chinese shift toward rejecting and challenging the status quo order might look like, and briefly review the debate over the trajectory of Chinese foreign policy. Second, I establish that China has outstanding status ambitions and delineate the specific rights that China seeks to have recognized. This section also explores the question of why the West might fail to accommodate Beijing's claims. Third, I argue that accommodation failure could produce demands for policies that reject and challenge the status quo order (indeed, some Chinese elites already make these kinds of demands), and that these demands could influence foreign policy.

The Liberal Order and the Rise of China

The most obvious feature of the status quo order that confronts the rising China is American dominance. While China's economy has grown rapidly over the past two and a half decades and Chinese military capabilities have advanced, the United States maintains a marked advantage in economic productivity, innovation, and wealth, has by far the world's most powerful military, and remains the only state with global power projection capabilities. The United States also maintains status and influence advantages by virtue of its central positions in security, political, and economic institutions. These are the distributive elements of the status quo order, and Chinese foreign policy is currently oriented toward narrowing many of these gaps.[3]

One of the most important questions at the heart of the debate over the rise of China is whether China's advance along these distributive dimensions (increases in power, wealth, and influence) will lead to an effort to

that China will adopt a *radically revisionist* foreign policy orientation – that it will oppose and seek to undo the liberal order, instead of working to increase its standing (and influence) inside of it. This would not only hamper attempts at joint Sino-American global governance, but could also contribute to the rise of a less restrained belligerence in Chinese foreign policy.

[3] On the robustness of American primacy, see Beckley (2011) and Brooks and Wohlforth (2015, 2016).

overthrow the normative elements of the status quo. These elements are the rules, norms, and institutions that constitute what Ikenberry has termed the "liberal international order."[4] In the years after World War II, the United States constructed a matrix of institutions whose purpose was to bind the United States to its allies and facilitate cooperation in the realms of security, politics, and economics. This order has persisted and evolved in the subsequent decades and consists now of formal and informal institutions, rules, and norms that constitute actors, help states to legitimate collective action, and regulate behavior. The liberal order is made up of formal institutions like the United Nations, the World Trade Organization, the World Bank, and the International Monetary Fund; less formal institutions like the G7; norms and principles that relate legitimacy to standards of representation and human rights; and rules about, for instance, what kinds of states can legitimately possess nuclear weapons.

There are three key characteristics of the liberal international order. The first is that it is aimed at maintaining open and rule-based relations between states as a way of maximizing the benefits of economic interaction, minimizing the risk of major conflict, and reducing fears about American adventurism. The second is that – at least in the post-Cold War era – it is purportedly universal. The liberal international order is not geographically bounded, although the extent to which it is effective varies geographically. The third is that it is underwritten by American leadership: the United States provides a number of public goods in both the economic and security spheres from whose consumption other states benefit. For instance, the US dollar provides a global reserve currency, and American military power facilitates the free flow of resources and commerce.

China currently participates more or less fully in these institutions, but scholars disagree about whether its rise will mean the end of the liberal international order. China could buy into the order's rules, norms, and institutions; its rise would accordingly change the order's distributive dimension but strengthen and reinforce (while perhaps reforming) its normative foundation. There would still be Sino-American competition over power, influence, and status, but it would be constrained by a common commitment to the rules of the international security, economic, and political games. This was, by and large, the outcome of the Anglo-American power transition.

Alternatively, China could pursue policies aimed at weakening and overthrowing the liberal international order.[5] This might entail open rule-

---

[4] See Ikenberry (2011).

[5] For discussions of what this might look like, see Ikenberry (2011), pp. 309–312 and Kupchan (2012), pp. 199–202.

breaking for the purpose of protesting or delegitimating the rules and norms of the liberal order; the construction of parallel institutions and groupings of states aimed at opposing the Western order; and (as difficult as it might be to imagine) withdrawal from the institutions of the liberal order.[6] An anti-liberal order foreign policy would be unlikely to involve an explicit commitment to military confrontation against the United States (especially given the dynamics of nuclear deterrence), but the pursuit of policies aimed at protest, delegitimation, and overthrow would contribute to Sino-American rivalry and could encourage leaders in Beijing to pursue other kinds of provocative policies (by lowering their costs and undercutting arguments against provocation). These might in turn raise the risk of Sino-American conflict.

The question of which of these paths China will choose is the subject of a lively debate among IR scholars. Rejectionists think there is little chance that China will integrate within the liberal international order. One strand of rejectionist reasoning emphasizes the supposed timeless dynamics of power transitions – rising states always seek more power, more influence, and more status, and they are not satisfied until they have achieved at least regional hegemony and reconstituted the international order on their own terms. This, for rejectionists, is the lesson of 1914.[7] Another strand of rejectionist thought emphasizes civilizational or ideological differences between China and the founders of the liberal international order. As China grows more powerful, it will seek to create an order that reflects its civilizational values, domestic political ideology, and conception of its proper role in the world.[8] This, for rejectionists, is one of the lessons of the fascist rising powers of interwar Europe and Asia.[9]

Integrationists, on the other hand, think that China can be persuaded that its interests lie in the persistence of the liberal international order. China benefits from the order's open, market-based economic system. The institutions of the liberal order are also, according to Ikenberry, open to accommodating the voice and ambitions of a rising power in a way that makes the Sino-American power transition unlike those from the first half of the twentieth century.[10] Moreover, challenging the order would entail significant costs stemming from the provocation of Western powers. Chinese leaders understand this, which is why, since the time of Deng

---

[6] See Pillsbury (2015), Chapter 9 for a full discussion.

[7] See especially Mearsheimer (2010); Kagan (2005); see also Betts (1994); Friedberg (1994, 2000, 2011); Bernstein and Munro (1997).

[8] See especially Pillsbury (2015), Chapter 1; Kupchan (2014a), p. 224; and Jacques (2009) p. 528.

[9] Kupchan (2014b), p. 26.

[10] Ikenberry (2011), pp. 343–345; see also Ikenberry and Wright (2008).

Xiaoping, they have sought to avoid giving the impression that China is a dissatisfied rising power.[11] Thus, if the United States can find ways to reassure China that the status quo order serves its interests (by, for instance, compromising on the status of Taiwan or taking greater account of the challenges China faces as a relatively poor, developing economy), China can be kept reasonably satisfied and perhaps even turned into a partner.[12]

Each of these perspectives captures an important piece of the picture. Rejectionists are right to emphasize the difficulty of accommodating a rising power within an order that it did not construct. Yet they neglect the role of politics and contingency in the stories of the twentieth-century revisionist rising powers, exaggerate the degree to which rising power necessarily drives deep dissatisfaction, and ignore the actual processes through which hardline preferences develop and influence decisionmaking. What this means is that the rejectionists are too pessimistic: a Chinese challenge to the liberal international order is no more inevitable from the perspective of 2017 than were the rise of Hitler or Japan's withdrawal from the League of Nations from the perspective of 1920.

The integrationists, though, are too optimistic. They are right to emphasize the material incentives that China faces to integrate within the liberal international order. But they miss other forces that might push Beijing toward radical revisionism. Each of the twentieth-century revisionists also had material incentives to behave moderately, and there were German and Japanese leaders that understood these incentives and wanted policy to reflect them. Yet in each case, moderate policies were defeated by hardline policies in part because of the social psychological and political consequences of status immobility – forces that are absent from optimistic integrationist analyses.[13]

Status Anxiety and the Rise of China

The remainder of this chapter contributes to the debate about the rise of China and the future of the liberal international order by exploring the implications of status immobility theory for the Sino-American power transition. Status immobility should not be understood as competing with the dynamics emphasized by extant rejectionist and integrationist

---

[11] Shambaugh and Xiao (2012), Kindle location 877. On China's "peaceful rise," see Zheng (2011), Chapter 6; and Guo (2006), Chapter 1.

[12] See, for instance, Glaser (2015), Goldstein (2015), Christensen (2015).

[13] Glaser (2015), p. 64, for instance, acknowledges that non-security motives are outside the bounds of his analysis, which, as a result, misses a critical potential obstacle to a Sino-American "grand bargain."

accounts, but instead as highlighting a commonly ignored set of forces that need to be taken on board by both. In particular, I argue that demands that Chinese foreign policy reject and challenge the liberal international order – which are already common among some Chinese elites – might become more resonant and widespread if the United States fails to accommodate China's status ambitions and signals that these are incompatible with the status quo. This could, in turn, influence policy by pressuring the more moderate elites who currently control the government.

This section has two purposes. First, I argue that China has outstanding status ambitions, and that its foreign policy is currently aimed – in part – at satisfying them. Chinese elites and the public care deeply about international respect, and this concern influences the way China behaves externally. Chinese policy appears to be staking a claim to "great power" status, the satisfaction of which requires behavior by the United States that signals that China has two particular rights: to a sphere of influence in East Asia, and to freedom from external interference in its domestic affairs. In other words, China is currently pursuing distributive revisionism aimed at adjusting the distribution of status in the system in its favor. Second, I explore potential obstacles to the accommodation of these claims by the United States. The upshot is that – contrary to the assessment of the integrationists – it is quite easy to imagine American foreign policy failing to accommodate Chinese status claims.

The Rise of China and the Rights of a Great Power

In two respects, China's current foreign policy bears a striking resemblance to Japan's Shidehara diplomacy and Germany's Locarno diplomacy. First, it is concerned with avoiding provocation and working within the extant international order to improve China's position. Second, it is aimed at enhancing China's status in the world. That status anxiety is one of the most salient features of Chinese foreign policy is widely supported by recent scholarship. One observer suggests that "China's status sensitivity appears unparalleled."[14] International social status (*Guoji Diwei*) has been a prominent part of Chinese foreign policy discourse since the middle of the 1990s, and leaders often treat it "as if it were the most desirable value, the one that leads to power, security, and respect."[15]

---

[14] Deng (2008), p. 9; see also Wolf (2014), p. 207; and Xuetong (2001).
[15] Deng (2008), p. 8.

And it is not just that leaders value status. A range of scholars notes that the Chinese public (at least the politically engaged portion of it) is watching and cares about China's standing.[16] According to Chinese IR scholar Yan Xuetong (in 2001), "most Chinese people merely hope that their nation can grow to be as rich as the United States and can secure proper respect in the international community."[17] Recent opinion surveys have shown that large numbers of politically active Chinese hope for at least "shared leadership" in the international system. According to one 2012 study, strong majorities of Chinese believe that the United States and important Asian allies like India, Vietnam, and Japan do not respect China and that "China is not receiving the due treatment it deserves on the international stage."[18] Another used experimental methods to demonstrate that "perceived humiliation threat" is a more important driver of Chinese attitudes about policy toward the United States than "perceived military threat."[19]

The status that China is seeking is somewhat ambiguous, but seems to be a particular understanding of membership in a "legitimate" great power club in which members – including the United States – have equal standing. Status-seeking is implicated in a variety of concrete policies, including China's accession to international organizations, its drive to host the Olympics, its participation in UN peacekeeping missions, and its pursuit of a fleet of aircraft carriers.[20] While one might argue that China has already achieved great power status (in light of its permanent seat on the UN Security Council), Beijing does not agree. In July 2010, in response to a series of Sino-American crises in which US behavior violated what Chinese elites apparently understand as appropriate standards of great power interaction, the *People's Daily* – a mouthpiece for the Communist Party of China – asked: "Is the United States ready to recognize China as a power on the world stage?"[21]

As is the case whenever a state seeks status, satisfaction comes not primarily from achieving status markers but rather from recognition. It is clear that Chinese leaders and the Chinese public do not believe that their claims have been adequately recognized. What recognition of great power status means to China today is somewhat uncertain, in part because Chinese leaders have often seemed hesitant to openly discuss

---

[16] Wolf (2014), pp. 207–209; Xuetong (2001); Shambaugh (2013), Chapters 2 and 3; Gries (2005a).

[17] Xuetong (2001), p. 36.   [18] Jung (2012), p. 14; see also Wolf (2014), fn. 74.

[19] Gries et al. (2011), p. 17.

[20] Deng (2008), p. 35; see also Larson and Shevchenko (2010); Goldstein (2005); Zhang and Tang (2005). On the Beijing Olympics, see Xu (2006); on the *Varyag*, see Ross (2009) and Pu and Schweller (2014).

[21] Zhong (2010).

specifics.[22] However, understanding great power status as carrying with it a bundle of rights and privileges yields some insight. Recognizing China's claim to great power status today would require the United States and others to acknowledge China's heightened position by 1) behaving in ways that seem to grant that China can take actions that are appropriate and legitimate for great powers to take; and 2) not behaving in ways that communicate that China does not have the same rights as other great powers.[23]

But what, exactly, are the rights that China claims? In 2012, then Vice President Xi Jinping introduced the concept of the "New Type of Great Power Relations" as a framework for reforming the Sino-American relationship.[24] This is the clearest indication yet that part of what China wants is recognition and respect, and provides important clues about the concrete rights that Beijing claims. According to one analyst, the point of the diplomatic effort is to convince "the American president to recognize that China is dramatically rising in military and economic ways," which will allow China to be "nicer" in a "very tense situation."[25] Cheng Li and Lucy Xu suggest that "China wants to be viewed as an equal. By using the term 'Great Power' to primarily, if not solely, refer to China and the United States, China aims to elevate itself to a level playing field."[26] Part of the reason for seeking recognition of equal status is domestic: "By strengthening China's view of itself as a recognized and respected power, Xi Jinping is able to foster stronger nationalistic pride under CCP leadership and gain political capital to consolidate his own power at home."[27]

Respect as an equal and recognition as a great power seem to refer to two related rights: an acknowledged geographical sphere of influence, and a set of interests that other states agree not to threaten.[28] At the center of Xi's proposal is the idea that China and the United States should respect each other's "core interests." Read in combination with previous assertions of the nature of China's core interests, this means, in more concrete terms, that China is demanding that the United States recognize a Chinese sphere of influence in East Asia (likely including the South

---

[22] Deng (2008), p. 13.

[23] On great power status as a bundle of rights and privileges, see Bull (1977), p. 196; Suzuki (2008), p. 47; Simpson (2004), pp. 68–71.

[24] See Lampton (2013) for a discussion.   [25] Perez (2013).   [26] Li and Xu (2014).

[27] Ibid.

[28] This is consistent with the English School's definition of "great power." For Bull (1977), two of the privileges that great powers have are 1) the "unilateral exercise of preponderance in particular areas of the world or among particular groups of states" (p. 207); and 2) the establishment of "spheres of influence, interest, or responsibility" (p. 212); see also Simpson (2004), pp. 70–71; and Heimann (2014).

China Sea), and make a commitment to respect China's sovereignty by dialing back the pressure on Chinese human rights abuses.[29]

There are, of course, other reasons for Chinese leaders to harbor these ambitions. Their demands may not be entirely or even primarily *driven* by status concerns. What matters is that – whatever the primary motivation – these demands *engage* status concerns because of the way that Chinese elites understand and talk about them. The official Chinese line is that the "New Type of Great Power Relations" is not about power maximization, but rather about "the principle of treating each other as equals," and constructing a relationship in which "neither side should see itself above the other side."[30] This means that these specific issues may come to be seen in China as tests of Washington's willingness to recognize Chinese claims to equal status, in the same way that the British response to the Morocco crises of 1905 and 1911 or the Western response to the Mukden Incident were seen as tests of British and American willingness to recognize German and Japanese status claims. This, in turn, raises the possibility that a failure to accommodate Chinese claims could produce forces similar to those that operated in the twentieth-century revisionists.

Why the West Might Not Accommodate China

But the liberal international order, according to the integrationists, is uniquely suited to accommodating the rise of new great powers. The open, rule-based order provides opportunities for Chinese status and influence over the governance of the system to be increased without destabilizing the order itself. This is true, and it is also true that declining powers do not invariably oppose rising challengers.

Still, the West's ability and inclination to accommodate Chinese status claims are more uncertain than the integrationists let on. This is partly because – to the extent that great power status involves a right to a sphere of influence – Chinese claims are unlikely to be fully satisfied by, for instance, increasing China's vote share in the IMF. But it is also because of the overlapping obstacles that often prevent status accommodation. The prospects for status accommodation of China by the United States face four distinct kinds of obstacles.

First, status accommodation of the rising power might conflict with the security interests of the declining power. This is not always true – many

---

[29] Mancinelli (2014), p. 15. On the claim that part of what China is demanding (or is likely to demand in the future) is a sphere of influence in East Asia, see Tiezzi (2014); Kupchan (2012), p. 200; Schweller (2014), Kindle location 1459; and Friedberg (2015), p. 143. On Chinese sensitivity to human rights rhetoric, see Carlson (2005), p. 239.

[30] Tankai and Hanzhao (2012), Section III.

British leaders did not think accommodating American status claims conflicted with the British Empire's vital security interests; and the Western powers could have done much more than they did to accommodate Japanese status claims without undermining American or British security. But sometimes accommodating the rights associated with a status category is incompatible with the way the established power defines its vital security interests. During the late nineteenth and twentieth centuries, the possession of large navies consisting of battleships was a marker of the status category "world power."[31] As Chapter 3 showed, while Germany's *Flottenpolitik* was primarily motivated by status and identity concerns, it threatened British security, which required naval superiority. The incompatibility of Germany's status claim with British security made it difficult if not impossible for the British to accede to German demands for recognition of the right to naval parity.

Are Chinese status claims likely to conflict with vital American security interests? This depends on what one thinks American interests are. If it is true that China's claim to great power status depends in part on acquiring a recognized sphere of influence in East Asia (a sort of Chinese Monroe Doctrine encompassing the South China Sea), then future American leaders will face a difficult choice: either accommodate Chinese claims by recognizing China's special role in East Asia, or commit to maintaining American dominance in East Asia at the risk of signaling status denial. I return to the implications of this dilemma for American grand strategy in the next chapter; for now it is enough to note that it is not clear that any American leader would be able to square China's claim to privilege in the South China Sea with the vital security interests of the United States, as they are currently understood – indeed even those who counsel accommodation of China do not go so far as to propose that the United States abandon its dominant role in East Asia.[32]

Second, the rising power's status claims might be incompatible with the established or declining power's understanding of its identity. This might be the case if the established power's dominant identity narrative depends upon a claim to superiority or to exceptionalism. Under these conditions, it might be difficult for a leader in the established power to sustainably acknowledge that another state belonged in the same status category or had access to equal rights. For instance, during the fifteenth, sixteenth, and seventeenth centuries, China refused to recognize first Japanese and then British claims to equal rights and status. Leaders in Edo and London

---

[31] Murray (2010); Steinberg (1965).

[32] Ikenberry (2011), p. 356; Kupchan (2012), p. 201. One important exception is Layne (2014).

were uncomfortable playing by the rules of the Sino-Centric order, which involved tribute and kowtowing to signal Chinese dominance and foreign submission.[33] Bending these rules was unthinkable to Ming and Qing leaders because China's identity narrative involved an exceptionalist claim to the divine origin and sanction of the emperor. Accommodating Japanese and British requests for immunity from the performance of the rituals that constituted Chinese dominance would have threatened not only China's status but also its self-understanding. According to Ringmar (writing about the Chinese refusal to recognize Great Britain's demand for formal equality): "the model that had placed the Chinese sun at its symbolic center could not easily be traded for a model in which China was merely one billiard ball among others following an independent path."[34]

There is good reason to be concerned that identity politics could hamper Sino-American accommodation. One problem is that American political discourse includes prominent claims to exceptionalism and indispensability. Even the Obama administration – which acknowledged a preference for "leading from behind" and was criticized from the right for abandoning exceptionalism – maintained a commitment to the United States' unique role in the world. The 2015 National Security Strategy reasserted a belief in an "American exceptionalism" rooted in "founding values," and argued that "there are no global problems that can be solved without the United States."[35] Exceptionalist identity narratives fit awkwardly with claims to equal rights by others. When Chinese leaders and the Chinese public wonder why the United States can exercise unilateral power abroad or maintain a sphere of influence in its periphery while acting and talking as if China does not have the same rights, responding that American founding values make the United States a unique force for good is unlikely to satisfy. A related problem is that to be an American leader is to support a range of values that are inconsistent with Chinese status claims. American official support, for instance, for human rights and liberal democracy violate Chinese understandings of what it means to respect sovereignty, let alone what it means to act appropriately toward another great power.[36]

The third obstacle is rooted in the domestic politics of the established power. Leaders in dominant states are sometimes constrained from taking steps to signal recognition of rising state status claims by concerns

---

[33] On the Sino-Centric order, see Fairbank (1968), Jansen (2000), Toby (1984), and Kang (2010).

[34] Ringmar (2012), p. 17.   [35] The White House (2015), pp. 2–3.

[36] See Deng (2008), Chapter 3 on this point. The 2015 National Security Strategy (The White House 2015, p. 19) makes clear that the United States is committed to "promoting universal values abroad."

about the reaction of important domestic groups. In certain types of domestic regimes, leaders might also be unable to prevent sub-state actors from taking steps that communicate status denial. The discussion of Japan's struggle for recognition in Chapter 4 provides several examples illustrating these dynamics. Australian Prime Minister Billy Hughes opposed the racial equality clause at the Paris Peace Conference in part because he knew that opposition was a political winner. Similarly, one of the reasons Woodrow Wilson ultimately opposed the clause was because of its political implications for domestic race relations. Indeed, the broader conflict between the West and Japan over immigration, which played such an important role in the story of failed accommodation, was driven largely by domestic politics, and in some cases even by local politics.[37]

American domestic politics could certainly pose an obstacle to accommodation of Chinese status claims. This goes beyond a general unwillingness to appear weak or to renegotiate international commitments out of a concern about the reaction of domestic audiences. There is also, according to many observers, a tradition of "China-bashing" during US election seasons.[38] As Ted Galen Carpenter notes, during campaigns "the major party candidates vie to see who can appear tougher on China" in what is "a quadrennial political ritual."[39] The rise of Chinese economic power coupled with American economic difficulties have combined recently to make China an even more attractive target for scapegoating. Chinese citizens have noticed, which has perhaps contributed to a recent decline in Chinese attitudes toward the United States.[40] In short, the pressures of domestic politics could make it difficult for leaders in the White House or Congress to support accommodation.

The fourth obstacle is alliance politics. Leaders are sometimes constrained from pursuing accommodation because they are concerned about the reactions of their allies. During the Paris Peace Conference, for instance, the primary reason that British leaders opposed the racial equality clause was that they knew the Dominion governments (especially the Australians) were against it. Similarly, while American and British

---

[37] For an overview, see Shimazu (1998).

[38] On China-bashing in 2012, see Oded Shenkar (2012); Madison Park (2012); Brower and Lerer (2012); Osnos (2012); Washington Post Editorial Board (2012).

[39] Carpenter (2012). This was even more evident during the 2016 election cycle, which saw Donald Trump accuse China of "raping" the American economy. Trump has also famously declared that climate change was a "hoax" concocted by Beijing to "make U.S. manufacturing non-competitive," though he did so via Twitter in 2012. See Diamond (May 2, 2016) and Wong (November 18, 2016).

[40] Park (2012); "Why China-Bashing Dominates U.S. Presidential Elections," People's Daily Online (2012).

leaders preferred a conciliatory settlement after World War I and tried at times after Versailles to accommodate German claims, they were constrained by French opposition.[41]

Alliance politics could also trouble Sino-American relations. Even if future American leaders decide to acknowledge, in some form, a Chinese sphere of influence in East Asia, they might still care about maintaining security relationships with countries like Japan and South Korea, since these arguably have benefits that go beyond containing China.[42] But this could prove impossible, since erstwhile East Asian allies might begin to doubt the credibility of American security guarantees. They are already nervous: in the face of a Chinese push to assert territorial claims in the South China Sea, American foreign policy has in recent years been oriented toward reassuring allies that the United States is committed to East Asia. Predictably, this has worsened Sino-American relations.[43] The upshot is that it is unclear whether accommodation of Chinese status claims and the maintenance of American alliance commitments in East Asia are compatible objectives.

None of this is to say that accommodation is *impossible*. But it is likely to be much more difficult than the integrationists – who focus primarily on the openness of the institutions of the liberal order – suggest. Effective accommodation would likely require the United States to make serious sacrifices not just in terms of giving up influence in international institutions, but also in terms of dramatically redefining the way it conceives of its role abroad. Accommodation may not ultimately be in the United States' best interest. But that is a conclusion that cannot be drawn without first considering the potential consequences of status denial, which is the question that occupies the rest of this chapter.

Status Immobility and Chinese Foreign Policy

There is not yet widespread support in China for policies aimed at rejecting the liberal international order. One 2012 opinion survey suggested that only fifteen percent of Chinese advocate creating a "new, alternative China-led world order and institutions," and, on the whole, the Chinese public remains optimistic about China's trajectory.[44]

Yet there are reasons to worry that the ground is fertile for the development and spread of beliefs that China faces a status "glass ceiling." One

[41] See Tooze (2014) for an overview of interwar haggling between the Allies.
[42] Brooks, Ikenberry, and Wohlforth (2013), pp. 40–50.
[43] On American reassurance and its consequences for Sino-American relations, see Ott (2014); Denyer (2014); and Ross (2012).
[44] Jung (2012), pp. 10–13.

is that China – like Imperial Japan – has a legacy of being humiliated by Western powers. This has resulted in a "victim mentality" that could make claims that great power status is unavailable particularly resonant.[45] According to Deng (who argues that China is the most status conscious country in the world), the "century of humiliation" that lasted from the Opium Wars to the end of World War II may explain China's status sensitivity; Yan Xuetong suggests that "the Chinese regard their rise as regaining China's lost international status rather than obtaining something new"; William Callahan argues that an important objective of Chinese foreign policy is to "cleanse National Humiliation," and that invocations of shame and humiliation at the hands of the West have played a central role in the development of Chinese nationalism; Christopher Hughes, similarly, claims that the Chinese Communist Party routinely promises to "deliver the nation from humiliation" as a way of legitimating its rule.[46] While leaders have so far used appeals to national humiliation instrumentally to mobilize and consolidate support for limited revisionist policies, the analysis throughout this book shows that this kind of sentiment can take on a life of its own. In combination with foreign behavior that seems to deny status claims, it might contribute to the emergence of political conditions that interfere with efforts to pursue moderate policies.[47]

A second reason to worry about the development of status immobility in China is the inherent tension between China's domestic political institutions and the way that Western leaders seem to understand the requirements for entry into the "responsible" great power club. In particular, Chinese leaders are wary of the fact that a commitment to democracy and respect for Western conceptions of human rights may be central markers of status in the contemporary international system.[48] One important objective of Chinese foreign policy has been to reduce the extent to which relevant others view China as disqualified from legitimate great power status on these grounds. It has done so in two ways: by improving perceptions of China's human rights record, and by altering the "standard of great power recognition" through an effort to change or

---

[45] For an analysis of the temporal component of Chinese status dissatisfaction, see Freedman (2016).

[46] Deng (2008), p. 41; Yan Xuetong (2001), p. 34; Callahan (2004), p. 205; Hughes (2006), p. 156; see also Li (2009), p. 183.

[47] See Wang (2008), p. 802; Gries et al. (2005b), p. 17; and Barme (1995), for analyses of these dynamics.

[48] See especially Deng (2008), Chapter 3; on democracy as a marker of status in the contemporary system, see Kim (2003); on human rights norms as markers of legitimacy or status, see Sikkink (1993); Risse and Sikkink (1999); Donnelly (1998); Clark (2005); and Krasner (1995).

reduce the salience of respect for human rights as a marker.[49] Deng notes that Chinese "compliance" behaviors – including accession to a series of human rights treaties – are attempts to enhance China's status through integration and emulation. At the same time, China has tried to "minimize human rights as a yardstick for international standing" by emphasizing the value of sovereignty and the cultural relativity of human rights standards.[50]

Chinese status sensitivity might seem to provide leverage for Western states to influence China's domestic institutions and behavior by holding out recognition of great power status as a carrot. But this could be dangerous. The more stridently Western leaders insist that China must "accept and contribute to the evolving international legal regime on issues such as human rights, [and] collective defense of democracy," the more convinced Chinese leaders and elites may become that it is impossible to achieve recognition of great power status without fundamentally undermining the regime.[51] In fact, some Chinese elites already seem to think that the Western focus on democracy promotion and human rights is a deliberate plot to prevent China's rise to great power status.[52]

A third reason to worry about status immobility in China is racial difference. While American foreign policy is not explicitly organized around racial distinctions like it was a century ago, Chinese observers could easily interpret slights by the United States and its leaders in racial terms. William Callahan has recently argued that contemporary Chinese conceptions of race bear a striking similarity to those of the nineteenth-century West. "In its racial nationalist form," he writes, "Chinese identity is part of a hierarchy, with Han Chinese at the top and blacks at the bottom."[53] The meaning of the term *Minzu* (which Chinese frequently use to refer to China) "is quite broad and ambiguous, ranging from ethnicity to nation to race."[54] This does not mean that Chinese view the world exclusively through the lens of race or think of international politics as a competition between racial groups. But racial interpretations remain prominently available to Chinese trying to make sense of international politics – as they were for Japanese in the 1920s and 1930s. This could be problematic for reasons explored in Chapter 4: an apparent racial

---

[49] Deng (2008), p. 89.   [50] Ibid., pp. 82–92.

[51] Castañeda (2011); Clunan (2014b), p. 295, makes a similar point about the dangers of forcing aspiring powers to conform to Western status criteria.

[52] See Bernstein (2012); and Lieberthal and Wang (2012). In his contribution to the coauthored report cited in this note, Wang (p. 12) even claims that "it is widely believed in the Chinese leadership that the Americans orchestrated awarding the Nobel Peace Prize to Liu Xiaobo in October 2010."

[53] Callahan (2013), p. 104.   [54] Ibid., p. 104.

obstacle could dampen Chinese optimism about the prospects of satisfying their international status ambitions.[55]

But even if a strong belief that China faces a status "glass ceiling" does develop, would it have an effect on Chinese foreign policy? In the remainder of this section, I argue that it is not difficult to imagine status immobility unleashing in China similar social psychological and political forces as it did in Wilhelmine Germany, Imperial Japan, and Weimar Germany.

Chinese Status Anxiety and Demands for Rejection

The foreign policy preferences of China's elite vary fairly widely. Shambaugh and Xiao have identified seven distinct orientations toward the status quo within Chinese foreign policy discourse. At the integrationist end of the spectrum are the Globalists, who believe that China should take on additional responsibility for global governance within the existing framework of institutions – in short, China should "act as a responsible power."[56] Chinese Globalists are much like Western "liberal institutionalists," and are thus generally supportive of the liberal order. Five other perspectives (which Shambaugh and Xiao identify as Selective Multilateralists, the Global South school, the Asia Firsters, the Major Powers School, and the Realists) are less sold on the liberal order, but at least agree that some degree of participation in its institutions, norms, and rules is necessary.[57]

But there is one group – the Nativists – that rejects participation in the liberal international order. The Nativists are "hyper-nationalist" Marxist ideologues who oppose domestic reforms aimed at producing openness and market capitalism. In the realm of foreign policy, they oppose participation in the liberal order because they "view international multilateral involvement as 'traps' (laid by the West) to embroil China in costly overseas commitments."[58] Nativists have multiple reasons for rejecting integration, not all of which have to do with status – for instance, they worry that participation in the Western order will destabilize the Communist Party. But they are also deeply concerned about China's status and are skeptical about the prospects of achieving their ambitions within an order dominated by Western powers. According to Shambaugh and Xiao, Nativists "regularly harp on the nationalist theme of the 'century of shame and

---

[55] Christensen, Johnston, and Ross (2006), p. 411, agree that the role of "racial stereotypes in the formulation and execution of foreign policy" – especially in China – is understudied but critical. See also Johnston's reply in Chen, Pu, and Johnston (2014).

[56] Shambaugh and Xiao (2012), Kindle location 1238.   [57] Ibid., Kindle location 1265.

[58] Ibid., Kindle location 1025.

humiliation' and argue that China is entitled to global respect (particularly by those powers that previously humiliated China)."[59]

Liu Mingfu's sensationally popular *China Dream* is a remarkably open call for a deep revisionist challenge to the liberal order. While Liu may not be a Nativist (according to Shambaugh's classification), his writing is worth considering as a modern Chinese manifestation of the kind of argument that Friedrich von Bernhardi popularized in Germany during the years before World War I. Liu's central proposition is that China should aim to become a "champion" nation – the global top dog or leader (as distinct from the hegemon, which to Liu implies a form of imperialism and military domination). As the "champion," China would "create a new world order that prefers peace, development, freedom, and cooperative civilization." This seems like a clear demand for China to – at some point – remake the international order.

What is significant is the source of the demand for radical revisionism, and its implications for China's participation in the liberal order. Liu links the need for a new order to the deficiencies of American hegemony, the "worst expression" of which is "its monopolization of its status as champion."[60] In other words, the United States will not accede willingly to China's attainment of a position of equality in a "multipolar" world. The book goes on to document and decry American efforts to contain the rise of China, considers lessons from the successful American defeat of two other potential "champions" (the Soviet Union and Japan), and makes a clear argument against integrating too deeply within the liberal order:

However, it cannot be denied that America has a clear upper hand in terms of control and power with China. China can be promoted to copilot to help the United States cope with risks, but this will only help America maintain its position as pilot. America allows opponents to board its plane, which is ultimately a higher degree of control and containment.[61]

Integrating within the liberal order would amount to becoming Washington's "copilot," which would do nothing more than strengthen the basis of a status hierarchy that the United States is intent upon preserving. This is reminiscent of the way that Bernhardi, militant pan-Asianists, and Weimar nationalists argued against participation in the pre-World War I and interwar orders. And Liu's book is hardly peripheral: in 2013, Xi Jinping began invoking the term "China Dream" to describe his vision for

---

[59] Ibid., Kindle location 1053. See also Shambaugh (2013), pp. 27–31. Other authors have also identified a deeply revisionist strand of Chinese foreign policy thought. Callahan (2013), p. 43, calls it "divergence"; and Schweller and Pu (2011), p. 61, identify a group who advocates that China construct a "new Chinese world order."

[60] Liu (2015), Kindle location 953.   [61] Ibid., Kindle location 3890.

China's future, and has reportedly been deeply influenced by the book's central argument.[62]

Nativists and other revisionists may not be ascendant in Chinese foreign policy decisionmaking, but their foreign policy preferences are not marginal either. While other schools of thought do not take such strident positions against participation in the liberal order, some share a sense of skepticism: Realists for instance, are also concerned that Western institutions are traps meant to keep China down.[63] And Chinese elites remain worried about Chinese status and link it to the terms of participation in the liberal order – they emphasize "equality of participation" over "governance" and chafe at the idea of complying with American standards in order to be recognized as a "responsible power."[64]

So while Chinese foreign policy is currently run mostly by proponents of intermediate and at least partially integrationist perspectives, Nativists and others like Liu constitute a loud and potentially influential voice for policies that reject the liberal international order – much like Pan-Asians or German radical nationalists spent the 1920s demanding policies of protest and delegitimation from the more moderate leaders who ran Taishō and Weimar foreign policy.[65] It is not difficult to imagine support for the Nativist perspective (not just among the elite but also in the public) growing along with developments that seem to confirm fears that Chinese status ambitions face an insurmountable, unjust obstacle imposed by the United States and the liberal order. Indeed, evidence suggests that Chinese "netizen" nationalists are hyper-aware of status issues and often mobilize in response to concerns about the way China is treated by foreign actors and what that treatment says about China's international standing.[66]

Status, Domestic Politics, and Chinese Foreign Policy

The question that remains is whether – in China's authoritarian system – pressure from outside the government for radical revisionist policies could have much influence. The government is (and likely will be for the foreseeable future) committed to foreign policy moderation: but what if developments appearing to confirm that China faces a status "glass ceiling" increase support for the Nativist position and lead to widespread demands for policies aimed at rejecting the liberal order? Could these forces impact Chinese policy in the same way that they impacted German

---

[62] Page (2013).   [63] Shambaugh and Xiao (2012), Kindle location 1116.
[64] Ibid., Kindle location 1274.
[65] Pillsbury (2015) argues that Chinese foreign policy is *already* fundamentally oriented toward overthrowing the liberal order.
[66] Shen and Breslin (2010), p. 265.

and Japanese policy? It is hard to know for sure, but there is good reason to think that the government is susceptible to influence from external pressure and that it may only become more so in the future.

While some scholars maintain that Chinese policymakers mostly effectively ignore public opinion, or that public opinion prompts short-term shifts in official rhetoric or policy but does not influence grand strategic direction, many others agree that "bottom-up" forces play a significant role in Chinese foreign policy.[67] Unofficial attitudes and preferences cannot influence policy through the mechanisms of electoral political competition, but this does not mean they are irrelevant. First, policy has to be at least somewhat responsive to the diversity of elite preferences – just as Bethmann Hollweg was constrained by the attitudes of the Kaiser, Tirpitz, and the Pan-Germans, Chinese leaders may be constrained by the preferences of Nativists and some status-sensitive and integration-skeptical Realists in the military and the Party.[68] Second, mass opinion can threaten China's elite through the dynamics of widespread popular protest. According to Weiss, mass protests may menace ruling elites by creating demonstration effects, tipping points, and information cascades; facilitating future mobilization against the regime; and fostering or exacerbating divisions within the leadership.[69] And while strong authoritarian states like China can prevent and manage anti-regime protests, there are costs and risks associated with doing so, especially when public opinion is aimed at forcing the regime to adopt a more aggressive foreign policy posture.[70] This means that the masses can be a potent weapon for anyone interested in forcing the government into adopting a more belligerent foreign policy; in turn, this means that any factor that makes it easier to mobilize anti-Western opinion (such as apparent evidence that the United States is unwilling to accommodate a Chinese claim to equal rights) may provide opportunities for Chinese proponents of challenging the liberal order.

This logic is supported by scholars of Chinese foreign policy who contend that public pressure has influenced policy in the past and will continue to do so. These analysts point to a series of episodes – including, among others, the 1985 Sino-Japanese dispute over Prime Minister Nakasone's visit to Yasukuni Shrine, the 2001 EP3 crisis, the 2003 decision to remove a contract to build a Chinese bullet train from the operator of Japan's Shinkansen, the 2005 crisis over Japan's attempt to win a permanent seat on the UN Security Council, and the 2012 Sino-Japanese Diaoyu-Senkaku

[67] For skeptical voices, see Shen (2004) and Reilly (2012), p. 5.
[68] Shambaugh and Xiao (2012), Kindle location 1302.
[69] Weiss (2014), p. 19; see also Weiss (2013).   [70] Weiss (2014), p. 19.

crisis – during which China's official policy became more aggressive in response to popular, nationalist pressure.[71]

There is nothing necessarily belligerent about Chinese public opinion, and not all scholars agree that it poses a challenge to the maintenance of moderate foreign policy.[72] But under the wrong circumstances, the role of the Chinese public could make it difficult for moderate leaders to avoid taking provocative steps that they might prefer not to. For instance, in the wake of a major crisis with the United States over the status of the South China Sea, nationalist popular opinion would be ripe for exploitation by hardline elites.[73] The result would likely be intense pressure on Chinese moderates to move away from integration within the liberal order – which, after all, is seen by Nativists and many Realists as nothing more than a tool to perpetuate the dominance of the United States by containing China. A crisis that seemed to validate this view would produce political resources for the proponents of a wide range of provocative policies.

And the role of the Chinese public is only likely to become more important in the future. The slow and uneven opening up of China's political system – a result of hesitant local-level democratization, increasingly influential media, and, most important, the growth of the internet as a site for political contestation – raises the possibility that China's elite may come under even more serious pressure from below.[74] Netizenship, in particular, has drawn a great deal of attention from China-watchers as a potential threat to the regime. Chinese online forums facilitate the publication and distribution of news and opinion, as well as popular mobilization.[75] Xin-An Lu attributes recently inflamed anti-Japan and anti-US public pressure in part to the internet; and while the Chinese regime has tools at its disposal to control online nationalist opinions, there are costs associated with using them.[76]

The upshot is that the regime may become more vulnerable to external pressure over the next several years.[77] This has a wide range of implications

---

[71] See Reilly (2012), pp. 69–70; Li (2005), p. 59; Hong (2005), p. 102; Weiss (2014), Chapters 6 and 8; and for a summary of a handful of other crises, see Lu (2005), pp. 114–116.

[72] See, for example, Lai (2010).

[73] On elite conflict and popular protest in China, see Fewsmith and Rosen (2001), pp. 172–175.

[74] See Wang (2006); Yu (2005); and on the internet see Junhao Hong (2005); Lu (2005); Shen and Breslin (2010); Lu (2009); John Lagerkvist (2010); Tai (2006); Qiang (2011); Shirk (2011); Hao and Hou (2009); Yu (2009); Wu (2007). For dissenting opinions about the influence of netizenship on Chinese politics, see MacKinnon (2008), and Feldman (2013).

[75] Hong (2005), p. 95.   [76] Lu (2005), p. 114; Shen and Breslin (2010), p. 275.

[77] Indeed, Shambaugh (2015) has recently suggested that the collapse of the Communist Party is imminent.

for the future of the liberal international order, one of which is that the social psychological and political forces that status immobility unleashed in Germany and Japan during the first half of the twentieth century could well operate in contemporary China as well.

Conclusion

There are, of course, also reasons for optimism. Younger members of the elite have more favorable attitudes toward the United States than do older generations; there are powerful Chinese groups (especially in coastal provinces) deeply invested in continued integration with the international economy and caution in foreign policy. According to Hongyi Lai, China's "primary domestic imperatives suggest that peaceful rise and prevention of a major war are in [its] best interests."[78] And, most importantly, Beijing continues to value caution and stability in foreign policy and still seems capable of managing nationalist frustrations without allowing them to dictate its course.[79] In short, the integrationists may be right.

Still, analysts and policymakers should not ignore Chinese status anxiety. Taking status seriously suggests that the integrationist and rejectionist perspectives are both inaccurate. Rejectionists ignore the dynamics of status immobility which blinds them to the possibility that the policy they promote could create the revisionist China whose development they think inevitable. Another way to put this is that rejectionists ignore the full costs of containment – these include not just the material and opportunity costs of military spending and the potential for security dilemma dynamics, but also the possibility of creating and empowering elites with preferences deeply opposed to the liberal international order.

Integrationists, on the other hand, underestimate the difficulty of successful accommodation. Recognizing China's status claims may require the United States to dramatically redefine the way it understands the role it plays in the world. The purpose of pointing this out is not to advocate accommodation, but to suggest that perhaps China cannot be bought off by increasing its influence in the institutions of the

---

[78] Lai (2010), p. 169; see also Lieberthal and Wang (2012); Hao and Su (2005), p. 30; and Chen (2005).

[79] For instance, Beijing's response to the recent Permanent Court of Arbitration rejection of its South China Sea claims has been encouragingly restrained, though the ruling prompted expressions of fury and resentment (including a call to prepare for a "people's war at sea") probably intended to signal resolve and satisfy nationalist demands for protest. See Wuthnow (2016).

liberal international order or even by facilitating the return of Taiwan to Beijing's control. Satisfying China's status claims may be much more painful than that. Whether doing so is ultimately worth it is an important debate – and one that requires a clear understanding of the potential costs of both accommodation and denial.

Conclusion

When rising powers openly challenge international order, they court disaster. This is why the moderate leadership of early twentieth-century rising powers – people like Theobald von Bethmann Hollweg, Kijurō Shidehara, and Gustav Stresemann – counseled patient caution and opposed unnecessarily provocative steps that would alienate and threaten their neighbors. Yet in these three cases, moderate counsel lost out to calls for policies that protested or aimed at overthrowing the status quo order.

Why? In this book, I have argued that traditional explanations – like material or security motives, domestic dysfunction, or ideology – do not adequately account for deeply revisionist shifts in the foreign policies of rising powers. Instead, a particular type of anxiety about status – the belief that the state's status ambitions were incompatible with the status quo order – played a key and underappreciated role in the origins of radical revisionism in Wilhelmine Germany, Imperial Japan, and interwar Germany. Status immobility produced preferences among some nationalists for policies that would protest, delegitimate, or overthrow status quo rules, norms, and institutions; and developments that seemed to validate claims about the existence of a status "glass ceiling" provided political resources that advantaged hardliners over moderates in domestic contests over the direction of foreign policy.

This argument represents a novel way of understanding the role of status in world politics. Instead of focusing on establishing that states care about status, or showing how status as a motive influences state behavior, this book has explicitly investigated the consequences of *not being able to* satisfy status ambitions. And it has done so by casting status concerns in a new role: as a phenomenon at least partially driven by processes at the level of the international system that influences the domestic political environment in ways that stack the deck in favor of proponents of provocative, aggressive policies.

The resulting explanatory framework – status immobility theory – is a step forward in the study of status in world politics. It also has implications for contemporary international relations, and in particular for American grand strategy in a world of rising and reemerging great powers.

In this concluding chapter, I first take stock of the value that focusing on status immobility adds to our explanations of the behavior of history's most disruptive rising powers. I then highlight the limitations of the theory, which in turn point toward potentially fruitful new avenues for future research on status in world politics. Finally, I unpack the argument's implications for American grand strategy.

Status Immobility and Revisionism in Historical Rising Powers

The case studies in Chapters 3, 4, and 5 each began by identifying important puzzles left outstanding by dominant narratives about the rise of revisionism in Wilhelmine Germany, Imperial Japan, and interwar Germany. The most prominent accounts of these cases typically overstate the degree to which their outcomes were driven by the deterministic effects of shifting power, geopolitical necessity, or the interests of militant groups, and obscure the extent to which viable alternatives to radical revisionist policies remained available and plausible in debates among elites.

German and Japanese challenges to order were the result of political contests between groups of leaders and elites who disagreed with each other about the direction of foreign policy. Bethmann Hollweg was a decided proponent of détente with Great Britain and was willing to give up the naval race in exchange for better relations. He was opposed by pan-Germans outside the government and militarists inside the government who wanted German policy to eschew cooperation with London and instead aim to undermine or overthrow the European balance of power. Shidehara, Saionji, and other Japanese moderates thought the best way to ensure Japanese security and prosperity was to uphold the interwar institutional order while expanding politically and economically in mainland East Asia. This remained their position even after the Mukden Incident and the League's condemnation. They were opposed by pan-Asianists and others who wanted to withdraw from or overturn the Western-dominated East Asian order. Gustav Stresemann and other German moderates of the Weimar period thought the best way to better Germany's position in Europe was to fulfill the terms of the Versailles settlement and thereby avoid antagonizing the great powers. They were opposed by the NSDAP and others on the German right who thought fulfillment bought nothing but humiliation.

In each of these cases, the hardliners ultimately silenced the moderates, and policy reflected the preferences of the former at the expense of the latter. Dominant accounts have trouble explaining two critical parts of these stories. First, why did some hardliners want to withdraw from, protest, or overthrow the order in the first place? Second, why did they prevail over moderates at these crucial junctures?

Status immobility's most valuable contribution to the study of international politics is to provide answers to these questions in a way that is theoretically grounded and consistent with the historical record. The most important existing answers to the question of why leaders sometimes become interested in overthrowing international order come from mainstream realist theories, and focus on security motives. Leaders in Wilhelmine Germany, according to one prominent interpretation, were willing to launch a major war in 1914 because they were terrified of the rise of Russia.[1] But a closer look at the logic of that argument and the record of German debates over prewar foreign policy reveals that this is not an adequate explanation. Many German leaders surely did fear the rise of Russia, but if they were only worried about the physical survival of the German state, there were other, cheaper and less risky, options – such as working for détente with the British. The problem was that many proponents of major war worried not only about the physical survival of the German state but also about its ability to take its rightful place in the international status hierarchy. This was what Bernhardi, for instance, meant when he wrote of a choice between "world power" and "decline," and it was why the Kaiser was unwilling to do what would have been necessary in order to foster Anglo-German détente.[2] The ambition for status – and the belief that its pursuit was unjustly obstructed – explains why certain options (détente with London) were unattractive, and why a fear of relative decline meant that an apocalyptic war seemed attractive. It was not German security requirements but German status ambitions that were incompatible with the European balance of power.

It is similarly impossible to understand pan-Asianist or interwar German nationalist opposition to the moderate policies of Shidehara and Stresemann without understanding that pan-Asians and German nationalists cared about much more than security. In both cases, preferences for deeply revisionist policies that would protest, undermine, or overthrow the status quo order were driven in large part by the belief that that order had been put together in a way that would unjustly thwart the state's attempt to attain or regain equal status alongside great powers like Great Britain, the United States, and France.[3]

---

[1] Copeland (2000), Chapters 4 and 5.   [2] See Chapter 3.   [3] See Chapters 4 and 5.

It is worth stopping here to underline one important point of contrast between the evidence presented in this book and the way many analysts have understood the way that status ambitions influence foreign policy. Previous work on status in world politics – like that of Deborah Larson and Alexei Shevchenko – has argued that states respond to apparently obstructed status ambitions by engaging in geopolitically competitive practices aimed, in the end, at securing recognition from relevant others.[4] My analysis of three separate cases of apparently obstructed status ambitions suggests a different – and darker – conclusion. German and Japanese nationalists who believed their state's status ambitions were incompatible with the status quo order demanded not further competition for status (which would, after all, have been bounded by the need to secure recognition from rivals) but rather policies aimed at protesting or overthrowing the order completely.

Existing explanations for early twentieth-century German and Japanese revisionism also have trouble explaining a second question: why did hardliners prevail over moderates in domestic contests over the direction of foreign policy? Mainstream realist accounts typically ignore this question completely, as do explanations that focus on ideological distance or content as a driver of foreign policy; interpretations that focus on domestic dysfunction do better by acknowledging that individual and sub-state interests were heterogeneous and problematizing the victory of hardliners over moderates.

Status immobility's value is to help account for the conditions that made those outcomes possible in a way that links international-level processes with domestic politics. In Wilhelmine Germany, the moderate Bethmann Hollweg was constrained by nationalist anger after the Second Morocco Crisis and by the kaiser's frustration with British obstructionism. In Imperial Japan, accumulating evidence of racial discrimination produced political and rhetorical resources that Japanese militarists used to silence moderate opposition to leaving the League of Nations and abrogating the Washington Naval Treaty. Similarly, increasing nationalist anger associated with Stresemann's apparent failure to restore German rights as a great power produced political conditions that helped Hitler move out of the margins of Weimar politics and become the standard-bearer of the German right by September 1930.

These insights are not new to historians, who for decades have noted the importance of the ambition for "world power" in Wilhelmine Germany, racial discrimination for Japan's turn against the interwar order, and the anger and shame of the Versailles settlement for the rise

---

[4] Larson and Shevchenko (2010, 2014a); see also Wolf (2014) and Malinova (2014).

of Hitler. But the discipline of international relations has had no framework for systematically understanding how these kinds of factors mattered – and may continue to matter – for foreign policy and international politics. This book's most important contribution is to develop and illustrate the utility of such a framework, which simultaneously challenges conventional wisdoms about these three important cases of revisionism and advances our knowledge of the way that status dynamics work in world politics.

Limitations, Extensions, and Directions for Future Research

This book's ambition has been to answer a very big question; in doing so it has raised others. In this section, I highlight two significant unanswered questions about the role of status in world politics: where do status ambitions come from? And why do declining powers often fail to accommodate the status ambitions of rising powers? These questions raise the possibility that the logic of my argument might extend further than the scope conditions that have structured the analysis in this book; they also constitute potentially fruitful areas for future research on the role of status concerns in the domestic politics of foreign policy making.

The Origins of Status Ambitions

My focus has been on the consequences of obstructed or thwarted status ambitions. I have – by design – not fully developed an argument about where status ambitions come from in the first place. This is not because the question is unimportant or uninteresting. It is, instead, because the question of the origins of status ambitions is *too* big. It actually encompasses at least two more specific questions, each of which could on its own support a robust stream of research.

The first issue relates to the *value* of status. Explaining the origins of status ambitions involves explaining why states – and the individuals who identify with them – care about it. One explanation – the one at the core of this book – is that status matters because people (especially those who identify most strongly with the state) care about being able to make positive social comparisons between their state and other states, and they want these positive comparisons to be acknowledged by relevant others. That is, states care about status because individuals care about status, and individuals care about status because it influences the part of their self-esteem that is related to social identity.

A second explanation – which is at the core of rational-materialist analyses of status-seeking – is that status is a resource which increases a state's influence, and thereby its security. Having higher status grants states certain rights that might be materially valuable; it allows states access to institutions within which they might be able to exercise leverage on important issues; and it might also boost material capabilities or produce advantages in interstate bargaining.[5]

The answer to the question of status' value matters a great deal because it influences the frequency with which we should expect status immobility to have the effects that I have highlighted in this book. In situations in which status is *only* valued for material reasons, status immobility should not produce social psychological and domestic political effects that drive states toward radical revisionism. These mechanisms *only work* when status is (at least partially) valued for reasons that go beyond its role as a security or power-enhancing resource. Thus exploring the value of status – and potential variation in the nature of its value (perhaps, for instance, different kinds of states value status for different reasons) – is a critical direction for future work.

The second issue relates to the origins of *expectations* about a state's proper position in the status hierarchy. Why do people sometimes feel that their state is entitled to a higher position? This is a question, ultimately, about imagination: when and why do individuals begin to conceive of their state as belonging in a particular status category or club?[6]

The analysis in this book is structured by the conventional claim that increasing material capabilities are one source of rising expectations about the state's standing in world politics, and thus a common cause of status ambitions in rising powers. But rising power is not *necessary* for the development of outstanding status ambitions. In fact, it is not difficult to identify cases in which a non-rising state's foreign policy expressed dissatisfaction with its international status. One example is early modern Japan. Some Japanese leaders during the Ashikaga and Tokugawa eras were deeply uncomfortable with Japan's subordinate position within the Sino-Centric East Asian Order. This was not due to an apparent material convergence between Japan and Ming and later Qing China, but rather to the implications of Shinto ideology and its incompatibility with a vision of order in which the Japanese emperor was a vassal of the Chinese emperor.[7]

---

[5] See Dafoe, Renshon, and Huth (2014); Renshon (2016, 2017); Sambanis, Skaperdas, and Wohlforth (2015).

[6] Larson and Shevchenko (2014a), p. 38.

[7] See Kang (2010), p. 77; Mizuno (2004), p. 140; Hawley (2005), p. 54; Earl (1964), p. 13; and Ringmar (2012b).

A second example is mid-nineteenth-century Paraguayan dictator Francisco Solano Lopéz. Lopéz developed delusions of grandeur following a tour of European capitals, which prompted him to try to convince his much larger neighbors Brazil and Argentina to treat Paraguay as a European-style great power.[8] Lopéz's status ambitions were not the result of rising expectations as a result of rising power, but the combined result of Lopéz's personality and his infatuation with the trappings of the European great power club.

A third example is post-Soviet Russia. Contemporary Russia is not a rising power and has not been one for decades, but for much of its post-Cold War history, Russian foreign policy has been aimed at reestablishing Russia's position as a great power. While Russia's initial grand strategic orientation after the Cold War was toward retrenchment and the abandonment of claims to great power status, this proved impossible to sustain, in part because it was inconsistent with collective understandings of Russia's historical identity and role in international politics.[9] By 1996, the "Primakov Doctrine" had officially reasserted Russia's claim to great power status, and the drive to satisfy this ambition has been implicated in a range of concrete projects, the most important of which is the reestablishment of a Russian sphere of influence in its near abroad. From this perspective, the threat to Russian status ambitions posed by the eastward expansion of NATO and the European Union was at the root of the 2008 crisis over Georgia and the 2014 crisis over Ukraine.[10] What is significant is that Moscow's status ambitions appear to have been generated not by rising power, but rather by the stickiness of historical memory and identity.

States at the top of international hierarchies sometimes also exhibit concerns about or ambitions to raise or restore their status. For instance, Musgrave and Nexon have shown that the voyages of Ming "treasure fleets" in the fifteenth century and American investment in the "space race" during the early Cold War both constituted attempts to shore up Chinese and American status in systems that those two powers already dominated.[11] And Donald Trump's critique of American foreign

---

[8] See Saeger (2007); Beverina (1973), Chapter 1; Zenequelli (1997), p. 20; Thompson (1869), pp. 21, 46; Whigham (2002), p. 177; Bray (1945), pp. 118–119.

[9] On this point, see Larson and Shevchenko (2010) and Clunan (2009). Russian sensitivity to status has a long history, and many scholars acknowledge its centrality in the formation of Russian foreign policy. See also Larson and Shevchenko (2003); Neumann (2005, 2008, 2014); Greenfeld (1990); Malinova (2014a); Clunan (2014a); Forsberg (2014); Heller (2014); Larson and Shevchenko (2014b); Tsygankov (2014); and Smith (2014).

[10] On the domestic unsustainability of giving up claims to great power status, see Clunan (2009), p. 126; on the Primakov Doctrine, see Ambrosio (2005), pp. 4–5; on status and the 2008 Georgia War, see Tsygankov (2012).

[11] Musgrave and Nexon (forthcoming).

policy – which has been remarkably consistent since the 1980s – reflects a paradoxical concern that the United States deserves higher status than it is accorded within an international order that it constructed and continues to sit atop.[12]

The heterogeneous sources of ambitions for higher status have two implications for the future study of status in world politics. First, the dynamics of status immobility could be relevant for a wide range of states beyond rising powers. Indeed, early modern Japan and Paraguay under López both confronted status "glass ceilings." In the former case, this was because China refused to treat Japan as more than a vassal; in the latter case, it was because Brazilian and Argentine leaders did not take López's claims to rights (especially the right to intervene in diplomatic conflicts that did not directly involve Paraguay) seriously. Tokugawa Japan responded by withdrawing from the Sino-Centric order, effectively refusing to participate in the rules, norms, and institutions that constituted the status quo.[13] López responded by launching a war to the death against Brazil, Argentina, and Uruguay.[14] And Trump's opposition to the liberal international order is fairly clearly linked, in part, to a sense that it is corrosive of and incompatible with American "greatness." Obstructed status ambitions could, in short, push a wide range of states – not just rising powers – to challenge international order through policies of protest and revolution.

The second implication is that we need to pay more attention to explaining the origins of status expectations. Most of the action in the literature on status in world politics (this book is no exception) is on its consequences for foreign policy. Yet understanding why states adopt the status ambitions that they do is also important, and the issue poses a number of interesting puzzles: why do some states (like Paraguay under López) adopt "outsized" or unrealistic status ambitions? Why do states whose status ambitions have been blocked not just adopt less ambitious ones? And what is the role of domestic political contestation in the formation of the state's status ambitions?

Status Accommodation and the Role of the Dominant or Declining Power

The second question that this book has raised but cannot fully answer relates to the role of the dominant or declining state in the process that

---

[12] See Simms and Laderman (2017) on Trump's worldview.

[13] See Toby (1984), pp. 29–89; Mizuno (2004), pp. 47–72; Jansen (1992), pp. 1–2).

[14] A variety of historians agree that anger resulting from denied status claims was one of the causes of López's aggression. See Saeger (2007); Leuchars (2002), p. 29; and Whigham (2002), p. 157.

generates apparent status "glass ceilings." If status immobility contributes to processes that push rising powers to challenge international order, then dominant states should have an interest in *accommodating*, not blocking, the satisfaction of the rising power's status ambitions. I highlighted the role that accommodation can play in managing the rise of a new power in Chapter 6: British accommodation of the United States after 1895 was critical to curtailing American anti-British sentiment, which could otherwise have pushed American foreign policy in a direction that might have made the decline of the British empire much more difficult and painful than it was.

Yet – as Chapters 3, 4, and 5 suggested – dominant powers often do not accommodate the status claims of rising powers. And the evidence from these cases suggests that this is not always because leaders fear that accommodation could accelerate the dominant state's decline or contribute to a greater threat from the riser. In other words, it is not always the case that status accommodation fails because the dominant state is committed to a policy aimed at containing the material threat from the rising power. The failure to accommodate Japanese claims to equality ran into opposition from Western racial attitudes and domestic political dynamics well before American or British leaders began to seriously worry about containing Japanese expansion in East Asia and the Western Pacific. And the Allied imposition of the Versailles Treaty and failure to satisfy Weimar Germany's early attempts to lift its most grating provisions was paired with a decided *unwillingness* to contain Germany's growing power.

The upshot is that explaining variation in dominant power treatment of rising power status claims is a potentially fruitful avenue for future research. Just as most work on status has been less interested in the origins of status ambitions than in their consequences, there has been far more attention to how states *gain* status than on when and how they give it up.[15] But there is no reason that the fear of losing status should be any less consequential for foreign policy – or the subject of less scholarly inquiry – than the desire to gain it or the belief that it is being unjustly withheld. And the social psychological and political dynamics at the core of this book could shed light on questions about, for instance, how the fear of losing status influences domestic contests over the direction of foreign policy within declining states. The great power graveyard is littered with states whose "place in the sun" ended decades or centuries ago – states like Sweden, Spain, Italy, Austria, Great Britain, and France. Did decline generate status anxiety? If so, how did leaders and other elites react to it?

[15] For the few exceptions, see Heimann (2014); Onea (2014); Paul and Shankar (2014); and Paul (2016).

What kind of policies did they promote in response? In what ways, if any, did the fear of falling influence domestic politics in the declining state? These questions are outside the purview of the present book, but a framework like the one developed within it might provide some analytical traction.

Status, American Grand Strategy, and the Rise of New Great Powers

In Chapter 7, I argued that the denial of Chinese status claims might activate forces that could push Chinese foreign policy toward protesting, delegitimating, or overthrowing the liberal international order. This, in turn, could increase the risk of Sino-American conflict and reduce the prospects for effective global governance. The argument that I have made in this book thus has implications for American grand strategy as the United States faces not just the rise of China but also a series of rising potential great powers who are likely to eventually demand recognition of higher status.

But deriving lessons for American grand strategy is more complicated than promoting across-the-board accommodation. Accommodation has costs, the severity of which depends upon the nature of the rising state's claims and the way in which the established state defines its interests. It is easy to suggest that China should be accommodated so long as the United States does not have to give up anything really important – like military superiority in the South China Sea.

As Chapter 7 suggested, though, satisfying Chinese status claims might require the United States to dramatically reimagine its role as a provider of security in East Asia. This means that accommodation would involve heavy costs, which is why one side of the debate over the future of Sino-American relations thinks that conflict is inevitable. What China wants, the United States will not give up without a fight. Thus the United States should prepare to contain rather than accommodate China's rise.

But what proponents of containment ignore is the argument at the center of this book: failing to accommodate has costs that go beyond the direct military expenses and opportunity costs associated with "pivoting to Asia" or the possibility of having defensive intentions misinterpreted as offensive ones. They also include the danger that containment will fundamentally alter political conditions inside China in a way that benefits actors with deeply revisionist preferences – the Nativists and their allies. Failing to accommodate China may help to create the China that proponents of containment fear.

It is well beyond the scope of this book to decide whether accommodating China is worth the sort of significant concessions that it might require. My aim in the rest of this chapter is merely to propose a framework that integrates insights about the consequences and dynamics of accommodation failure into debates about American grand strategy. This should help to shed new light on some of the calculations that American decision-makers will have to make in the coming decades.

The framework I develop is premised upon the idea – introduced in Chapter 2 – that containment and accommodation are not opposite positions along the same dimension of policy, but rather describe different positions on separate policy dimensions. Containment refers to a commitment to preventing a state from materially dominating its region. Its opposite is not accommodation but retrenchment, a policy that withdraws or lessens security commitments abroad and tacitly acquiesces to the material rise of another state.

Accommodation, on the other hand, refers to a policy aimed at recognizing the status claims of another state. Its opposite is not containment but rather status denial: taking steps that signal that the aspiring power does not have legitimate access to the rights and privileges that it claims.

The material and status dimensions sometimes coincide, but they do not always and there is value in keeping them analytically separate. For instance, Ming and Qing China could have accommodated Ashikaga and Tokugawa Japan's status claims without acquiescing in its material domination of East Asia. Similarly, the Western denial of Imperial Japan's status claims in the form of the Lytton Report had no effect on Japan's ability to materially dominate mainland Asia – it was merely a symbolic move that denied the legitimacy of Japan's claim to a sphere of influence.

Combining these two dimensions yields four ideal-typical established-power grand strategic orientations. The first combines accommodation and retrenchment; the second combines accommodation and containment; the third combines status denial and retrenchment; and the fourth combines status denial and containment. Only the first and last of these are likely to be viable long-term American approaches to the rise of China, which will present American policymakers with a difficult choice. The rest of the chapter explains why the others – accommodation/containment and status denial/ retrenchment – are unlikely to be effective and outlines the difficult choice between accommodation/retrenchment and status denial/containment.

The Illusions of Cost-Free Denial and Sacrifice-Free Accommodation

The second and third strategies often seem attractive because, in different ways, they seem to promise important benefits while allowing the

established state to avoid incurring serious costs or making serious sacrifices. Status denial/retrenchment does this by denying the status claims of
the rising power, but at the same time retrenching in order to avoid paying
the costs of containing the rising power. In other words, this combination
completely ignores the possibility that denial will produce a deeply revisionist rising power that will then need to be contained – at much greater
cost – later. This was the mistake that the Allied powers made in imposing
the Versailles settlement on Germany without being willing to prevent the
renewed rise of German power. Versailles activated forces that contributed
to the rise of Hitler, yet Allied leaders were unwilling to take steps to reduce
potential German power (as they did after World War II).

There is some danger that the American approach to the rise of China
could approximate a status denial/retrenchment strategy. In spite of the
recent "pivot to Asia," American attention remains divided among other
regions, in particular the Middle East and Eastern Europe. And attitudes
toward security commitments abroad among the American public are
ambivalent at best, as the victory of the quasi-isolationist Donald Trump
in the 2016 presidential election dramatically highlighted.[16] At the same
time, there is little indication that the United States is ready to seriously
accommodate Chinese demands for equal status and rights. Indeed,
Trump's erratic approach to foreign policy could lead him to send salient
and damaging signals of status denial without even realizing it – after all, one
of his first moves as president-elect was to have a direct phone conversation
with the president of Taiwan.[17] And if Ikenberry is right about the salutary
effects of the "open" nature of the liberal order on the prospects for accommodating rising powers, the possible disintegration of the order at the hands
of the Trump administration will only make effective accommodation
harder.[18] This is a troubling combination. Accommodation failure is likely
to help create a China that will need to be confronted, but the United States'
commitment to preparing for that confrontation by strengthening relationships with East Asian allies is shaky at best.

Accommodation/containment is also unlikely to work, but for
a different reason. This is a hedging strategy. It acknowledges that the
rising power's orientation toward the status quo depends upon its treatment by the established power, and thus it seeks to accommodate the
rising power wherever possible. At the same time, it is committed to
defending against the possibility that the rising power may turn aggressive, and thus pairs accommodation with the maintenance of a robust

---

[16] For attempts to make sense of Trump's foreign policy, see Wright (2016) and Dueck
(2015).
[17] Charlie Campbell (December 2, 2016).
[18] Ikenberry (2011); Ikenberry and Wright (2008).

military presence in the rising state's region in order to limit the riser's influence and power.

This approximates a commonly promoted approach to managing the rise of China – so-called congagement. Advocates of congagement argue that China should be engaged economically, socially, and politically (to tie China to the liberal international order), while being deterred militarily through a robust American military presence in East Asia.[19] This combination is supposed to shape China's orientation toward the status quo by simultaneously showing its leaders the benefits of cooperation and the costs of confrontation, while also hedging against the possibility that China could become aggressive in the future.

In principle, there is nothing wrong with accommodation/containment. If the rising power's status claims do not include the demand for an exclusive sphere of influence in its near abroad, then containment and accommodation can be pursued simultaneously. Unfortunately, that may not be true of China's status ambitions. China's claim to great power status does seem likely to include a demand for some kind of sphere of influence in East Asia. This means that it is unlikely that China can be completely bought off by increasing its influence in status quo institutions – or even, as Glaser proposes, by acceding to its reunification with Taiwan.[20] It also means that pursuing the goal of containment is likely to undermine the pursuit of the goal of accommodation.[21] Accommodating China probably requires that the United States dramatically reduce its presence and influence in China's backyard. Anything less would leave status ambitions unsatisfied, which would provide fodder for Chinese hardliners to harness the political advantages that come along with evidence of status "glass ceilings." This is why a "grand bargain" in which the United States gives Beijing its support for Taiwan reunification in exchange for China's approval of a long-term American military presence in East Asia is unrealistic: it fails to acknowledge the nature of China's status ambitions and thus the scope of the sacrifice that accommodating them would require.

Accommodation and Retrenchment or Denial and Containment?

Because of the problems with the two intermediate strategic combinations, in the long-run American decisionmakers may have to choose

---

[19] For two recent arguments in favor of this sort of approach, see Christensen (2015) and Glaser (2015). See also Goldstein (2005), Nye (2006), Ikenberry (2011), and Etzioni (2011).

[20] Glaser (2015).

[21] For a similar argument about the strategic inconsistency at the heart of "congagement," see Logan (2013).

between the two extremes: accommodate Chinese status claims while retrenching, or deny Chinese status claims while committing to maintain American dominance in East Asia, thereby containing the rise of Chinese power. In short, the choice is whether to commit to creating a Chinese partner while accepting the reduction in American influence that would likely require, or contribute – with eyes wide open – to the creation of a deeply revisionist Chinese rival while embracing the costs of confronting that reality.

The latter approach is much like the one preferred by Chapter 7's rejectionists.[22] Chinese ambitions are bound to run up against American interests, and it is no use pretending otherwise. The United States must begin to see China as a long-term strategic rival and prepare accordingly. From this perspective, there is no reason to attempt accommodation, because accommodation would require sacrifices inconsistent with either American vital interests or non-negotiable values. This would be an expensive and risky approach to managing Sino-American relations, but it at least does not suffer from the illusion that the United States can maintain its privileged position in international politics without confronting a challenge from a dissatisfied China.

The former approach is one that few policymakers and scholars openly promote.[23] If the United States is interested in avoiding the creation of a deeply revisionist, anti-Western China, it needs to accommodate China's status claims. Since these likely include the right to a sphere of influence in East Asia, accommodation would likely have to involve a reduction of the American military presence and American influence in that region. This does not mean conceding global leadership to China. Rather, the aim would be to acknowledge that China, as a great power, deserves the same rights that the United States does in world politics – including the right to manage East Asia and the South China Sea the way that the United States manages Latin America and the Caribbean.

This approach carries with it great risks and costs as well. What would be the effect on navigation and trade through the South China Sea? Would important American allies like Japan and South Korea turn into Beijing's vassals? What if an American withdrawal from East Asia produces a regional arms race? And what if China grows more ambitious rather than more satisfied as the United States withdraws overseas?

But accommodation/retrenchment also has some important advantages. Foremost among them is that it avoids antagonizing Beijing: it is premised

---

[22] See especially Pillsbury (2015); Mearsheimer (2010); Friedberg (2011); Kagan (1997, 2005); and Luttwak (2012).

[23] Layne (2014, 2015); Shapiro (2015); and Goldstein (2015, pp. 17–18) are notable recent exceptions.

upon the idea that, all else equal, accommodation is preferable to denial because denial activates forces that empower hardliners. Accommodation holds out the possibility of empowering moderates and facilitating China's integration within a reformed version of the liberal international order that has served its economic interests well. Another advantage is that accommodation/retrenchment is cheaper than any approach involving containment. Retrenchment would reduce American military expenditures while simultaneously creating incentives for other regional powers to bear a greater share of their defense burdens. The United States could return to an offshore balancing posture, which would allow it to redeploy to the region only if China tried to overthrow the new version of the status quo order by, say launching a war in East Asia. But by not signaling status denial, Washington would short circuit one of the major causes of radical revisionist challenges in history, thereby reducing the likelihood that active *onshore* balancing would be necessary.

It is worth emphasizing once again that accommodation would very likely have to involve the abandonment of the role that the United States has played in East Asian politics since the end of World War II. The idea that the United States has a right to exercise power in East Asia without consulting China is incompatible with Chinese status claims just as the idea that the British had a right to exercise power in the Americas without consulting the United States was inconsistent with American status claims in the late nineteenth century. The accommodation/retrenchment combination requires painful sacrifices just as the status denial/containment combination carries with it high costs and risks of Sino-American conflict.

Whether the former is more attractive than the latter depends upon answers to two difficult questions. First, is maintaining American dominance in East Asia a vital interest? Is it worth the high military spending that confronting a dissatisfied China would require and the heightened risk of Sino-American conflict that this course would likely run? Second, is American dominance in East Asia sustainable over the long run? For how long can the United States rely on the American military to provide security in the region and to guarantee freedom of navigation in the South China Sea?

Reasonable people can disagree about the answers to these questions. But too often (both in the past and in current debates over American policy toward China), leaders have sought to avoid engaging them because they are difficult. This is the danger of the intermediate strategic approaches, which are attractive precisely because they do not acknowledge that the rise of new great powers typically requires either painful or costly and risky adjustments by established powers. This book's most important implication for American grand strategy is that leaders should not put this debate off. China – if it continues to rise – will have to be either accommodated seriously or denied and contained. Analysts and policymakers must disabuse themselves of the comforting notion that China can be accommodated without making significant sacrifices or denied without paying the costs of confronting a deeply revisionist rising power.

References

Abel, Theodore. 1986. *Why Hitler Came into Power*. Cambridge, MA: Harvard University Press.

Abrams, Dominic, and Peter Grant. 2012. "Testing the Social Identity Relative Deprivation (SIRD) Model of Social Change: The Political Rise of Scottish Nationalism." *British Journal of Social Psychology* 51: 674–689.

Adler-Nissen, Rebecca. 2014. "Stigma Management in International Relations: Transgressive Identities, Norms, and Order in International Society." *International Organization* 68: 143–176.

Allen, William. 1965. *The Nazi Seizure of Power*. Chicago: Franklin Watts.

Ambrosio, Thomas. 2005. *Challenging America's Global Preeminence: Russia's Quest for Multipolarity*. Hampshire, UK: Ashgate.

Andelman, David. 2008. *A Shattered Peace: Versailles 1919 and the Price We Pay Today*. Hoboken, NJ: Wiley & Sons.

Anderson, Stuart. 1981. *Race and Rapprochement: Anglo-Saxonism and Anglo-American Relations, 1895–1904*. Rutherford, NJ: Fairleigh Dickinson University Press.

Art, Robert. 2003. *A Grand Strategy for America*. Ithaca, NY: Cornell University Press.

Asada, Sadao. 1973. "The Japanese Navy and the United States." In *Pearl Harbor as History: Japanese-American Relations 1931–1941*, eds. Dorothy Borg and Shumpei Okamoto. New York: Columbia University Press.

2014. "The London Conference and the Tragedy of the Imperial Japanese Navy." In *At the Crossroads between Peace and War*, eds. John Maurer and Christopher Bell. Annapolis, MD: Naval Institute Press.

Asagawa, K. 1908. "Japan in Manchuria." *Yale Review* 17: 268–302.

Aydin, Cemil. 2007. *The Politics of Anti-Westernism in Asia: Visions of World Order in Pan-Islamic and Pan-Asian Thought*. New York: Columbia University Press.

Bailey, Thomas. 1934. *Theodore Roosevelt and the Japanese-American Crises*. London: Oxford University Press.

Barme, Geremie. 1995. "To Screw Foreigners Is Patriotic: China's Avant-Garde Nationalists." *The China Journal* 34: 209–234.

Barnett, Michael, and Raymond Duvall. 2005. "Power in International Politics." *International Organization* 59: 39–75.

Barnhart, Joslyn. 2016. "Status Competition and Territorial Aggression: Evidence from the Scramble for Africa." *Security Studies* 25(3): 385–419.

Barnhart, Michael. 1987. *Japan Prepares for Total War: The Search for Economic Security, 1919–1924.* Ithaca: Cornell University Press.

Baynes, Norman, ed. 1942. *The Speeches of Adolf Hitler: April 1922–August 1939.* London: Oxford University Press.

Beasley, William G. 1955. *Select Documents in Japanese Foreign Policy, 1853–1868.* Oxford: Oxford University Press.

1963. *The Modern History of Japan.* New York: St. Martin's Press.

Beckley, Michael. 2015. "China's Century? Why America's Edge Will Endure." *International Security* 36: 41–78.

Beisner, Robert. 1975. *From the Old Diplomacy to the New, 1865–1900.* New York: Thomas Y. Crowell.

Bell, Duncan. 2007. *The Idea of Greater Britain: Empire and the Future of World Order, 1860–1900.* Princeton: Princeton University Press.

Bendersky, Joseph. 2014. *A Concise History of Nazi Germany.* Lanham, MD: Rowman & Littlefield.

Bennett, Andrew, and Colin Elman. 2006. "Complex Causal Relations and Case Study Methods: The Example of Path Dependence." *Political Analysis* 14: 250–267.

Bennett, Edward. 1979. *German Rearmament and the West, 1932–1933.* Princeton, NJ: Princeton University Press.

Berger, Gordon. 1977. *Parties Out of Power in Japan, 1931–1941.* Princeton: Princeton University Press.

Berger, Joseph, Murray Webster Jr., Cecilia Ridgeway, and Susan J. Rosenholtz. 1998. "Status Cues, Expectations, and Behavior." In *Status, Power, and Legitimacy: Strategies and Theories,* eds. Joseph Berger and Morris Zelditch Jr. New Brunswick and London: Transaction.

Berger, Joseph, and Morris Zelditch, eds. 1998. *Status, Power, and Legitimacy: Strategies and Theories.* New Brunswick, NJ: Transaction.

Berghahn, Volker R. 1973. *Germany and the Approach of War 1914.* New York: St. Martin's Press.

Bernhardi, Friedrich. 1914a. *Britain as Germany's Vassal.* London: Wm. Dawson & Sons Ltd.

1914b. *Germany and the Next War.* New York: Longman, Greens, and Co.

Bernstein, Richard. February 23, 2012. "The Chinese Are Coming!" *The New York Review of Books.* Available at www.nybooks.com/articles/2012/02/23/chinese-are-coming/.

Bernstein, Richard, and Ross Munro. 1997. "The Coming Conflict with America." *Foreign Affairs* 76: 18–32.

Betts, Richard. 1994. "Wealth, Power, and Instability: East Asia and the United States after the Cold War." *International Security* 18: 34–77.

Beverina, Juan. 1973. *La Guerra del Paraguay: 1865–1870.* Buenos Aires: Circulo Militar.

Bezerra, Paul, Jacob Cramer, Megan Hauser, Jennifer Miller, and Thomas J. Volgy. 2015. "Going for the Gold versus Distributing the Green: Foreign

Policy Substitutability and Complementarity in Status Enhancement Strategies." *Foreign Policy Analysis* 11: 253–272.

Bially Mattern, Janice, and Ayşe Zarakol. 2016. "Hierarchies in World Politics." *International Organization* 70: 623–654.

Bix, Herbert. 2000. *Hirohito and the Making of Modern Japan*. New York: HarperCollins.

Blanz, M., A. Mummenedey, R. Mielke, and A. Klink. 1998. "Responding to Negative Social Identity: A Taxonomy of Identity Management Strategies." *European Journal of Social Psychology* 28: 697–729.

Boen, Filip, and Norbert Vanbeselaere. 1998. "Reactions Upon a Failed Attempt to Enter a High Status Group: An Experimental Test of the Five-Stage Model." *European Journal of Social Psychology* 28: 689–696.

2000. "Responding to Membership of a Low-Status Group: The Effects of Stability, Permeability and Individual Ability." *Group Processes and Intergroup Relations* 3: 41–62.

Boltho, Andrea. 1996. "Was Japanese Growth Export-Led?" *Oxford Economic Papers* 48: 415–432.

Bourne, Kenneth. 1967. *Britain and the Balance of Power in North America, 1815–1908*. Berkeley, CA: University of California Press.

Boyle, T. 1978. "The Venezuela Crisis and the Liberal Opposition, 1895–96." *The Journal of Modern History* 50: D1185–D1212.

Bracher, Karl. 1991. *The German Dictatorship: The Origins, Structure, and Consequences of National Socialism*. London: Penguin Books.

Brands, H.W., ed. 2001. *The Selected Letters of Theodore Roosevelt*. New York: Cooper Square Press.

Brands, Hal. 2014. *What Good Is Grand Strategy? Power and Purpose in American Statecraft from Harry S. Truman to George W. Bush*. Ithaca: Cornell University Press.

Branscombe, N.R., and D.L. Wann. 1994. "Collective Self-Esteem Consequences of Outgroup Derogation When a Valued Social Identity Is on Trial." *European Journal of Social Psychology* 24: 641–657.

Bray, Arturo. 1945. *Solano Lopéz: Soldado de la Gloria y del Infortunio*. Buenos Aires: Guillermo Kraft.

Breslin, Shaun, and Simon Shen. 2010. "Online Chinese Nationalism(s): Comparisons and Findings." In *Online Chinese Nationalism and China's Bilateral Relations*, eds. Simon Shen and Shaun Breslin. Lanham: Rowman and Littlefield.

Bretton, Henry. 1953. *Stresemann and the Revision of Versailles*. Stanford, CA: Stanford University Press.

Brooks, Stephen, G. John Ikenberry, and William Wohlforth. 2013. "Don't Come Home, America: The Case Against Retrenchment." *International Security* 37: 7–51.

Brooks, Stephen, and William Wohlforth. 2015. "The Rise and Fall of the Great Powers in the Twenty-First Century: China's Rise and the Fate of America's Global Position." *International Security* 40: 7–53.

2016. *America Abroad: The United States' Global Role in the 21st Century*. New York: Oxford University Press.

Brower, Kate Anderson, and Lisa Lerer. June 13, 2012. "China-Bashing as Campaign Rhetoric Binds Obama to Romney." *Bloomberg*. Available at www.bloomberg.com/news/articles/2012–06–04/china-bashing-binds-obama-to-romney-with-trade-imbalance-as-foil.

Bukovansky, Mlada. 2002. *Legitimacy and Power Politics: The American and French Revolutions in International Political Culture*. Princeton, NJ: Princeton University Press.

Bull, Hedley. 1977. *The Anarchical Society: A Study of Order in World Politics*. New York: Columbia University Press.

Bullock, Alan. 1971. *Hitler: A Study in Tyranny*. New York: HarperCollins.

Bülow, Bernhard von. 1931. *Memoirs of Prince Von Bulow: From the Morocco Crisis to Resignation, 1903–1909*. Vol. II. Boston: Little, Brown, and Company.

Burk, Kathleen. 1985. *Britain, America, and the Sinews of War, 1914–1918*. New York: Harper Collins.

Burkman, Thomas W. 2008. *Japan and the League of Nations*. Honolulu: University of Hawaii Press.

Burleigh, Michael. 2000. *The Third Reich: A New History*. New York: Hill and Wang.

Buzan, Barry. 1991. *People, States and Fear*. Hemel Hempstead: Wheatsheaf.

2010. "China in International Society: Is 'Peaceful Rise' Possible?" *The Chinese Journal of International Politics* 3: 5–36.

Buzas, Zoltan. 2013. "The Color of Threat: Race, Threat Perception, and the Demise of the Anglo-Japanese Alliance (1902–1923)." *Security Studies* 22: 573–606.

Callahan, William. 2004. "National Insecurities: Humiliation, Salvation, and Chinese Nationalism." *Alternatives* 29: 199–218.

2013. *China Dreams: 20 Visions of the Future*. New York: Oxford University Press.

Campbell, Charles. 1957. *Anglo-American Understanding: 1898–1903*. Baltimore: Johns Hopkins Press.

1974. *From Revolution to Rapprochement: The United States and Great Britain, 1783–1900*. New York: John Wiley & Sons.

1976. *The Transformation of American Foreign Relations, 1865–1900*. New York: Harper & Row.

Campbell, Charlie. December 2, 2016. "Donald Trump Angers China with Historic Phone Call to Taiwan's President." *Time*. Available at http://time.com/4589641/donald-trump-china-taiwan-call/.

Campbell, D.A. 2007. *Unlikely Allies: Britain, America, and the Victorian Origins of the Special Relationship*. London: Hambledon Continuum.

"The Capture of Manila" and "The Fate of the Philippines," May 7, 1898. *The Spectator*, No. 3,645: 645–646.

Carlson, Allen. 2005. *Unifying China, Integrating with the World*. Stanford, CA: Stanford University Press.

Carpenter, Ted Galen. October 11, 2012. "China Bashing: A U.S. Political Tradition." *Reuters*. Available at http://blogs.reuters.com/great-debate/2012/10/11/china-bashing-a-political-tradition/.

Carr, E.H. 1946. *The Twenty Years' Crisis, 1919–1938: An Introduction to the Study of International Relations*. New York: Harper.

Carroll, Eber Malcolm. 1966. *Germany and the Great Powers, 1866–1914: A Study in Public Opinion and Foreign Policy*. Hamden, CT: Archon Books.

Castañeda, Jorge. 2011. "The Trouble with the Brics." *Foreign Policy*. Available at http://foreignpolicy.com/2011/03/14/the-trouble-with-the-brics/.

Chan, Steve. 2004. "Can't Get No Satisfaction? The Recognition of Revisionist States." *International Relations of the Asia Pacific* 4: 207–238.

Chen, Dingding, Xiaoyu Pu, and Alastair Iain Johnston. 2014. "Debating China's Assertiveness." *International Security* 38: 176–183.

Chen, Zhimin. 2005. "Coastal Provinces and China's Foreign Policy Making." In *China's Foreign Policy Making: Societal Force and Chinese American Policy*, eds. Yufan Hao and Lin Su. Hampshire, UK: Ashgate.

Chickering, Roger. 1984. *We Men Who Feel Most German: A Cultural Study of the Pan-German League, 1886–1914*. Boston: George Allen & Unwin.

Childers, Thomas. 1983. *The Nazi Voter: The Social Foundations of Fascism in Germany, 1919–1933*. Chapel Hill, NC: University of North Carolina Press.

Chong, Ja Ian, and Todd Hall. 2014. "The Lessons of 1914 for East Asia Today: Missing the Trees for the Forest." *International Security* 39: 7–43.

Christensen, Thomas. 1996. *Useful Adversaries: Grand Strategy, Domestic Mobilization, and Sino-American Conflict, 1947–1958*. Princeton: Princeton University Press.

2015. *The China Challenge: Shaping the Choices of a Rising Power*. New York: W. W. Norton.

Christensen, Thomas, Alastair Iain Johnston, and Robert Ross. 2006. "Conclusions and Future Directions." In *New Directions in the Study of China's Foreign Policy*, eds. Alastair Iain Johnston and Robert Ross. Stanford, CA: Stanford University Press.

Christensen, Thomas, and Jack Snyder. 1990. "Chain Gangs and Passed Bucks: Alliance Patterns in Multipolarity." *International Organization* 44: 137–168.

Clark, Christopher. 2012. *The Sleepwalkers: How Europe Went to War in 1914*. New York: Harper.

Clark, Ian. 2011. *Hegemony in International Society*. Oxford: Oxford University Press.

2005. *Legitimacy in International Society*. Oxford: Oxford University Press.

Clunan, Anne. 2009. *The Social Construction of Russia's Resurgence: Aspirations, Identity, and Security Interests*. Baltimore: The Johns Hopkins University Press.

2014a. "Historical Aspirations and the Domestic Politics of Russia's Pursuit of International Status." *Communist and Post-Communist Studies* 47: 281–290.

2014b. "Why Status Matters in World Politics." In *Status in World Politics*, eds. William Wohlforth, Deborah Larson and T.V. Paul. New York: Cambridge University Press.

Cohrs, Patrick. 2006. *The Unfinished Peace After World War I: America, Britain and the Stabilisation of Europe, 1919–1932*. Cambridge: Cambridge University Press.

Collar, Peter. 2013. *The Propaganda War in the Rhineland: Weimar Germany, Race and Occupation after World War I*. London: I.B. Tauris.

Conroy, Hilary. 1951. "Government Versus "Patriot": The Background of Japan's Asiatic Expansion." *Pacific Historical Review* 20: 31–42.

Cooper, John Milton. 2009. *Woodrow Wilson: A Biography*. New York: Random House.

Copeland, Dale C. 2000. *The Origins of Major War*. Ithaca: Cornell University Press.

   2011. "A Tragic Choice: Japanese Preventive Motivations and the Origins of the Pacific War." *International Interactions* 37: 116–126.

   2014. *Economic Interdependence and War*. Princeton: Princeton University Press.

Craig, Albert. 1968. "Fukuzawa Yukichi: The Philosophical Foundations of Meiji Nationalism." In *Political Development in Modern Japan*, ed. Robert Ward. Princeton: Princeton University Press.

Cramb, J.A. 1914. *Germany and England*. London: John Murray.

Crisp, Richard, Catriona Stone, and Natalie Hall. 2006. "Recategorization and Subgroup Identification: Predicting and Preventing Threats from Common Ingroups." *Personality and Social Psychology Bulletin* 32: 230–243.

Cronon, E. David, ed. 1963. *The Cabinet Diaries of Josephus Daniels, 1913–1921*. Lincoln, NE: University of Nebraska Press.

Crowley, James. 1966. *Japan's Quest for Autonomy*. Princeton: Princeton University Press.

   1974. "Japan's Military Foreign Policies." In *Japan's Foreign Policy, 1868–1941: A Research Guide*, ed. James Morley. New York: Columbia University Press.

Daase, Christopher, Caroline Fehl, Anna Geis, and Georgios Kolliarakis, eds. 2015. *Recognition in International Relations: Rethinking a Political Concept in a Global Context*. New York: Palgrave Macmillan.

Dafoe, Allan, Jonathan Renshon, and Paul Huth. 2014. "Reputation and Status as Motives for War." *Annual Review of Political Science* 17: 371–393.

Daniels, Roger. 1988. *Asian America: Chinese and Japanese in the United States since 1850*. Seattle: University of Washington Press.

Davidson, Jason. 2006. *The Origins of Revisionist and Status-Quo States*. New York: Palgrave Macmillan.

de Bary, William Theodore, Carol Gluck, and Arthur Tiedemann, eds. 2005. *Sources of Japanese Tradition, 1600–2000*, Second Edition. Vol. 2. New York: Columbia University Press.

de Carvalho, Benjamin, and Jon Harald Sande Lie. 2015. "A Great Power Performance: Norway, Status and the Policy of Involvement." In *Small State Status Seeking: Norway's Quest for International Standing*, eds. Iver Neumann and Benjamin de Carvalho. London: Routledge.

de Carvalho, Benjamin, and Iver Neumann, eds. 2015. *Small State Status Seeking: Norway's Quest for International Standing*. London: Routledge.

De la Rey, Cheryl, and Patricia Raju. 1996. "Group Relative Deprivation: Cognitive Versus Affective Components and Protest Orientation among Indian South Africans." *The Journal of Social Psychology* 136: 579–588.

Degrelle, Leon. 1987. *Hitler: Born at Versailles*. Costa Mesa, CA: Institute for Historical Review.

Deng, Yong. 2008. *China's Struggle for Status: The Realignment of International Relations*. Cambridge: Cambridge University Press.

Denyer, Simon. July 7, 2014. "China's Rise and Asian Tensions Send U.S. Relations into Downward Spiral." *Washington Post*. Available at www.was hingtonpost.com/world/asia_pacific/chinas-rise-and-asian-tensions-send-us -relations-into-downward-spiral/2014/07/07/f371cfaa-d5cd-4dd2-925c-24 6c099f04ed_story.html?utm_term=.1769c8ac3fa1.

DGFP. 1918–1945. *Documents on German Foreign Policy*. Series C (1933–1937): vol. I [January 30–October 14 1933].

Diamond, Jeremy. May 2, 2016. "Trump: 'We Can't Allow China to Rape Our Country.'" *CNN*. Available at www.cnn.com/2016/05/01/politics/donald-trump-china-rape/index.html.

Dobson, Alan. 1995. *Anglo-American Relations in the Twentieth Century*. London: Routledge.

Dobson, John. 1978. *America's Ascent: The United States Becomes a Great Power, 1880–1914*. DeKalb, IL: Northern Illinois University Press.

Doenecke, Justus. 2011. *Nothing Less Than War: A New History of America's Entry into World War I*. Lexington, KY: The University Press of Kentucky.

Donnelly, Jack. 1998. "Human Rights: A New Standard of Civilization?" *International Affairs* 74: 1–23.

Doosje, B., Naomi Ellemers, and R. Spears. 1995. "Perceived Intragroup Variability as a Function of Group Status and Identification." *Journal of Experimental Social Psychology* 31: 410–436.

Druckman, Daniel. 1994. "Nationalism, Patriotism, and Group Loyalty: A Social Psychological Perspective." *Mershon International Studies Review* 38: 43–68.

Dube, L., and S. Guimond. 1986. "Relative Deprivation and Social Protest: The Personal Group Issue." In *Relative Deprivation and Social Comparison*, eds. J. M. Olson, C.P. Herman and M.P. Zanna. Hillsdale, NJ: Erlbaum.

Dudden, Alexis. 1975. *Japan's Colonization of Korea: Discourse and Power*. Honolulu: University of Hawaii Press.

Dueck, Colin. 2015. "Donald Trump, American Nationalist." *The National Interest*. Available at http://nationalinterest.org/feature/donald-trump-ameri can-nationalist-14237.

Dugdale, E.T.S. 1930. *German Diplomatic Documents, 1871–1914*. Vol. III. London: Methuen & Co., Ltd.

    1931. *German Diplomatic Documents, 1871–1914*. Vol. IV. London: Methuen & Co., Ltd.

Duus, Peter. 1989. *The Cambridge History of Japan*, Vol. 6. Cambridge, UK: Cambridge University Press.

Earl, David. 1964. *Emperor and Nation in Japan: Political Thinkers of the Tokugawa Period*. Seattle: University of Washington Press.

East, Maurice. 1972. "Status Discrepancy and Violence in the International System: An Empirical Analysis." In *The Analysis of International Politics: Essays in Honor of Harold and Margaret Sprout*, eds. J.N. Rosenau, V. Davis and M.A. East. New York: Free Press.

Eatwell, Roger. 1995. *Fascism: A History*. London: Random House.

Eckstein, Harry. 1975. "Case Studies in Political Science." In *Handbook of Political Science*, eds. Fred Greenstein and Nelson Polsby. Vol. 7. Reading, MA: Addison-Wesley.

Eden, Anthony. 1962. *Facing the Dictators: The Eden Memoirs*. Boston: Houghton-Mifflin.

Eggert, Gerald. 1974. *Richard Olney: Evolution of a Statesman*. University Park, PA: The Pennsylvania State University Press.

Einstein, Lewis. 1918. *A Prophecy of the War*. New York: Columbia University Press.

Ellemers, Naomi, R. Spears, and B. Doosje. 1997. "Sticking Together or Falling Apart: Group Identification as a Psychological Determinant of Group Commitment Versus Individual Mobility." *Journal of Personality and Social Psychology* 72: 617–626.

Eller, Anja, and Dominic Abrams. 2004. "Come Together: Longitudinal Comparisons of Pettigrew's Reformulated Intergroup Contact Model in Anglo-French and Mexican-American Contexts." *European Journal of Social Psychology* 34: 229–256.

Elvert, Jurgen. 2003. "Why Did the Approaches to Conclude an Anglo-German Alliance Fail? Foreign Policy, British Public Opinion, and the Anglo-German Explorations from 1898 to 1900." In *Debating Foreign Affairs: The Public and British Foreign Policy since 1867*, ed. Christian Haase. Berlin: Philo.

Etzioni, Amitai. 1962. *The Hard Way to Peace: A New Strategy*. New York: Cromwell-Collier Press.

2011. "China: Making an Adversary." *International Politics* 48: 647–666.

2016. "Freedom of Navigation Assertions: The United States as the World's Policeman." *Armed Forces & Society* 42: 501–517.

Evangelista, Matthew. 1993. "Internal and External Constraints on Grand Strategy: The Soviet Case." In *The Domestic Bases of Grand Strategy*, eds. Richard Rosecrance and Arthur Stein. Ithaca: Cornell University Press.

Evans, Richard. 2004. *The Coming of the Third Reich*. New York: Penguin Press.

"Exciting Scenes in Washington." December 18, 1895. *New York Times*. pp. 1–2.

Eyck, Erich. 1962a. *A History of the Weimar Republic*, Vol. 1. Cambridge, MA: Harvard University Press.

1962b. *A History of the Weimar Republic*. Vol. 2. Cambridge, MA: Harvard University Press.

Fairbank, John, ed. 1968. *The Chinese World Order: Traditional China's Foreign Relations*. Cambridge, MA: Harvard University Press.

Fearon, James D. 1991. "Counterfactuals and Hypothesis Testing in Political Science." *World Politics* 43: 169–195.

Feldman, Noah. 2013. *Cool War: The Future of Global Competition*. New York: Random House.

Ferguson, John. 1939. *American Diplomacy and the Boer War*. Philadelphia: University of Pennsylvania Press.

Ferguson, Niall. 1998. *The Pity of War: Explaining World War I*. New York: Basic Books.

Feuchtwanger, E.J. 1993. *From Weimar to Hitler: Germany, 1918–1933*. New York: St. Martin's Press.

Fewsmith, Joseph, and Stanley Rosen. 2001. "The Domestic Context of Chinese Foreign Policy: Does 'Public Opinion' Matter?" In *The Making of Chinese Foreign and Security Policy in the Era of Reform*, ed. David Lampton. Stanford, CA: Stanford University Press.

Fikenscher, Sven-Eric, Lena Jaschob, and Rienhard Wolf. 2015. "Seeking Status Recognition through Military Symbols: German and Indian Armament Policies between Strategic Rationalizations and Prestige Motives." In *Recognition in International Relations: Rethinking a Political Concept in a Global Context*, eds. Christopher Daase, Caroline Fehl, Anna Geis, and Georgios Kolliarakis. New York: Palgrave Macmillan.

Fischer, Conan, ed. 1996. *The Rise of National Socialism and the Working Classes in Weimar Germany*. Oxford, UK: Berghahn Books.

Fischer, Fritz. 1961. *Germany's Aims in the First World War*. New York: W.W. Norton.

1965. *World Power or Decline: The Controversy Over Germany's Aims in the First World War*. New York: W.W. Norton.

1969. *War of Illusions: German Policies from 1911 to 1914*. New York: W.W. Norton.

Forsberg, Tuomas. 2014. "Status Conflicts Between Russia and the West: Perceptions and Emotional Biases." *Communist and Post-Communist Studies* 47: 323–331.

Frank, Robert. 1985. *Choosing the Right Pond: Human Behavior and the Quest for Status*. Oxford: Oxford University Press.

Freedman, Joshua. 2016. "Status Insecurity and Temporality in World Politics." *European Journal of International Relations* 22: 797–822.

Freeman, Joanne. 2001. *Affairs of Honor: National Politics in the New Republic*. New Haven, CT: Yale University Press.

Friedberg, Aaron. 1988. *The Weary Titan: Britain and the Experience of Relative Decline, 1895–1905*. Princeton, NJ: Princeton University Press.

1994. "Ripe for Rivalry: Prospects for Peace in a Multipolar Asia." *International Security* 18: 5–33.

2000. "The Struggle for Mastery in Asia." *Commentary* 110: 17–26.

2011. *A Contest for Supremacy: China, America, and the Struggle for Mastery in Asia*. New York: W.W. Norton.

2015. "The Sources of Chinese Conduct: Explaining Beijing's Assertiveness." *The Washington Quarterly* 37: 133–150.

Fritz, Stephen. 1987. "The NSDAP as Volkspartei? A Look at the Social Basis of the Nazi Voter." *The History Teacher* 20: 379–399.

FRUS. 1895. *Papers Relating to the Foreign Relations of the United States, Part I*. Washington, DC: Government Printing Office.

1920. *Papers Relating the Foreign Relations of the United States*. Washington, DC: Government Printing Office.

Fulda, Bernharda. 2009. *Press and Politics in the Weimar Republic*. Oxford, UK: Oxford University Press.

Gaertner, Sameul, and John Dovidio. 2005. "Understanding and Addressing Contemporary Racism: From Aversive Racism to the Common Ingroup Identity Model." *Journal of Social Issues* 61: 615–639.

Galtung, Johan. 1964. "A Structural Theory of Aggression." *Journal of Peace Research* 1: 95–119.

Garrett, F. Edmund. 1897. *The Story of an African Crisis*. Westminster, UK: Archibald Constable.

Gatzke, Hans. 1954. *Stresemann and the Rearmament of Germany*. Baltimore: Johns Hopkins University Press.

Geiss, Imanuel. 1967. *July 1914: The Outbreak of the First World War, Selected Documents*. New York: Charles Scribner's Sons.

1976. *German Foreign Policy, 1871–1914*. London: Routledge.

Gelber, Lionel. 1938. *The Rise of Anglo-American Friendship: A Study in World Politics, 1898–1906*. London: Oxford University Press.

George, Alexander, and Andrew Bennett. 2004. *Case Studies and Theory Development in the Social Sciences*. Cambridge: MIT Press.

Gest, Justin. 2016. *The New Minority: White Working Class Politics in an Age of Immigration and Inequality*. New York: Oxford University Press.

Gilpin, Robert. 1981. *War and Change in World Politics*. Cambridge: Cambridge University Press.

Glaser, Charles. 2004. "When Are Arms Races Dangerous? Rational versus Suboptimal Arming." *International Security* 24: 44–84.

2015. "A U.S.-China Grand Bargain? The Hard Choice between Military Competition and Accommodation." *International Security* 39: 49–90.

Gochman, Charles. 1980. "Status, Capabilities, and Major Power Conflict." In *The Correlates of War II: Testing Some Realpolitik Models*, ed. J. David Singer. New York: Free Press.

Goddard, Stacie E. 2009. "When Right Makes Might: How Prussia Overturned the European Balance of Power." *International Security* 33: 110–142.

Goddard, Stacie E., and Ronald Krebs. 2015. "Rhetoric, Legitimation, and Grand Strategy." *Security Studies* 24: 5–36.

Goethals, George, and John Darley. 1987. "Social Comparison Theory: Self-Evaluation and Group Life." In *Theories of Group Behavior*, eds. George Goethals and Brian Mullen. New York: Springer-Verlag.

Goldstein, Avery. 2005. *Rising to the Challenge: China's Grand Strategy and International Security*. Palo Alto, CA: Stanford University Press.

Goldstein, Lyle. 2015. *Meeting China Halfway: How to Defuse the Emerging US-China Rivalry*. Washington, DC: Georgetown University Press.

Gong, Gerrit. 1984. *The Standard of Civilization in International Society*. Oxford: Oxford University Press.

Gould, R.V. 2003. *Collision of Wills: How Ambiguity About Social Rank Breeds Conflict*. Chicago: University of Chicago Press.

Gourevitch, Peter. 1978. "The Second Image Reversed: The International Sources of Domestic Politics." *International Organization* 32: 881–912.

Graebner, Norman, and Edward Bennett. 2011. *The Versailles Treaty and Its Legacy: The Failure of the Wilsonian Vision*. New York: Cambridge University Press.

Graeger, Nina. 2015. "From 'Forces for Good' to 'Forces for Status'? Small State Military Status Seeking." In *Small State Status Seeking: Norway's Quest for International Standing*, eds. Iver Neumann and Benjamin de Carvalho. London: Routledge.

Grant, Peter. 2008. "The Protest Intentions of Skilled Immigrants with Credentialing Problems: A Test of a Model Integrating Relative Deprivation Theory with Social Identity Theory." *British Journal of Social Psychology* 47: 687–705.

Grant, Peter, and Rupert Brown. 1995. "From Ethnocentrism to Collective Protest: Reponses to Relative Deprivation and Threats to Social Identity." *Social Psychology Quarterly* 58: 195–212.

Grathwol, Robert. 1968. DNVP and European Reconciliation, 1924–1928: A Study of the Conflict between Party Politics and Government Foreign Policy in Weimar Germany. PhD Dissertation, University of Chicago.

1980. *Stresemann and the DNVP: Reconciliation or Revenge in German Foreign Policy, 1924–1928*. Lawrence, KS: The Regents Press of Kansas.

Greenberg, David. 2006. *Calvin Coolidge*. New York: Times Books.

Greenfeld, Liah. 1990. "The Formation of the Russian National Identity: The Role of Status Insecurity and Ressentiment." *Comparative Studies in Society and History* 32: 549–591.

Grenville, J.A.S. 1955 "Great Britain and the Isthmian Canal, 1898–1901." *American Historical Review* 61: 48–69.

1964. *Lord Salisbury and Foreign Policy, the Close of the Nineteenth Century*. London: Athlone.

Grenville, J.A.S., and George Young. 1966. *Politics, Strategy, and American Diplomacy*. New Haven: Yale University Press.

Grew, Joseph. 1944. *Ten Years in Japan*. New York: Simon and Schuster.

Gries, Peter Hays. 2005a. *China's New Nationalism: Pride, Politics, and Diplomacy*. Berkeley: University of California Press.

2005b. "Nationalism and Chinese Foreign Policy." In *China Rising: Power and Motivation in Chinese Foreign Policy*, eds. Yong Deng and Fei-Ling Wang. New York: Rowman and Littlefield.

Gries, Peter Hays, Qingmin Zhang, H. Michael Crowson, and Huajian Cai. 2011. "Patriotism, Nationalism, and China's U.S. Policy: Structures and Consequences of Chinese National Identity." *The China Quarterly* 205: 1–17.

Grynaviski, Eric. 2013. "Contrasts, Counterfactuals, and Causes." *European Journal of International Relations* 19: 823–846.

Guo, Sujian, ed. 2006. *China's "Peaceful Rise" in the 21st Century: Domestic and International Conditions*. Hampshire: Ashgate.

Gurr, Ted Robert. 1970. *Why Men Rebel*. Princeton: Princeton University Press.

Gwynn, Stephen, ed. 1929. *The Letters and Friendships of Sir Cecil Spring Rice*. 2 vols. Boston: Houghton Mifflin.

Haas, Mark. 2005. *The Ideological Origins of Great Power Politics, 1789–1989*. Ithaca, NY: Cornell University Press.

Halstead, Murat. September 1897. "American Annexation and Armament." *The Forum* 24: 56–66.

Hamilton, Richard. 1982. *Who Voted for Hitler?* Princeton, NJ: Princeton University Press.

Hao, Yufan, and Ying Hou. 2009. "Chinese Foreign Policy Making: A Comparative Perspective." *Public Administration Review* 69: S136–S141.

Hao, Yufan, and Lin Su. 2005. "Contending Views: Emerging Chinese Elites's Perception of America." In *China's Foreign Policy Making: Societal Force and Chinese American Policy*, eds. Yufan Hao and Lin Su. Hampshire, UK: Ashgate.

Harada, Kumao. 1978. *The Saionji-Harada Memoirs, 1931–1940: Complete Translation into English*. Washington, DC: University Publications of America.

Hast, Susanna. 2014. *Spheres of Influence in International Relations: History, Theory and Politics*. Surrey: Ashgate.

Hausrath, Adolf. 1914. *Treitschke: His Doctrine of German Destiny and of International Relations, Together with a Study of His Life and Work*. New York: G.P. Putnam's Sons.

Hawley, Samuel. 2005. *The Imjin War: Japan's Sixteenth Century Invasion of Korea and Attempt to Conquer China*. Seoul: The Royal Asiatic Society.

Heiber, Helmut. 1993. *The Weimar Republic*. Oxford, UK: Blackwell Publishers.

Heimann, Gadi. 2014. "What Does It Take to Be a Great Power? The Story of France Joining the Big Five." *Review of International Studies*. DOI: 10.1017/S0260210514000126.

Helbich, Wolfgang. 1959. "Between Stresemann and Hitler: The Foreign Policy of the Brüning Government." *World Politics* 12: 24–44.

Heller, Regina. 2014. "Russia's Quest for Respect in the International Conflict Management in Kosovo." *Communist and Post-Communist Studies* 47: 333–343.

Herring, George. 2008. *From Colony to Superpower: U.S. Foreign Relations since 1776*. Oxford: Oxford University Press.

Hertzman, Lewis. 1963. *DNVP: Right-Wing Opposition in the Weimar Republic, 1918–1924*. Lincoln, NE: University of Nebraska Press.

Hilgruber, Andreas. 1981. *Germany and the Two World Wars*. Cambridge, MA: Harvard University Press.

Hirobe, Izumi. 2001. *Japanese Pride, American Prejudice: Modifying the Exclusion Clause of the 1924 Immigration Act*. Stanford, CA: Stanford University Press.

Hobbes, Thomas. 1985. *Leviathan*, Introduction by C.B. Macpherson. New York: Penguin.

Hogg, Michael, and Dominic Abrams. 1988. *Social Identifications: A Social Psychology of Intergroup Relations and Group Processes*. London and New York: Routledge.

Holsti, K.J. 1992. "Governance without Government: Polyarchy in Nineteenth-Century European International Politics." In *Governance without Government: Order and Change in World Politics*, eds. James Rosenau and Ernst-Otto Czempiel. Cambridge: Cambridge University Press.

Hong, Junhao. 2005. "The Internet and China's Foreign Policy Making: The Impact of Online Public Opinions as a New Societal Force." In *China's*

Foreign Policy Making: Societal Force and Chinese American Policy, eds. Yufan Hao and Lin Su. Hampshire, UK: Ashgate.

Hornsey, Matthew, and Michael Hogg. 2000. "Subgroup Relations: A Comparison of Mutual Intergroup Differentiation and Common Ingroup Identity Models of Prejudice Reduction." *Personality and Social Psychology Bulletin* 26: 242–256.

Hotta, Eri. 2007. *Pan-Asianism and Japan's War 1931–1945*. New York: Palgrave Macmillan.

———. 2011. "Konoe Fumimaro: 'A Call to Reject the Anglo-American Centered Peace,' 1918." In *Pan-Asianism, a Documentary History, Volume 1: 1850–1920*, eds. Sven Saaler and Christopher Szpilman. Lanham: Rowman and Littlefield.

Hughes, Christopher. 2006. *Chinese Nationalism in the Global Era*. New York: Routledge.

Hull, Isabel. 2015. "Official and Unofficial Nationalism in Imperial Germany's Leap to War in 1914." Ithaca: Cornell University.

Hummel, Alexandre. 2016. "Recognition, the Non-Proliferation Regime, and Proliferation Crises." In *The International Politics of Recognition*, eds. Thomas Lindemann and Erik Ringmar. New York: Routledge.

Humphreys, R.A. 1967. "Presidential Address: Anglo-American Rivalries and the Venezuela Crisis of 1895." *Transactions of the Royal Historical Society* 17: 131–164.

Hurd, Douglas. 1997. *The Search for Peace: A Century of Peace Diplomacy*. New York: Little Brown.

Ikenberry, G. John. 2001. *After Victory: Institutions, Strategic Restraint, and Rebuilding of Order after Major Wars*. Princeton, NJ: Princeton University Press.

———. 2011. *Liberal Leviathan: The Origins, Crisis, and Transformation of the American World Order*. Princeton, NJ: Princeton University Press.

———. 2014. "The Logic of Order: Westphalia, Liberalism, and the Evolution of International Order in the Modern Era." In *Power, Order, and Change in World Politics*, ed. G. John Ikenberry. Cambridge, UK: Cambridge University Press.

Ikenberry, G. John, and Thomas Wright. 2008. "Rising Powers and Global Institutions." A Century Foundation Report. New York: The Century Foundation.

Ilchman, Warren. 1961. *Professional Diplomacy in the United States, 1779–1939: A Study in Administrative History*. Chicago: University of Chicago Press.

Iriye, Akira. 1965. *After Imperialism: The Search for a New Order in the Far East, 1921–1931*. Cambridge, MA: Harvard University Press.

Iriye, Akira. 1972. *Pacific Estrangement: Japanese and American Expansion, 1897–1911*. Cambridge, MA: Harvard University Press.

Ito, Takashi. 1973. "The Role of Right-Wing Organizations in Japan." In *Pearl Harbor as History: Japanese-American Relations 1931–1941*, eds. Dorothy Borg and Shumpei Okamoto. New York: Columbia University Press.

Jackel, Eberhard. 1972. *Hitler's Weltanschauung*. Middletown, CT: Wesleyan University Press.

Jackisch, Barry. 2012. *The Pan-German League and Radical Nationalist Politics in Interwar Germany, 1919–1939.* Surrey: Ashgate.

Jackson, Patrick T. 2011. *The Conduct of Inquiry in International Relations: Philosophy of Science and Its Implications for the Study of World Politics.* New York: Routledge.

Jackson, Patrick Thaddeus. 2006. *Civilizing the Enemy: German Reconstruction and the Invention of the West.* Ann Arbor: University of Michigan Press.

Jacobson, Jon. 1972. *Locarno Diplomacy: Germany and the West, 1925–1929.* Princeton, NJ: Princeton University Press.

1994. *When the Soviet Union Entered World Politics.* Berkeley: University of California Press.

Jacques, Martin. 2009. *When China Rules the World: The End of the Western World and the Birth of a New Global Order.* New York: Penguin.

Jansen, Marius. 1992. *China in the Tokugawa World.* Cambridge, MA: Harvard University Press.

2000. *The Making of Modern Japan.* Cambridge, MA: Harvard University Press.

Jarausch, Konrad. 1972. *The Enigmatic Chancellor: Bethmann Hollweg and the Hubris of Imperial Germany.* New Haven: Yale University Press.

Jervis, Robert. 1978. "Cooperation under the Security Dilemma." *World Politics* 30: 167–214.

"John Bull Is Angry." December 18, 1895. *New York Sun.* p. 1.

Jung, Joo-Youn. 2012. "Rising China and the Chinese Public's Security Perceptions." EAI Asia Security Initiative Working Paper 23. Available at www.eai.or.kr/data/bbs/eng_report/2012051516284649.pdf.

Kagan, Donald. 1995. *The Origins of War and the Preservation of Peace.* New York: Doubleday Publishing.

Kagan, Robert. January 20, 1997. "What China Knows That We Don't: The Case for a New Strategy of Containment." *Weekly Standard.* Available at www.weeklystandard.com/what-china-knows-that-we-dont/article/9599.

Kagan, Robert. May 15, 2005. "The Illusion of 'Managing' China." *Washington Post.* Available at www.washingtonpost.com/wp-dyn/content/article/2005/05/13/AR2005051301405.html.

Kakegawa, Tomiko. 1973. "The Press and Public Opinion in Japan, 1931–1941." In *Pearl Harbor as History: Japanese-American Relations 1931–1941,* eds. Dorothy Borg and Shumpei Okamoto. New York: Columbia University Press.

Kang, David. 2010. *East Asia before the West.* New York: Columbia University Press.

Kater, Michael. 1983. *The Nazi Party: A Social Profile of Members and Leaders, 1919–1945.* Cambridge, MA: Harvard University Press.

Kaufman, Edy. 1976. *The Superpowers and Their Spheres of Influence: The United States and the Soviet Union in Eastern Europe and Latin America.* London: Croom Helm.

Kawakami, K.K., and Kenneth L. Dion. 1995. "Social Identity and Affect as Determinants of Collective Action: Toward an Integration of Relative Deprivation and Social Identity Theories." *Theory & Psychology* 5: 551–577.

Kennan, George. 1996. *At a Century's Ending: Reflections, 1982–1995*. New York: W.W. Norton.

Kennedy, Paul. 1970. "Tirpitz, England, and the Second Navy Law of 1900: A Strategical Critique." *Militargeschichtliche Mitteilungen* 2: 33–57.

1980. *The Rise of the Anglo-German Antagonism 1860–1914*. London: George Allen and Unwin.

1981. *The Realities Behind Diplomacy: Background Influences on British External Policy, 1865–1980*. London: George Allen & Unwin.

Keohane, Robert. 1984. *After Hegemony: Cooperation and Discord in the World Political Economy*. Princeton: Princeton University Press.

Kershaw, Ian. 1998. *Hitler, 1889–1936: Hubris*. New York: W.W. Norton.

Kim, Samuel. 2003. "China's Path to Great Power Status in the Globalization Era." *Asian Perspective* 27: 35–75.

Kimmich, Christoph. 1976. *Germany and the League of Nations*. Chicago: University of Chicago Press.

King, Gary, Robert Keohane, and Sidney Verba. 1994. *Designing Social Inquiry: Scientific Inference in Qualitative Research*. Princeton: Princeton University Press.

Kinzer, Stephen. 2017. *The True Flag: Theodore Roosevelt, Mark Twain, and the Birth of American Empire*. New York: Henry Holt and Company.

Kirshner, Jonathan. 2007. *Appeasing Bankers: Financial Caution on the Road to War*. Princeton: Princeton University Press.

2014. "Gilpin Approaches War and Change: A Classical Realist in Structural Drag." In *Power, Order, and Change in World Politics*, ed. G. John Ikenberry. Cambridge, UK: Cambridge University Press.

Kissinger, Henry. 1957. *A World Restored: Metternich, Castlereagh, and the Problems of Peace, 1812–22*. London: Weidenfeld and Nicolson.

1994. *Diplomacy*. New York: Simon and Schuster.

2014. *World Order*. New York: Penguin Press.

Kolb, Eberhard. 1988. *The Weimar Republic*. London: Unwin Hyman.

Krasner, Stephen. 1982a. "Regimes and the Limits of Realism: Regimes as Autonomous Variables." *International Organization* 36: 497–510.

1982b. "Structural Causes and Regime Consequences." *International Organization* 36: 185–205.

1995. "Sovereignty, Regimes, and Human Rights." In *Regime Theory and International Relations*, eds. Volker Rittenberger and Peter Mayer. Oxford: Clarendon Press.

Krebs, Ronald. 2015a. *Narrative and the Making of US National Security*. Cambridge: Cambridge University Press.

2015b. "Tell Me a Story: FDR, Narrative, and the Making of the Second World War." *Security Studies* 24: 131–170.

Krebs, Ronald, and Patrick Thaddeus Jackson. 2007. "Twisting Tongues and Twisting Arms: The Power of Political Rhetoric." *European Journal of International Relations* 13: 35–66.

Krebs, Ronald, and Jennifer Lobasz. 2007. "Fixing the Meaning of 9/11: Hegemony, Coercion, and the Road to War in Iraq." *Security Studies* 16: 409–451.

Kupchan, Charles. 1996. *The Vulnerability of Empire*. Ithaca: Cornell University Press.

2010. *How Enemies Become Friends: The Sources of Stable Peace*. Princeton, NJ: Princeton University Press.

2012. *No One's World: The West, the Rising Rest, and the Coming Global Turn*. Oxford: Oxford University Press.

2014a. "The Normative Foundations of Hegemony and the Coming Challenge to Pax Americana." *Security Studies* 23: 219–257.

2014b. "Unpacking Hegemony: The Social Foundations of Hierarchical Order." In *Power, Order, and Change in World Politics*, ed. G. John Ikenberry. Cambridge, UK: Cambridge University Press.

Kydd, Andrew. 1997. "Sheep in Sheep's Clothing: Why Security-Seekers Do Not Fight Each Other." *Security Studies* 7: 114–155.

Laderman, Charlie, and Brendan Simms. 2017. *Donald Trump: The Making of a Worldview*. Endeavour Press.

LaFeber, Walter. 1963. *The New Empire: An Interpretation of American Expansion, 1860–1898*. Ithaca, NY: Cornell University Press.

Lagerkvist, Johan. 2010. *After the Internet, before Democracy: Competing Norms in Chinese Media and Society*. Bern: Peter Lang Publishers.

Lai, Hongyi. 2010. *The Domestic Sources of China's Foreign Policy: Regimes, Leadership, Priorities, and Process*. London: Routledge.

Lampton, David. 2013. "A New Type of Major-Power Relationship: Seeking a Durable Foundation for U.S.-China Ties." *Asia Policy* 16: 51–68.

Langhorne, Richard. 1973. "Anglo-German Negotiations Concerning the Future of the Portuguese Colonies, 1911–1914." *The Historical Journal* 16: 361–387.

Larson, Deborah, T.V. Paul, and William Wohlforth. 2014. "Status and World Order." In *Status in World Politics*, eds. T.V. Paul, Deborah Larson and William Wohlforth. New York: Cambridge University Press.

Larson, Deborah, and Alexei Shevchenko. 2003. "Shortcut to Greatness: The New Thinking and the Revolution in Soviet Foreign Policy." *International Organization* 57: 77–109.

2010. "Status Seekers: Chinese and Russian Responses to U.S. Primacy." *International Security* 34: 63–95.

2014b. "Russia Says No: Power, Status, and Emotions in Foreign Policy." *Communist and Post-Communist Studies* 47: 269–279.

2014a. "Managing Rising Powers: The Role of Status Concerns." In *Status in World Politics*, eds. T.V. Paul, Deborah Larson and William Wohlforth. New York: Cambridge University Press.

Lawson-Tancred, HC. 1991. *Aristotle: The Art of Rhetoric*. London: Penguin.

Layne, Christopher. 1994. "Kant or Cant: The Myth of the Democratic Peace." *International Security* 19: 5–49.

August 26, 2014. "US Must Acknowledge China's Ambition." *Boston Globe*. Available at www.bostonglobe.com/opinion/2014/08/26/avoid-conflict-must-acknowledge-china-ambition/sNHyMDZR7rtXwUi1bqpx8K/story.html.

2015. "China and America: Sleepwalking to War?" *The National Interest* (May–June). Available at http://nationalinterest.org/feature/china-america-sleep walking-war-12685.

Lebow, Richard Ned. 2008. *A Cultural Theory of International Relations.* Cambridge: Cambridge University Press.

2010a. *Forbidden Fruit: Counterfactuals and International Relations.* Princeton, NJ: Princeton University Press.

2010b. *Why Nations Fight: Past and Future Motives for War.* Cambridge: Cambridge University Press.

Lee, James Jungbok. 2016. "Will China's Rise Be Peaceful? A Social Psychological Perspective." *Asian Security* 12: 29–52.

Lee, Marshall, and Wolfgang Michalka. 1987. *German Foreign Policy, 1917–1933.* New York: St. Martin's Press.

Legro, Jeffrey. 2005. *Rethinking the World: Great Power Strategies and International Order.* Ithaca, NY: Cornell University Press.

Lenski, Gerhard E. 1954. "Status Crystallization: A Non-Vertical Dimension of Social Status." *American Sociological Review* 19: 405–413.

Leopold, John. 1977. *Alfred Hugenberg: The Radical Nationalist Campaign against the Weimar Republic.* New Haven, CT: Yale University Press.

Leuchars, Chris. 2002. *To the Bitter End: Paraguay and the War of the Triple Alliance.* Westport, CT: Greenwood Press.

Levy, Jack. 2014. "The Sources of Preventive Logic in German Decision-Making in 1914." In *The Outbreak of the First World War: Structure, Politics, and Decision-Making*, eds. Jack Levy and John Vasquez. New York: Cambridge University Press.

Li, Chenghong, and Lucy Xu. December 4, 2014. "Chinese Enthusiasm and American Cynicism over the 'New Type of Great Power Relations'." *Brookings.* Available at www.brookings.edu/opinions/chinese-enthusiasm-and-american-cynicism-over-the-new-type-of-great-power-relations/.

Li, Hongshan. 2005. "Recent 'Anti-Americanism' in China: Historical Roots and Impact." In *China's Foreign Policy Making: Societal Force and Chinese American Policy*, eds. Yufan Hao and Lin Su. Hampshire, UK: Ashgate.

Li, Rex. 2009. *A Rising China and Security in East Asia: Identity Construction and Security Discourse.* New York: Routledge.

Lieberthal, Kenneth, and Jisi Wang. March 2012. "Addressing U.S.-China Strategic Distrust." John L. Thornton China Center Monograph Series 4.

Lindemann, Thomas. 2010. *Causes of War: The Struggle for Recognition.* Colchester, UK: ECPR Press.

Lindemann, Thomas, and Erik Ringmar, eds. 2016. *The International Politics of Recognition.* New York: Routledge.

Little, Richard. 2007. *The Balance of Power in International Relations: Metaphors, Myths, and Models.* Cambridge, UK: Cambridge University Press.

Liu, Mingfu. 2015. *The China Dream: Great Power Thinking and Strategic Posture in the Post-American Era.* New York: CN Times Books, Inc.

Lobell, Steven E. 2016. "Realism, Balance of Power, and Power Transitions." In *Accommodating Rising Powers: Past, Present, and Future*, ed. T.V. Paul. Cambridge: Cambridge University Press.

Loch, C., M. Yaziji, and C. Langen. 2001. "The Fight for the Alpha Position: Channeling Status Competition in Organizations." *European Management Journal* 19: 16–25.

"Lodge Indorses Cleveland," December 18, 1895. *San Francisco Call*. p. 2.

Logan, Justin. 2013. "China, America, and the Pivot to Asia." Cato Institute *Policy Analysis* paper no. 717.

Lu, Xin-An. 2005. "Ministry of Foreign Affairs in the Age of the Internet." In *China's Foreign Policy Making: Societal Force and Chinese American Policy*, eds. Yufan Hao and Lin Su. Hampshire, UK: Ashgate.

Lu, Yiyi. 2009. "Online Protests in China: Internet Manhunts." *The World Today* 65(8/9): 16–17.

Luttwak, Edward. 2012. *The Rise of China vs. the Logic of Strategy*. Cambridge: Harvard Belknap.

MacDonald, Paul, and Joseph Parent. 2011. "Graceful Decline? The Surprising Success of Great Power Retrenchment." *International Security* 35: 7–44.

MacDonogh, Giles. 2000. *The Last Kaiser: The Life of Wilhelm II*. New York: St. Martin's Press.

Machiavelli, Niccolo. 1996. *Discourses on Livy, Translated and Edited by Harvey C. Mansfield, Jr. And Nathan Tarcov*. Chicago: University of Chicago Press.

1998. *The Prince*, Translated by Harvey C. Mansfield. Second ed. Chicago: University of Chicago Press.

MacKinnon, Rebecca. 2008. "Flatter World and Thicker Walls? Blogs, Censorship, and Civil Discourse in China." *Public Choice* 134: 31–46.

MacMillan, Margaret. 2013. *The War That Ended Peace: The Road to 1914*. New York: Random House.

Mahan, Alfred Thayer. 1890. *The Influence of Sea Power Upon History*. Boston: Little, Brown and Company.

2009 [1910]. *The Interest of America in International Conditions*. Brunswick, NJ: Transaction Publishers.

Malinova, Olga. 2014. "Obsession with Status and Ressentiment: Historical Backgrounds of the Russian Discursive Identity Construction." *Communist and Post-Communist Studies*. Available at http://dx.doi.org/10.1016/j.postcomstud.2014.07.001.

Mancinelli, Paul. 2014. "Conceptualizing 'New Type Great Power Relations': The Sino-Russian Model." *China Brief* 14: 12–15.

Marder, AJ. 1961. *From Dreadnoughts to Scapa Flow*. Vol. I. Oxford: Oxford University Press.

1964. *The Anatomy of British Sea Power: A History of British Naval Policy in the Pre-Dreadnought Era, 1880–1905*. Hamden, CT: Archon Books.

Markey, Daniel. 1999. "Prestige and the Origins of Major War: Returning to Realism's Roots." *Security Studies* 8: 126–172.

2000. "The Prestige Motive in International Relations." Ph.D. Dissertation, Princeton University.

Marks, Sally. 1976. *The Illusion of Peace: International Relations in Europe 1918–1933*. New York: St. Martin's Press.

2013. "Mistakes and Myths: The Allies, Germany, and the Versailles Treaty, 1918–1921." *The Journal of Modern History* 85: 632–659.

Martel, Gordon. 2014. *The Month That Changed the World: July 1914*. Oxford, UK: Oxford University Press.

Martineau, John. 1908. *The Life of Henry Pelham, Fifth Duke of Newcastle, 1811–1864*. London: J. Murray.

Matthias, Eric. 1971. "The Influence of the Versailles Treaty on the Internal Development of the Third Reich." In *German Democracy and the Triumph of Hitler: Essay in Recent German History*, eds. A.J. Nicholls and Eric Matthias. London: George Allen and Unwin.

Mayo, Marlene. 1966. "Rationality in the Meiji Restoration: The Iwakura Embassy." In *Modern Japanese Leadership: Transition and Change*, eds. Bernard Silberman and Harry Harootunian. Tucson, AZ: University of Arizona Press.

McCormick, Thomas. 1967. *China Market: America's Quest for Informal Empire, 1893–1901*. Chicago: Quadrangle Books.

McGowan, Lee. 2003. *The Radical Right in Germany: 1870 to the Present*. New York: Routledge.

McMeekin, Sean. 2013. *July 1914: Countdown to War*. New York: Basic Books.

Mearsheimer, John. 2010. "The Gathering Storm: China's Challenge to U.S. Power in Asia." Paper presented at the Fourth Annual Michael Hintze Lecture in International Security, University of Sydney, August 4.

Mearsheimer, John J. 2001. *The Tragedy of Great Power Politics*. New York: Norton.

Mercer, Jonathan. 2017. "The Illusion of International Prestige." *International Security* 41(4): 133–168.

Merkl, Peter. 1975. *Political Violence under the Swastika: 581 Early Nazis*. Princeton, NJ: Princeton University Press.

Miller, Jennifer, Jacob Cramer, Thomas J. Volgy, Paul Bezerra, Megan Hauser, and Christina Sciabarra. 2015. "Norms, Behavioral Compliance, and Status Attribution in International Politics." *International Interactions* 41: 779–804.

Minohara, Tosh. 2014. "The Clash of Pride and Prejudice: The Immigration Issue and US-Japan Relations in the 1910s." In *The Decade of the Great War: Japan and the Wider World in the 1910s*, eds. Tosh Minohara, Tze-ki Hon and Evan Dawley. Leiden: Brill.

Mitcham, Samuel. 1996. *Why Hitler? The Genesis of the Nazi Reich*. Westport, CT: Praeger.

Mitzen, Jennifer. 2013. *Power in Concert: The Nineteenth-Century Origins of Global Governance*. Chicago: University of Chicago Press.

Mizuno, Norihito. 2004. "Japan and Its East Asian Neighbors: Japan's Perception of China and Korea and the Making of Foreign Policy from the Seventeenth to the Nineteenth Century." PhD Dissertation, The Ohio State University.

Mombauer, Annika, ed. 2013. *The Origins of the First World War: Diplomatic and Military Documents*. Manchester, UK: Manchester University Press.

Mommsen, Wolfgang. 1984. *Max Weber and German Politics, 1890–1920*. Chicago: University of Chicago Press.

1995. *Imperial Germany 1865–1918*. London: Arnold.

Morgenthau, Hans. 1948. *Politics among Nations: The Struggle for Power and Peace*. New York: McGraw-Hill.

Morris, Warren. 1982. *The Weimar Republic and Nazi Germany*. Chicago: Nelson-Hall.

Muhlberger, Detlef. 2004. *Hitler's Voice: The Volkischer Beobachter, 1920–1933*. Vol. 1. Bern: Peter Lang.

Mulligan, William. 2010. *The Origins of the First World War*. Cambridge: Cambridge University Press.

Mummenedey, Amelie, Thomas Kessler, Andreas Klink, and Rosemarie Mielke. 1999. "Strategies to Cope with Negative Social Identity: Predictions by Social Identity Theory and Relative Deprivation Theory." *Journal of Personality and Social Psychology* 76: 229–245.

Murray, Michelle. 2010. "Identity, Insecurity, and Great Power Politics: The Tragedy of German Naval Ambition before the First World War." *Security Studies* 19.

2016. "Recognition, Disrespect, and the Struggle for Morocco: Rethinking Imperial Germany's Security Dilemma." In *The International Politics of Recognition*, eds. Thomas Lindemann and Erik Ringmar. New York: Routledge.

Murray, Williamson. 1984. *The Change in the European Balance of Power, 1938–1939: The Path to Ruin*. Princeton, NJ: Princeton University Press.

Musgrave, Paul, and Daniel Nexon. Forthcoming. "Defending Hierarchy from the Moon to the Indian Ocean: Symbolic Capital and Political Dominance in Early Modern China and the Cold War." *International Organization*.

Nanto, Dick, and Shinji Takagi. 1985. "Korekiyo Takahashi and Japan's Recovery from the Great Depression." *The American Economic Review* 75: 369–374.

Narsimhan, Sushila. 1999. *Japanese Perceptions of China in the Nineteenth Century*. New Delhi: Phoenix Publishing House.

"National Honor and Pride." December 22, 1895. *Wichita Daily Eagle*. p. 12.

Nau, Henry. 2013. *Conservative Internationalism: Armed Diplomacy under Jefferson, Polk, Truman, and Reagan*. Princeton: Princeton University Press.

Neu, Charles. 1967. *An Uncertain Friendship: Theodore Roosevelt and Japan, 1906–1909*. Cambridge, MA: Harvard University Press.

1975. *The Troubled Encounter: The United States and Japan*. New York: John Wiley & Sons.

Neumann, Iver. 2005. "Russia as a Great Power." In *Russia as a Great Power: Dimensions of Security under Putin*, eds. Jakob Hedenskog, Vilhelm Konnander, Bertil Nygren, Ingmar Oldberg, and Christer Pursiainen. London: Routledge.

2008. "Russia as a Great Power, 1815–2007." *Journal of International Relations and Development* 11: 128–151.

2014. "Status Is Cultural: Durkheiman Poles and Weberian Russians Seek Great-Power Status." In *Status in World Politics*, eds. William Wohlforth, Deborah Larson, and T.V. Paul. New York: Cambridge University Press.

Neumann, Iver, and Benjamin de Carvalho. 2015. "Introduction: Small States and Status." In *Small State Status Seeking: Norways Quest for International Standing*, eds. Benjamin de Carvalho and Iver Neumann. London: Routledge.

Nicholls, A.J. 1968. *Weimar and the Rise of Hitler*. New York: St. Martin's Press.

Nish, Ian. 1993. *Japan's Struggle with Internationalism: Japan, China, and the League of Nations, 1931–1933*. New York: Kegan Paul International.

2002. *Japanese Foreign Policy in the Interwar Period*. Westport, CT: Praeger Publishers.

Nye, Joseph. 2006. "The Challenge of China." In *How to Make America Safe: New Policies for National Security*, ed. Stephen Van Evera. Cambridge, MA: The Tobin Project.

Ogata, Sadako. 1964. *Defiance in Manchuria: The Making of Japanese Foreign Policy 1931–1932*. Berkeley: University of California Press.

Onea, Tudor. 2014. "Between Dominance and Decline: Status Anxiety and Great Power Rivalry." *Review of International Studies* 40: 125–152.

Onuf, Nicholas. 1989. *World of Our Making: Rules and Rule in Social Theory and International Relations*. Columbia, SC: University of South Carolina Press.

Orlow, Dietrich. 1969. *The History of the Nazi Party: 1919–1933*. Pittsburgh: University of Pittsburgh Press.

Osgood, Charles Egerton. 1962. *An Alternative to War or Surrender*. Urbana, IL: University Illinois Press.

Osnos, Evan. November 6, 2012. "The Year China-Bashing Went Mainstream." *The New Yorker*. Available at www.newyorker.com/news/evan-osnos/the-year-china-bashing-went-mainstream.

Ott, Marvin. April 24, 2014. "Obama's Goal in Asia: Reassure Nervous Allies." *The National Interest*. Available at http://nationalinterest.org/feature/obamas-goal-asia-reassure-nervous-allies-10303.

Otte, T.G. 2014a. *July Crisis: The World's Descent into War, Summer 1914*. Cambridge, UK: Cambridge University Press.

2014b. "War, Revolution, and the Uncertain Primacy of Domestic Politics." In *The Next Great War? The Roots of World War I and the Risk of U.S.-China Conflict*, eds. Richard Rosecrance and Steven Miller. Cambridge, MA: The MIT Press.

Owen, John. 2010. *The Clash of Ideas in World Politics: Transnational Networks, States, and Regime Change, 1510–2010*. Princeton: Princeton University Press.

Page, Jeremy. March 13, 2013. "For Xi, a 'China Dream' of Military Power." *Wall Street Journal*. Available at www.wsj.com/articles/SB10001424127887324128504578348774040546346.

Park, Madison. October 22, 2012. "Obama, Romney's 'China-Bashing' Grates Chinese Netizens." *CNN*. Available at www.cnn.com/2012/10/22/world/asia/china-us-debates-comments/index.html.

Pash, Sidney. 2014. *The Currents of War: A New History of American-Japanese Relations, 1899–1941.* Lexington, KY: The University Press of Kentucky.

Paul, T.V. 2016. "The Accommodation of Rising Powers in World Politics." In *Accommodating Rising Powers: Past, Present, and Future*, ed. T.V. Paul. Cambridge: Cambridge University Press.

Paul, T.V., and Mahesh Shankar. 2014. "Status Accommodation through Institutional Means: India's Rise and the Global Order." In *Status in World Politics*, eds. William Wohlforth, Deborah Larson and T.V. Paul. New York: Cambridge University Press.

Peattie, Mark. 1975. *Ishiwara Kanji and Japan's Confrontation with the West.* Princeton: Princeton University Press.

1984. "Introduction." In *The Japanese Colonial Empire, 1895–1945*, eds. Ramon Hawley Myers and Mark Peattie. Princeton: Princeton University Press.

Pelz, Stephen. 1974. *Race to Pearl Harbor: The Failure of the Second London Naval Conference and the Onset of World War II.* Cambridge, MA: Harvard University Press.

Perez, Jane. May 28, 2013. "Chinese President to Seek New Relationship with U. S. In Talks." *New York Times.* Available at www.nytimes.com/2013/05/29/world/asia/china-to-seek-more-equal-footing-with-us-in-talks.html.

Perkins, Bradford. 1968. *The Great Rapprochement: England and the United States, 1895–1914.* New York: Atheneum.

1994. "Interests, Values, and the Prism: The Sources of American Foreign Policy." *Journal of the Early Republic* 14: 458–466.

Pillsbury, Michael. 2015. *The Hundred-Year Marathon: China's Secret Strategy to Replace America as the Global Superpower.* New York: Henry Holt and Company.

Pinson, K.S. 1966. *Modern Germany.* London: Macmillan.

Pogge von Strandman, Hartmut, ed. 1985. *Walter Rathenau, Industrialist, Banker, Intellectual, and Politician: Notes and Diaries 1907–1922.* Oxford, UK: Clarendon Press.

Pouliot, Vincent. 2014. "Setting Status in Stone: The Negotiation of International Institutional Privileges." In *Status in World Politics*, eds. William Wohlforth, Deborah Larson and T.V. Paul. New York: Cambridge University Press.

Presseisen, Ernst. 1969. *Germany and Japan: A Study in Totalitarian Diplomacy.* New York: H. Fertig.

Proctor, J.R. 1898. "Isolation or Imperialism?" *The Forum* 26: 14–26.

Pyle, Kenneth. 2007. *Japan Rising: The Resurgence of Japanese Power and Purpose.* New York: PublicAffairs.

Qiang, Xiao. 2011. "The Rise of Online Public Opinion and Its Political Impact." In *Changing Media, Changing China*, ed. Susan Shirk. New York: Oxford University Press.

Ray, James. L. 1974. "Status Inconsistency and War-Involvement in Europe, 1816–1970." *Peace Science Society Papers* 23: 69–80.

Reilly, James. 2012. *Strong Society, Smart State: The Rise of Public Opinion in China's Japan Policy.* New York: Columbia University Press.

Renshon, Jonathan. 2015 "Losing Face and Sinking Costs: Experimental Evidence on the Judgment of Political and Military Leaders." *International Organization* 69: 659–695.

2016. "Status Deficits and War." *International Organization* 70(3): 513–550.

2017. *Fighting for Status: Hierarchy and Conflict in World Politics*. Princeton, NJ: Princeton University Press.

Reus-Smit, Christian. 1999. *The Moral Purpose of the State: Culture, Social Identity, and Institutional Rationality in International Relations*. Princeton, NJ: Princeton University Press.

Rhamey, Patrick, and Bryan Early. 2013. "Going for the Gold: Status-Seeking Behavior and Olympic Performance." *International Area Studies Review* 16: 244–261.

Rhodes, Edward. 1995. "Constructing Peace and War: An Analysis of the Power of Ideas to Shape American Military Power." *Millennium* 24: 53–85.

1999. "Constructing Power: Cultural Transformation and Strategic Adjustment in the 1890s." In *The Politics of Strategic Adjustment: Ideas, Institutions, and Interests*, eds. Peter Trubowitz, Emily Goldman and Edward Rhodes. New York: Columbia University Press.

Ringmar, Erik. 1996. *Identity, Interest, and Action: A Cultural Explanation of Sweden's Intervention in the Thirty Years War*. Cambridge, UK: Cambridge University Press.

2012. "Performing International Systems: Two East-Asian Alternatives to the Westphalian Order." *International Organization* 66: 1–25.

Risse, Thomas, and Kathryn Sikkink. 1999. "The Socialization of Human Rights Norms." In *The Power of Human Rights: International Norms and Domestic Change*, eds. Stephen Robb and Kathryn Sikkink. New York: Cambridge University Press.

Roberts, Andrew. 2003. "The Whale against the Wolf: The Anglo-American War of 1896." In *What Ifs? Of American History: Eminent Historians Imagine What Might Have Been*, ed. Robert Cowley. New York: G.P. Putnam's Sons.

Rock, Stephen. 1989. *Why Peace Breaks Out: Great Power Rapprochement in Historical Perspective*. Chapel Hill: University of North Carolina Press.

Röhl, John. 2001. *Wilhelm II: The Kaiser's Personal Monarchy, 1888–1900*. Cambridge: Cambridge University Press.

2014. *Wilhelm II: Into the Abyss of War and Exile 1900–1941*. Cambridge, UK: Cambridge University Press.

2015. "Goodbye to All That (Again)? The Fischer Thesis, the New Revisionism, and the Meaning of the First World War." *International Affairs* 91: 153–166.

Roosevelt, Theodore. October 27, 1906. "*Letter from Theodore Roosevelt to Kermit Roosevelt*." Thedore Roosevelt Collection, Harvard College Library.

Ross, Robert. 2009. "China's Naval Nationalism: Sources, Prospects, and the U.S. Response." *International Security* 34: 46–81.

2012. "The Problem with the Pivot: Obama's New Asia Policy Is Unnecessary and Counterproductive." *Foreign Affairs* 91: 70–82.

Rousseau, Jean-Jacques. 1991. "Fragments on War." In *Rousseau on International Relations*, eds. Stanley Hoffman and David P. Fidler. Oxford: Clarendon Press.

Rubarth, Edgar Stern. 1939. *Three Men Tried: Austen Chamberlain, Stresemann, Briand and Their Fight for a New Europe*. London: Duckworth.

Ruggie, John G. 1993. "Territoriality and Beyond: Problematizing Modernity in International Relations." *International Organization* 47: 139–174.

Runciman, W.G. 1966. *Relative Deprivation and Social Justice: A Study of Attitudes to Social Inequality in Twentieth Century England*. Berkeley, CA: University of California Press.

Saaler, Sven, and Christopher Szpilman. 2011. "Introduction: The Emergence of Pan-Asianism as an Ideal of Asian Identity and Solidarity, 1850–2008." In *Pan-Asianism, a Documentary History, Volume 2: 1920-Present*, eds. Sven Saaler and Christopher Szpilman. Lanham: Rowman and Littlefield.

Saeger, James Schofield. 2007. *Francisco Solano Lopéz and the Ruination of Paraguay: Honor and Egocentrism*. Lanham, MD: Rowman & Littlefield.

Sagan, Scott. 1988. "The Origins of the Pacific War." *Journal of Interdisciplinary History* 18: 893–922.

Sambanis, Nicholas, Stergios Skaperdas, and William Wohlforth. 2015. "Nation-Building through War." *American Political Science Review* 109: 279–296.

Samuels, Richard. 2007. *Securing Japan: Tokyo's Grand Strategy and the Future of East Asia*. Ithaca: Cornell University Press.

Scheck, Raffael. 1998. *Alfred Von Tirpitz and German Right-Wing Politics, 1914–1930*. Atlantic Highlands: Humanities Press.

Scheidemann, Philipp. 1929. *Memoirs of a Social Democrat*. Vol. 2. London: Hodder and Stoughton.

Schierbrand, Wolf von. 1902. *German: The Welding of a World Power*. New York: Doubleday, Page & Co.

Schlichtmann, Klaus. 2009. *Japan in the World: Shidehara Kijurō, Pacifism, and the Abolition of War, Volume II*. Lanham: Rowman and Littlefield.

Schmokel, Wolfe. 1964. *Dream of Empire: German Colonialism, 1919–1945*. New Haven, CT: Yale University Press.

Schwarz, Wolfgang. 1931. "Germany and the League of Nations: Address Given at Chatham House on February 11, 1931." *International Affairs* 10: 197–207.

Schweller, Randall L. 1998. *Deadly Imbalances: Tripolarity and Hitler's Strategy of World Conquest*. New York: Columbia University Press.

2006. *Unanswered Threats: Political Constraints on the Balance of Power, Princeton Studies in International History and Politics*. Princeton, N.J.: Princeton University Press.

2014. *Maxwell's Demon and the Golden Apple: Global Discord in the New Milennium*. Baltimore: Johns Hopkins University Press.

Schweller, Randall L., and Xiaoyu Pu. 2011. "After Unipolarity: China's Visions of International Order in an Era of U.S. Decline." *International Security* 36: 41–72.

2014. "Status Signaling, Multiple Audiences, and China's Blue-Water Naval Ambition." In *Status in World Politics*, eds. William Wohlforth, Deborah Larson and T.V. Paul. New York: Cambridge University Press.

Seager II, Robert, and Doris Maguire, eds. 1975. *Letters and Papers of Alfred Thayer Mahan*. 2 vols. Annapolis, MD: Naval Institute Press.

Shambaugh, David. 2013. *China Goes Global: The Partial Power*. New York: Oxford University Press.

March 6, 2015. "The Coming Chinese Crackup." *The Wall Street Journal*. Available at www.wsj.com/articles/the-coming-chinese-crack-up-1425659198.

Shambaugh, David, and Ren Xiao. 2012. "China: The Conflicted Rising Power." In *Worldviews of Aspiring Powers: Domestic Foreign Policy Debates in China, India, Iran, Japan, and Russia*, eds. Henry Nau and Deepa Ollapally. Oxford: Oxford University Press.

Shapiro, Jeremy. March 11, 2015. "Defending the Defensible: The Value of Spheres of Influence in U.S. Foreign Policy." *Brookings*. Available at www.brookings.edu/blog/order-from-chaos/2015/03/11/defending-the-defensible-the-value-of-spheres-of-influence-in-u-s-foreign-policy/.

Sharp, Alan. 2010. *Consequences of Peace: The Versailles Settlement, Aftermath and Legacy 1919–2010*. London: Haus Publishing.

Shen, Simon. 2004. "Nationalism or Nationalist Foreign Policy? Contemporary Chinese Nationalism and Its Role in Shaping Chinese Foreign Policy in Response to the Belgrade Embassy Bombing." *Politics* 24: 122–130.

Shenkar, Oded. September 21, 2012. "Elections Bring China-Bashing Season." *CNN*. Available at www.cnn.com/2012/09/21/opinion/shenkar-china-trade/index.html.

Shimazu, Naoko. 1998. *Japan, Race and Equality*. London: Routledge.

Shirk, Susan. 2011. "Changing Media, Changing Foreign Policy." In *Changing Media, Changing China*, ed. Susan Shirk. New York: Oxford University Press.

Shlaes, Amity. 2014. *Coolidge*. New York: HarperCollins.

Sikkink, Kathryn. 1993. "Human Rights, Principled Issue-Networks, and Sovereignty in Latin America." *International Organization* 47: 411–441.

Simpson, Gerry. 2004. *Great Powers and Outlaw States: Unequal Sovereigns in the International Legal Order*. Cambridge, UK: Cambridge University Press.

Singer, J. David, and Melvin Small. 1966. "The Composition and Status Ordering of the International System: 1815–1940." *World Politics* 18: 236–282.

Sissons, D.C.S. 1971. "The Immigration Question in Australian Diplomatic Relations with Japan, 1875–1919." Prepared for the meeting of the Australian and New Zealand Association for the Advancement of Science. Available via the Papers of David Sissons, National Library of Australia, MS 3092, Series 1.2, Folder 15.

Slomp, Gabriella. 1990. "Hobbes, Thucydides and the Three Greatest Things." *History of Political Thought* 11: 565–586.

Small, Melvin and J. David Singer. 1973. "The Diplomatic Importance of States, 1816–1970: An Extension and Refinement of the Indicator." *World Politics* 25: 577–599.

Smith, Hanna. 2014. "Russia as a Great Power: Status Inconsistency and the Two Chechen Wars." *Communist and Post-Communist Studies* 47: 355–363.

Snyder, Jack. 1987. "The Gorbachev Revolution: A Waning of Soviet Expansionism?" *International Security* 12: 93–131.

   1989. "International Leverage on Soviet Domestic Change." *International Security* 42: 1–30.

   1991. *Myths of Empire: Domestic Politics and International Ambition.* Ithaca: Cornell University Press.

Snyder, Louis. 1966. *The Weimar Republic.* New York: D. Van Nostrand Company.

Spears, R., B. Doosje, and Naomi Ellemers. 1997. "Self-Stereotyping in the Face of Threats to Group Status and Distinctiveness: The Role of Group Identification." *Personality and Social Psychology Bulletin* 23: 538–553.

Stein, Janice Gross. 1991. "Reassurance in International Conflict Management." *Political Science Quarterly* 106: 431–451.

Steinberg, James, and Michael O'Hanlon. 2014. *Strategic Reassurance and Resolve: U.S.-China Relations in the Twenty-First Century.* Princeton: Princeton University Press.

Steinberg, Jonathan. 1965. *Yesterday's Deterrent: Tirpitz and the Birth of the German Battle Fleet.* New York: The Macmillan Company.

Stekelenburg, Jacquelien, Bert Klandermans, and Wilco Van Dijk. 2011. "Combining Motivations and Emotion: The Motivational Dynamics of Protest Participation." *Revist Psicologia Social* 26: 91–104.

Storry, Richard. 1957. *The Double Patriots: A Study of Japanese Nationalism.* Boston: Houghton Mifflin.

   1979. *Japan and the Decline of the West in Asia 1894–1943.* New York: St. Martin's Press.

Strachan, Hew. 2001. *The First World War, Volume I: To Arms.* Oxford: Oxford University Press.

   2004. The Outbreak of *the* First World War. Oxford: Oxford University Press.

Strikwerda, Carl. 2013. "Imagining a Global World: Imperialism, Nationalism, and the Tragedy of Great Power Politics in the First Era of Globalization, 1870–1914." In *Culture and Civilization,* ed. Gabriel Ricci. Vol. 5. New Brunswick, NJ: Transaction Publishers.

Stryker, Sheldon, and Anne Statham Macke. 1978. "Status Inconsistency and Role Conflict." *Annual Review of Sociology* 4: 57–90.

Sumner, Charles. April 13, 1869. "Our Claims on England." *Congressional Globe,* Senate, 41st Congress, 1st Session, Appendix, p. 21.

Sutton, Eric, ed. 1937. *Gustav Stresemann: His Diaries, Letters, and Papers.* Vol. II. New York: The Macmillan Company.

Suzuki, Shogo. 2005. "Japan's Socialization into Janus-Faced European International Society." *European Journal of International Relations* 11: 137–164.

2008. "Seeking 'Legitimate' Great Power Status in Post-Cold War International Society: China's and Japan's Participation in Unpko." *International Relations* 22: 45–63.

Szpilman, Christopher. 2011a. "Mori Kaku: 'Extraordinary Means for Extraordinary Times,' 1932." In *Pan-Asianism, a Documentary History, Volume 2: 1920-Present*, eds. Sven Saaler and Christopher Szpilman. Lanham: Rowman and Littlefield.

2011b. "Ōkawa Shūmei: 'Various Problems of Asia in Revival,' 1922." In *Pan-Asianism, a Documentary History, Volume 2: 1920-Present*, eds. Sven Saaler and Christopher Szpilman. Lanham: Rowman and Littlefield.

Taft, William Howard. January 17, 1911. "Letter from William H. Taft to Theodore Roosevelt." Theodore Roosevelt Papers, Library of Congress Manuscript Division.

Tai, Zixue. 2006. *The Internet in China: Cyberspace and Civil Society*. New York: Routledge.

Tajfel, Henri. 1978a. "Interindividual Behaviour and Intergroup Behaviour." In *Differentiation between Social Groups: Studies in the Social Psychology of Intergroup Relations*, ed. Henri Tajfel. New York: Academic Press, Inc.

1978b. "Social Categorization, Social Identity, and Social Comparison." In *Differentiation between Social Groups: Studies in the Social Psychology of Intergroup Relations*, ed. Henri Tajfel. New York: Academic Press, Inc.

ed. 1982. *Social Identity and Intergroup Relations*. Cambridge: Cambridge University Press.

Tajfel, Henri, and John C. Turner. 1979. "An Integrative Theory of Intergroup Conflict." In *The Social Psychology of Intergroup Relations*, eds. William Austin and Stephen Worchel. Monterey, CA: Brooks/Cole.

Takaki, Yasaka. 1932. "World Peace Machinery and the Asia Monroe Doctrine." *Pacific Affairs* 5: 941–953.

Takemoto, Toru. 1978. *Failure of Liberalism in Japan: Shidehara Kijurō's Encounter with Anti-Liberals*. Washington, DC: University Press of America.

Taliaferro, Jeffrey W. 2009. "Neoclassical Realism and Resource Extraction: State Building for Future War." In *Neoclassical Realism, the State, and Foreign Policy*, eds. Steven E. Lobell, Norrin M. Ripsmann and Jeffrey W. Taliaferro. Cambridge, UK: Cambridge University Press.

Tankai, Cui, and Pang Hanzhao. 2012. "China-U.S. Relations in China's Overall Diplomacy in the New Era: On China and U.S. Working Together to Build a New-Type Relationship between Major Countries." Ministry of Foreign Affairs of the People's Republic of China. Beijing. Available at www.fmprc.gov.cn/mfa_eng/wjb_663304/zzjg_663340/bmdyzs_664814/xwlb_664816/t953682.shtml.

Tankha, Brij. 2006. *Kita Ikki and the Making of Modern Japan: A Vision of Empire*. Honolulu: University of Hawaii Press.

Taylor, A.J.P. 1973. "The Immediate Circumstances." In *The Nazi Revolution: Hitler's Dictatorship and the German Nation*, ed. John Snell. Lexington, MA: D.C. Heath and Co.

Taylor, D.M., I. Gamble, and E. Zeller. 1987. "Disadvantaged Group Responses to Perceived Inequity: From Passive Acceptance to Collective Action." *Journal of Social Psychology* 127: 259–272.

Taylor, D.M., and D.J. McKirnan. 1984. "A Five-Stage Model of Intergroup Relations." *British Journal of Social Psychology* 23: 291–300.

Taylor, Frederick. 2013. *The Downfall of Money: Germany's Hyperinflation and the Destruction of the Middle Class*. New York: Bloomsbury Press.

Tetlock, Philip, and Aaron Belkin. 1996. "Counterfactual Thought Experiments in World Politics: Logical, Methodological, and Psychological Perspectives." In *Counterfactual Thought Experiments in World Politics: Logical, Methodological, and Psychological Perspectives*, eds. Philip Tetlock and Aaron Belkin. Princeton, NJ: Princeton University Press.

The White House. 2015. National Security Strategy of the United States. Washington, DC. Available at http://nssarchive.us/wp-content/uploads/2015/02/2015.pdf.

Thies, Jochen. 2012. *Hitler's Plans for Global Domination: Nazi Architecture and Ultimate War Aims*. New York: Berghahn Books.

Thompson, George. 1869. *The War in Paraguay*. London: Longmans, Green, and Co.

Thompson, Wayne. 1980. *In the Eye of the Storm: Kurt Riezler and the Crises of Modern Germany*. Iowa City: University of Iowa Press.

Thompson, William R. 1999. "The Evolution of a Great Power Rivalry: The Anglo-American Case." In *Great Power Rivalries*, ed. William R. Thompson. Columbia, SC: University of South Carolina Press.

Thucydides. 1972. *History of the Peloponnesian War*, Translated by Rex Warner, Introduced by M.I. Finley. London: Penguin.

Tiezzi, Shannon. September 10, 2014. "NSA Susan Rice in China: Rethinking 'New Type Great Power Relations'." *The Diplomat*. Available at http://thedi plomat.com/2014/09/nsa-susan-rice-in-china-rethinking-new-type-great-po wer-relations/.

Toby, Ronald. 1984. *State and Diplomacy in Early Modern Japan: Asia in the Development of the Tokugawa Bakufu*. Princeton, NJ: Princeton University Press.

Tooze, Adam. 2014. *The Deluge: The Great War, America, and the Remaking of the Global Order, 1916–1931*. New York: Viking.

Towns, Ann. 2009. "The Status of Women as a Standard of 'Civilization.'" *European Journal of International Relations* 15: 681–706.

2010. *Women and States: Norms and Hierarchies in International Society*. Cambridge, UK: Cambridge University Press.

2012. "Norms and Social Hierarchies: Understanding International Policy Diffusion 'From Below.'" *International Organization* 66: 179–209.

Townsend, Mary. 1938. "The German Colonies and the Third Reich." *Political Science Quarterly* 53: 186–206.

Tracy, Benjamin. 1890. "Letter from the Secretary of the Navy Transmitting, in Compliance with Senate Resolution January 27, 1890, the Report of the So-called Policy Board." United States Senate executive document, 51st Congress, 1st Session, no. 43.

Tsunoda, Ryusaku, William Theodore de Bary, and Donald Keene. 1958. *Sources of Japanese Tradition*. Vol. 2. New York: Columbia University Press.

Tsygankov, Andrei. 2012. *Russia and the West from Alexander to Putin: Honor in International Relations*. New York: Cambridge University Press.

2014. "The Frustrating Partnership: Honor, Status, and Emotions in Russia's Discourses of the West." *Communist and Post-Communist Studies* 47: 345–354.

Tucker, Robert, and David Hendrickson. 1990. "Thomas Jefferson and American Foreign Policy." *Foreign Affairs* 69: 135–156.

Turner, Henry. 1963. *Stresemann and the Politics of the Weimar Republic*. Princeton, NJ: Princeton University Press.

Vincent, R.J. 1974. *Nonintervention and International Order*. Princeton: Princeton University Press.

Vitalis, Robert. 2010. "The Noble American Science of Imperial Relations and Its Laws of Race Development." *Comparative Studies in Society and History* 52: 909–938.

2015. *White World Order, Black Power Politics: The Birth of American International Relations*. Ithaca: Cornell University Press.

Voeten, Erik. 2005. "The Political Origins of the UN Security Council's Ability to Legitimize the Use of Force." *International Organization* 59: 527–557.

Volgy, Thomas J., Renato Corbetta, Patrick Rhamey, Ryan Baird, and Keith Grant. 2014. "Status Considerations in International Politics and the Rise of Regional Powers." In *Status in World Politics*, eds. Deborah Larson, T.V. Paul and William Wohlforth. Cambridge: Cambridge University Press.

Volgy, Thomas J., and S. Mayhall. 1995. "Status Inconsistency and International War: Exploring the Effects of Systemic Change." *International Studies Quarterly* 39: 67–84.

Vucetic, Srdjan. 2011. *The Anglosphere: A Genealogy of a Racialized Identity in International Relations*. Palo Alto: Stanford University Press.

Walker, Iain, and Leon Mann. 1987. "Unemployment, Relative Deprivation, and Social Protest." *Personality and Social Psychology Bulletin* 13: 275–283.

Walker, Iain, and Thomas Pettigrew. 1984. "Relative Deprivation Theory: An Overview and Conceptual Critique." *British Journal of Social Psychology* 23: 301–310.

Wallace, Michael. 1971. "Power, Status, and International War." *Journal of Peace Research* 8: 23–35.

1973. *War and Rank among Nations*. Lexington, MA: D.C. Heath.

Waltz, Kenneth N. 1979. *Theory of International Politics*. 1st ed. Boston, MA: McGraw-Hill.

Wang, Yan. 2008. "Analyzing Features in China's 'New' Diplomacy: Strategic Dialogues and Multilateral Diplomacy." In *China's "New" Diplomacy*, eds. Pauline Kerr, Stuart Harris and Yaqing Qin. New York: St. Martin's Press.

Wang, Zhengxu. 2006. "Hybrid Regime and Peaceful Development in China." In *China's "Peaceful Rise" in the 21st Century*, ed. Sujian Guo. Hampshire: Ashgate.

"War on Every Lip." December 18, 1895. *Chicago Daily Tribune*. p. 1.

Ward, Steven. 2013. "Race, Status, and Japanese Revisionism in the Early 1930s." *Security Studies* 22: 607–639.

Forthcoming. "Lost in Translation: Social Identity Theory and the Study of Status in World Politics." *International Studies Quarterly.*

Washington Post Editorial Board. October 17, 2012. "It's China-Bashing Time Again." *The Washington Post.* Available at www.washingtonpost.com/opinions/its-china-bashing-time-again/2012/10/17/589a603c-1879-11e2-8bfd-12e2ee90dcf2_story.html?utm_term=.25fa81c2c387.

Watson, Adam. 1992. *The Evolution of International Society: A Comparative Historical Analysis.* New York: Routledge.

Watson, Alexander. 2014. *Ring of Steel: Germany and Austria-Hungary in World War I.* New York: Basic Books.

Weisiger, Alex. 2013. *Logics of War: Explanations for Limited and Unlimited Conflicts.* Ithaca: Cornell University Press.

Weiss, Jessica. 2013. "Authoritarian Signaling, Mass Audiences, and Nationalist Protest in China." *International Organization* 67: 1–35.

2014. *Powerful Patriots: Nationalist Protest in China's Foreign Relations.* New York: Oxford University Press.

Welch, David. 1993. *Justice and the Genesis of War.* New York: Cambridge University Press.

Wendt, Alexander E. 1998. "On Constitution and Causation in International Relations." *Review of International Studies* 24: 101–118.

Whigham, Thomas. 2002. *The Paraguayan War: Volume I, Causes and Early Conflict.* Lincoln, NE: University of Nebraska Press.

White, Hugh. 2012. *The China Choice: Why We Should Share Power.* Oxford: Oxford University Press.

"Why China-Bashing Dominates U.S. Presidential Elections." October 27, 2012. *People's Daily Online.* Available at http://en.people.cn/90883/7993732.html.

Wight, Martin. 1977. *Systems of States.* Leicester: Leicester University Press.

Williams, Michael. 2003. "Words, Images, Enemies: Securitization and International Politics." *International Studies Quarterly* 47: 511–531.

Williams, William A. 1970. *The Roots of the Modern American Empire: A Study of the Growth and Shaping of Social Consciousness in a Marketplace Society.* London: Vintage Books.

Wilson, Sandra. 2002. *The Manchurian Crisis and Japanese Society, 1931–1933.* London: Routledge.

Wohlforth, William. 2015. "Conclusion: A Small Middle Power." In *Small State Status Seeking: Norway's Quest for International Standing,* eds. Iver Neumann and Benjamin de Carvalho. London: Routledge.

Wohlforth, William. 2014. "Status Dilemmas and Interstate Conflict." In *Status in World Politics,* eds. William Wohlforth, Deborah Larson and T.V. Paul. New York: Cambridge University Press.

Wohlforth, William. 2009. "Unipolarity, Status Competition, and Great Power War." *World Politics* 61: 28–57.

Wolf, Reinhard. 2014. "Rising Powers, Status Ambitions, and the Need to Reassure: What China Could Learn from Imperial Germany's Failures." *The Chinese Journal of International Politics* 7: 185–219.

Wolfers, Arnold. 1962. *Discord and Collaboration*. Baltimore: Johns Hopkins University Press.

———. 1966. *Britain and France between Two Wars*. New York: W.W. Norton.

Wong, Edward. November 18, 2016. "Trump Has Called Climate Change a Chinese Hoax. Beijing Says It Is Anything But." *New York Times*. Available at www.nytimes.com/2016/11/19/world/asia/china-trump-climate-change .html?_r=0.

Wood, Graeme. March 2015. "What ISIS Really Wants." *The Atlantic*. Available at www.theatlantic.com/magazine/archive/2015/03/what-isis-really-wants/3 84980/.

Woodward, David. 1993. *Trial by Friendship: Anglo-American Relations, 1917–1918*. Lexington, KY: The University Press of Kentucky.

Wright, Jonathan. 2002. *Gustav Stresemann: Weimar's Greatest Statesman*. Oxford: Oxford University Press.

Wright, Stephen, Donald Taylor, and Fathali Moghaddam. 1990. "Responding to Membership in a Disadvantaged Group: From Acceptance to Collective Protest." *Journal of Personality and Social Psychology* 58: 994–1003.

Wright, Thomas. 2016. "Trump's 19th Century Foreign Policy." *Politico*. Available at www.politico.com/magazine/story/2016/01/donald-trump-for eign-policy-213546.

Wu, Xu. 2007. *Chinese Cyber Nationalism: Evolution, Characteristics, and Implications*. Lanham: Lexington Books.

Wuthnow, Joel. 2016. "China's Calibrated Response to the South China Sea Is Firm (yet Flexible)." *The National Interest*. Available at http://nationalinter est.org/feature/chinas-calibrated-response-the-south-china-sea-firm-yet-17386.

Xu, Xin. 2006. "Modernizing China in the Olympic Spotlight: China's National Identity and the 2008 Beijing Olympiad." *The Sociological Review* 54: 90–107.

Xuetong, Yan. 2001. "The Rise of China in Chinese Eyes." *Journal of Contemporary China* 10: 33–39.

Yarwood, A.T. 1964. *Asian Migration to Australia: The Background to Exclusion, 1896–1923*. Melbourne: Melbourne University Press.

Yasuba, Yasukichi. 1996. "Did Japan Ever Suffer from a Shortage of Natural Resources before World War II?" *The Journal of Economic History* 56: 543–560.

Yearwood, Peter. 2009. *Guarantee of Peace: The League of Nations in British Policy, 1914–1925*. Oxford: Oxford University Press.

Young, George. 1942. "Intervention under the Monroe Doctrine: The Olney Corollary." *Political Science Quarterly* 57: 247–280.

Young, Kenneth. 1934. *Arthur James Balfour: The Happy Life of the Politician, Prime Minister, Statesman, and Philosopher, 1848–1914*. New York: Columbia University Press.

Yu, Haiqing. 2009. *Media and Cultural Transformation in China*. New York: Routledge.

Yu, Yanmin. 2005. "The Role of the Media: A Case Study of China's Media Coverage of the U.S. War in Iraq." In *China's Foreign Policy Making: Societal*

Force and Chinese American Policy, eds. Yufan Hao and Lin Su. Hampshire, UK: Ashgate.

Zakaria, Fareed. 1998. *From Wealth to Power: The Unusual Origins of America's World Role*. Princeton, NJ: Princeton University Press.

Zarakol, Ayşe. 2011. *After Defeat: How the East Learned to Live with the West*. New York: Cambridge University Press.

Zenequelli, Lilia. 1997. *Cronica De Una Guerra: La Triple Alianza, 1865–1870*. Buenos Aires: Ediciones Dunken.

Zhang, Yunling, and Shiping Tang. 2005. "China's Regional Strategy." In *Power Shift: China and Asia's New Dynamics*, ed. David Shambaugh. Berkeley: University of California Press.

Zheng, Bijian. 2011. *China's Road to Peaceful Rise: Observations on Its Cause, Basis, Connotations, and Prospects*. New York: Routledge.

Zhong, Sheng. July 29, 2010. "Is US Ready to Recognize China as World Power?" *People's Daily*. Available at http://en.people.cn/90001/90780/91343/7085804.html.

Index